e Foundations of the Market Economy

Mario J. Rizzo
iversity
H. White
University

eme in this series is the importance of understanding and assessing economy from a perspective broader than the static economics ompetition and Pareto optimality. Such a perspective sees markets ocesses generated by the preferences, expectations and beliefs of gents. The creative acts of entrepreneurship that uncover new about preferences, prices and technology are central to these ith respect to their ability to promote the discovery and use of n society.

et economy consists of a set of institutions that facilitate voluntary and exchange among individuals. These institutions include the hical framework as well as more narrowly "economic" patterns eraction. Thus the law, legal institutions and cultural and ethical ell as ordinary business practices and monetary phenomena, fall nalytical domain of the economist.

and Political Change after Crisis
r Government, Liberty, and the Rule of Law
phen H. Balch and Benjamin Powell

on and Free Trade

Freedom and Prosperity
and Maintenance of Liberalization
njamin Powell

and Inequality
f State and Market
P. Manish and Stephen C. Miller

formation about this series, please visit www.routledge.com/series/

Capitalism and Inequa

Capitalism and Inequality rejects the popular
in inequality to a failure of market instit
original research from established scholars
in a free market from an economic and h
the question of whether the recent increas
capitalism and government intervention is

The book features sections on theoret
political economy of inequality, and the m
explore several key questions such as the
market-driven inequality and the inequality
how the inequality created by regulation
and whether the economic growth that ac
always benefits an elite minority while lea
main policy conclusions that emerge fro
that are currently popular. The authors in
role of markets and reducing the extent of
inequality while ensuring greater material

This key text makes an invaluable contrib
and markets and is essential reading for stu

G.P. Manish is Associate Professor of Econ
BB&T Professor of Economic Freedom at
Political Economy, Troy University, USA.

Stephen C. Miller is Associate Professo
USA, and Adams-Bibby Chair of Free En
Center for Political Economy, Troy Univer

Routledg
Edited by
New York U
Lawrence
George Mas

A central t
the market
of perfect c
as causal p
Economic
informatio
processes v
knowledge

The ma
cooperatio
legal and
of social i
norms, as
within the

Economi
Prospects f
Edited by S

Competit
Pascal Salin

Economi
The Origi
Edited by E

Capitalis
The Role
Edited by C

For more i
SE0104

Capitalism and Inequality

The Role of State and Market

Edited by G.P. Manish and Stephen C. Miller

Routledge
Taylor & Francis Group
LONDON AND NEW YORK

First published 2021
by Routledge
2 Park Square, Milton Park, Abingdon, Oxon OX14 4RN

and by Routledge
52 Vanderbilt Avenue, New York, NY 10017

Routledge is an imprint of the Taylor & Francis Group, an informa business

British Library Cataloguing-in-Publication Data
A catalogue record for this book is available from the British Library

Library of Congress Cataloging-in-Publication Data
A catalog record for this book has been requested

ISBN: 978-0-367-46746-3 (hbk)
ISBN: 978-1-003-03080-5 (ebk)

Typeset in Bembo
by Apex CoVantage, LLC

Contents

Contributors

Peter J. Boettke is University Professor of Economics and Philosophy at George Mason University, USA. He is also Director of the F.A. Hayek Program for Advanced Study in Philosophy, Politics and Economics and BB&T Professor for the Study of Capitalism at the Mercatus Center, George Mason University, USA.

Donald J. Boudreaux is Professor of Economics at George Mason University, USA. He is also Senior Fellow with the F.A. Hayek Program for Advanced Study in Philosophy, Politics and Economics and holds the Martha and Nelson Getchell Chair for the Study of Free Market Capitalism at the Mercatus Center, George Mason University, USA.

Rosolino A. Candela is Associate Director of Academic & Student Programs and Senior Fellow with the F.A. Hayek Program for Advanced Study in Philosophy, Politics, and Economics at the Mercatus Center, George Mason University, USA.

Vincent Geloso is Assistant Professor of Economics at King's University College, Canada, and is Senior Fellow at the American Institute of Economic Research, USA.

Randall G. Holcombe is DeVoe Moore Professor of Economics at Florida State University, USA.

Steven Horwitz is Distinguished Professor of Free Enterprise in the Department of Economics in the Miller College of Business, Ball State University, USA. He is also Affiliated Senior Scholar at the Mercatus Center in Arlington, VA, and Senior Fellow at the Fraser Institute of Canada.

Phillip W. Magness is Senior Research Fellow at the American Institute of Economic Research, USA.

G.P. Manish is Associate Professor of Economics at Troy University, USA, and BB&T Professor of Economic Freedom at the Manuel H. Johnson Center for Political Economy, Troy University, USA.

Stephen C. Miller is Associate Professor of Economics at Troy University, USA, and Adams-Bibby Chair of Free Enterprise at the Manuel H. Johnson Center for Political Economy, Troy University, USA.

Robert P. Murphy is Research Fellow at the Independent Institute, USA, Senior Economist with the Institute for Energy Research, USA, and Senior Fellow at the Mises Institute, USA.

Richard Vedder is Distinguished Professor of Economics Emeritus at Ohio University, USA, and Senior Fellow at the Independent Institute, USA.

Kaitlyn Woltz is a Ph.D. candidate in Economics at George Mason University, USA, and is a PhD fellow and a Graduate Fellow with the F.A. Hayek Program for Advanced Study in Philosophy, Politics and Economics at the Mercatus Center, George Mason University, USA.

Acknowledgments

We would like to thank Dr. Manuel Johnson and the Manuel H. Johnson Center for Political Economy at Troy University for supporting and funding this project. We are grateful to Troy University for providing administrative and institutional support. We would also like to thank our student, Asem Abdelfattah, for his valuable research assistance.

We are grateful to the authors who participated in this project. They were a pleasure to work with and we would like to thank them for their excellent contributions. The final product is more comprehensive and insightful than anything that we could have possibly written on our own.

We thank Edward Stringham, Phillip Magness, and the American Institute of Economic Research for organizing a manuscript workshop where drafts of the chapters were discussed. David Henderson and the other participants in this workshop provided valuable suggestions that helped improve the book, and for this we are grateful. We would also like to thank Benjamin Powell and Peter Boettke for feedback and support over the course of this project.

Finally, we would like to thank Andrew Humphries at Routledge for supporting the publication of this book and Emma Morley at Routledge for providing editorial assistance while preparing the manuscript.

Introduction

G.P. Manish and Stephen C. Miller

Of late, a growing consensus has emerged regarding the growth of inequality in the United States and in other developed countries such as the United Kingdom, Canada, and Australia (Piketty and Saez 2003, 2006; Atkinson et al. 2011). It is now established opinion, both among academics and policymakers, that there has been a steep increase in the level of income inequality in these countries over the last three decades. The most obvious and troubling manifestation of this rising inequality is the ever-growing share of the economic pie that has been flowing to individuals and households at the top of the income distribution.

What explains this surge in the levels of inequality? Several eminent economists have grappled with this question. The most prominent among them is French economist Thomas Piketty, whose international bestseller, *Capital in the 21st Century* (Piketty 2014), tries to provide an answer. In this book, Piketty pinpoints the increasing concentration of wealth as the source of the recent surge in income inequality. As capital is accumulated, market forces ensure that this growing stock of productive wealth is distributed unequally, with a large portion of it concentrated in the hands of a few households. Those who earn most of their income in the form of interest on investments can thus get by with doing little or no work, whereas the bulk of the population, who own little wealth, are forced to rely on work and wages for most of their income.

When the rate of return on investments in capital and wealth (*r*) exceeds the rate of growth of output and wages (*g*), as has been the case through most of human history and for the past 30 years in many parts of the developed world (Piketty 2014: 350–358; Piketty and Saez 2014), then this concentration of wealth that is inherent to a market economy is reinforced and results in a sharp increase in income inequality. For the few households that own most of the wealth now see their incomes grow at the higher rate *r*, enabling them to capture a growing share of the economic pie and to accumulate a larger chunk of productive wealth. The rest of the population, who see a more meager increase in their wages at the rate of *g*, receives a dwindling share of the pie and have little room to save, invest, and increase their ownership of wealth. Thus, the natural tendency of capitalist societies, i.e., societies that allow private investors and entrepreneurs to allocate capital, is toward greater and greater inequality; and this inequality, if left unchecked, can lead to oligarchy and civil unrest.

Piketty's analysis of the growth of inequality has won over many prominent economists, including Nobel Laureates such as Joseph Stiglitz (Stiglitz 2012), Paul Krugman (Krugman 2014), and Robert Solow (Solow 2014). In fact, in his *New York Times* bestselling book on the subject, *The Price of Inequality* (Stiglitz 2012), Stiglitz takes Piketty's analysis a step further. The tendency for wealth and capital to concentrate in a few hands in a market economy, Stiglitz argues, is strengthened by the fact that the elite superrich are able to use their wealth to influence and control the political process. They use this political influence to frame and enforce the "rules of the game" that help maintain and enhance their privileged economic status (Stiglitz 2012: 35–64).

In addition to discussing the inegalitarian implications of the concentration of productive wealth, Stiglitz also focuses on the increasing inequality of income from labor caused by market forces (Stiglitz 2012: 66–80). Both the significant increase in the extent of globalization over the last three decades and the rapid technological changes ushered in by the digital revolution, he argues, have benefited the skilled sections of the workforce in the developed world and have hurt those who are relatively unskilled. The more skilled workers have seen their incomes grow at a fast clip, whereas those who are less skilled and less well-off to begin with have been left further behind.

This Piketty–Stiglitz perspective on the causes of rising income inequality is characterized by its adherence to three key tenets. The *first* of these is that market forces are overwhelmingly responsible for increasing inequality. Whether this increasing inequality stems from the concentration of the ownership of wealth, or from the greater inequality of the incomes earned from work, it is caused by the voluntary interactions of buyers and sellers on the free market. *Second*, economic growth, when it is accompanied by such market-driven increases in inequality, primarily benefits the rich. The poorer sections of society are left behind: the rising tide of growth does not lift all boats when it is accompanied by market-driven increases in inequality.

The *third* tenet deals with the role of government regulation. In the Piketty–Stiglitz view, such interventions are never the cause of rising inequality. Instead, the primary role of the government is to reduce high levels of inequality by redistributing income and wealth from those at the top of the distribution to those at the bottom. Moreover, such interventions do not stifle productivity and growth. They ensure that economic progress benefits all sections of society and not just a narrow elite.

Piketty, for example, emphasizes the important role that a more progressive tax on income and wealth can play in fighting the rising tide of inequality (Piketty 2014: 493–539). Stiglitz, meanwhile, in addition to tax reform, also emphasizes more stringent financial regulations, a more vigorous enforcement of antitrust regulations, labor market reforms in the form of a higher minimum wage and an increased role for labor unions, and a host of other interventions to help reduce inequality and promote more equitable economic growth (Stiglitz 2012: 332–363).

The overarching goal of this book is to critically analyze this Piketty–Stiglitz perspective on inequality. It aims to ask questions and to analyze issues that do not fit into the dominant narrative and are thus relatively underexplored. Are market forces solely responsible for the recent rise in income inequality or have government regulations also contributed their fair share to this phenomenon? Can we differentiate between the effects of market-driven inequality and the inequality caused by government intervention? Does the economic growth that accompanies market-driven inequality always benefit only the elite while leaving the relatively poorer sections of society behind? How does the inequality created by regulation affect those who are less well-off? And does the current discussion on inequality rest on solid empirical foundations? These are some of the important questions that the chapters in this book try to analyze, in the hope of broadening the debate on inequality and adding more nuance and subtlety to discussions on the subject.

The first four chapters of the book analyze these questions from a more theoretical perspective. In Chapter 1, "Capitalism, cronyism and inequality," Randall Holcombe focuses on the relationship between political institutions and income inequality. Over the last three decades, Holcombe notes, the economic and political elite, both part of the 1%, have exercised significant control over the shaping of public policy in America. They have used this power to craft economic policies that benefit them at the expense of the masses, or the 99%. This capture of American political institutions by the 1% and the resulting cronyism, Holcombe argues, has played a significant role in the recent increase in income and wealth inequality.

In Chapter 2, "Globalization and inequality: does anyone lose from free trade?" Donald Boudreaux addresses the much-discussed question of the relationship between free trade and inequality. According to the mainstream perspective on the subject, Boudreaux notes, opening up an economy to international competition creates winners and losers, with the latter consisting primarily of individuals at the lower ends of the income distribution. In this chapter, Boudreaux subjects this claim to critical scrutiny and argues against the notion that there are individuals and households that lose economically from free trade.

The 20th century saw a significant transformation in economic thought: the earlier focus of Classical economists such as Adam Smith and David Hume on the entrepreneurial process of competition gave way to a preoccupation with analyzing states of equilibrium, devoid of uncertainty, entrepreneurship, and dynamic competition. Has this transformation in economic thought had an influence on how economists analyze the benefits of income redistribution? In Chapter 3, "The institutional justice of the market process: entrepreneurship, increasing returns, and income distribution," Peter Boettke, Rosolino A. Candela and Kaitlyn Woltz address this important question. They argue that excluding uncertainty and entrepreneurship from economic analysis has made economists lose sight of how market forces open up new economic opportunities for the poor and of the egalitarian implications of entrepreneurial competition; and that this, in turn, has made economists more open to calls for redistribution.

In Chapter 4, "Growth, inequality, and unfairness: comparing the progressive and classical liberal perspectives," Steven Horwitz examines whether the growth generated by the American economy over the last three decades has benefited the poorer sections of American society. As Horwitz notes, adherents of the Progressive perspective on this issue call for government-led redistribution and a more egalitarian distribution of wealth and income. According to them, redistribution is justified because the economic growth and the accompanying income inequality over the last 30 years has largely benefited a rich minority while leaving the poor behind. Horwitz, however, presents the case for the opposing Classical Liberal perspective on this issue, arguing that households at the lower ends of the income distribution have seen significant improvements in their living standards over the past three decades. Moreover, Horwitz also makes the important point that several forces that increase inequality are actually the product, not of the operation of market forces, but of government interventions into the American economy.

Chapters 5–8 analyze the questions surrounding income inequality through the lens of political economy: they adopt an approach that is more empirical and historical. In Chapter 5, "Government labor policies and the law of unintended consequences," Richard Vedder focuses on a very important question: Have the various government interventions into the American labor market, put in place primarily to help the economically vulnerable sections of society, actually achieved their objective? Vedder argues that, although well-intentioned, policies such as the minimum wage, public assistance programs for the poor, and unemployment insurance benefits have served largely to increase levels of poverty and inequality, primarily by throwing unskilled, low-wage workers out of work and by restricting their access to well-paying jobs.

In Chapter 6, "Government and the economic history of American income inequality," Vincent Geloso subjects the dominant U-curve narrative on income inequality to critical scrutiny. According to this narrative, promoted by prominent scholars of the subject like Piketty and Emmanuel Saez (Piketty and Saez 2003, 2006, 2014; Piketty 2014), high levels of income inequality prevailed in the American economy during the early years of the 20th century, followed by a decline of inequality during the period stretching from the Great Depression to the mid-1970s, and a subsequent sharp increase that commenced in the 1980s. The periods of rising inequality are the result, they argue, of reduced government regulation and a reduction in top tax rates, whereas the sustained decline in the post–World War II era was the result of greater government intervention and a more progressive tax code.

In his chapter, Geloso makes three broad points that pose significant problems for this narrative. First, he argues that it rests on shaky empirical foundations. Second, he shows that, in many instances, the operation of market forces in the postwar era actually helped reduce the gap in living standards between the rich and the poor. And third, he argues that certain government regulations have played an important role in shaping the trend of rising inequality since the early 1980s.

In Chapter 7, "Inequality, monetary policy, and the gold standard," Robert Murphy also criticizes certain aspects of the U-curve narrative on inequality. Whereas proponents of this narrative date the beginning of the upward trend in inequality to sometime around the mid-1980s, Murphy argues that a closer look at the data shows that the level of income inequality began to increase much earlier, during the early 1970s. Keeping this in mind, he makes the case that the significant changes in monetary policy that occurred during that period, particularly Richard Nixon's decision to close the gold window, had significant inegalitarian consequences for the distribution of income. The loosening of monetary policy made possible by the decision to leave the gold standard and provide more discretionary powers to the Federal Reserve, Murphy argues, set in motion economic forces that have made the rich richer while leaving the poor poorer.

In Chapter 8, "Market liberalization and the poor: measuring economic inequality through consumption," G.P. Manish analyzes the impact of economic liberalization on the poorer sections of society in India. After noting that, according to most estimates, the first two decades of liberalization have seen an increase in inequality, especially in urban India, Manish takes a closer look at four consumer goods industries that have been extensively liberalized since reforms began in the early 1990s: televisions, electric fans, mobile phones and cellular services, and scooters and motorcycles. In each of these cases, he finds that a substantial reduction in regulation and an unshackling of competition resulted in a significant increase in the average ownership levels of these goods, especially among households in the lower and middle deciles of the distribution of consumption expenditure, with the increase being especially pronounced in the urban areas. Moreover, this increase in ownership levels was accompanied by significant qualitative improvements in the case of televisions, mobile phones and cellular services, and scooter and motorcycles. Based on this evidence, Manish concludes that, at least in the case of these four industries, the forces of competition have worked to improve the lives of the masses in India.

The last two chapters of the book take a closer look at the empirical foundations that underlie most of the public discourse on inequality. In Chapter 9, "The economic history of taxation and inequality in the United States," Phillip Magness presents a critical analysis of the empirical foundations of the U-curve narrative on income inequality that dominates the work of Piketty. As Magness notes, this narrative rests on the trend of the share of income flowing to the top 1% in the American economy, as calculated by Piketty and others like Emmanuel Saez and Gabriel Zucman from federal income tax data. Magness argues that the U-curve trend in income shares calculated from this data, far from reflecting actual changes in the income distribution, merely reflects changes that have taken place to federal income tax liability and to the overall federal tax base over the course of the 20th century. He thus concludes that many of Piketty's policy proposals, such as moving to a more progressive income tax system, are built on flimsy empirical foundations.

In Chapter 10, "The measurement of income distribution and the measurement of inequality: a critical analysis," Stephen C. Miller takes a closer look at the three main measures used in research on income and wealth inequality: Gini coefficients, income and wealth shares flowing to different quantiles of the population, and measures of income and wealth mobility. The goal of constructing these measures, Miller notes, is to help us measure changes in the underlying economic inequality or in the gap in living standards between individuals or groups of people. In the chapter, Miller argues that these standard measures of inequality fail to necessarily capture and reflect these changes in economic inequality: an argument that has significant implications for how economists use these measures in their research on income and wealth inequality.

The contributions to this volume point to some potentially fruitful lines of future research. The first of these involves a deeper analysis of the impact of market-driven economic growth on the poor. What has the impact of such growth been on the living standards of the relatively poorer sections of society? Have the poor benefited significantly from the recent liberalization that has swept through India, China, and other developing countries? Can they now access a bigger bundle of consumer goods of better quality as compared to the pre-reform era? Similar questions can also be asked of other important market-led episodes of robust economic growth, such as the Industrial Revolution and the recent growth experienced by the United States and the United Kingdom in the era after the reforms ushered in by Reagan and Thatcher. While some of the chapters in this book, especially the ones by Steve Horwitz and G.P. Manish, analyze these questions, much more research is needed to provide a definitive answer to them.

A second line of research revolves around the impact of regulation on the poorer sections of society. Do many common government interventions have effects that are regressive, affecting the poor adversely while having a much smaller negative impact on the rich, or even, in many cases, benefiting the latter economically? While this is a growing area of research, as suggested by many of the chapters in this book, more research on this question can help provide a clearer picture on the impact that regulation has on growth and inequality. Moreover, this question can also be analyzed in a historical manner, with research that focuses on the impact that growth in planned economies like the erstwhile Soviet Union, or in pre-reform India and China, had on the less economically fortunate. Such historical analysis can also facilitate a comparison of how growth in a highly regulated and centrally planned environment has differed from episodes of market-led growth in its impact on the material well-being of all sections of society.

Moreover, some of the contributions to this book, especially the chapter by Randall Holcombe, suggest another line of future research that focuses on the political implications of growing inequality. Both Piketty (2014) and Stiglitz

(2012) suggest that the inherent tendency of market forces to increase income and wealth inequality serves to undermine representative political institutions. This leads them to conclude that unfettered capitalism is incompatible with democracy. But does the source of the problem lie in the economic institutions of capitalism or in the political institutions of a representative democracy? Holcombe, in his chapter, draws on the literature in the field of public choice and argues that representative institutions provide incentives for rampant cronyism and the capture of political institutions by an economic and political elite. There is much research to be done to analyze which of these opposing views is more robust, and on the more fundamental question of whether the institutions of capitalism and democracy are, in fact, incompatible in the face of growing inequality.

Over the past decade, the Piketty–Stiglitz perspective has come to dominate public discourse about economic inequality. Both on the political left and on the right, there are now influential factions that subscribe to some or all of its important tenets. On the left, there was the Occupy Wall Street movement that emerged in the aftermath of the financial crisis of 2008, driven by the belief in a growing divide between the elite of American society and the rest, between the wealthy 1% and the other 99%. The rallying cry of this movement, echoed in the Presidential campaigns of Senator Sanders and Senator Warren, and in the burgeoning Democratic Socialist movement, is to bridge this divide by greater economic regulation and government-led redistribution. On the other side of the political spectrum, meanwhile, several prominent politicians, including President Trump, and a number of important intellectuals are convinced of the inegalitarian implications of globalization. The free movement of goods and services, and the free flow of labor across borders, they argue, harms the least well-off in the American economy.

The chapters in this book offer a different perspective on inequality, and in their main conclusions, differ markedly from the views that currently dominate public discourse on the subject. The implications for public policy that follow from them differ significantly from those that are popular today. Whereas the dominant perspective today calls for increased regulation and significant income and wealth redistribution as the solution to the problems posed by the recent growth of inequality, the chapters in this book suggest that increasing the role of markets and reducing the extent of regulation is the best way to lower inequality while ensuring greater material well-being for all sections of society. In providing this alternative perspective, we hope that this book highlights a fresh and thought-provoking point of view on the subject. And while the readers of this book may not always agree with the conclusions presented in these chapters, we hope that they serve to broaden the discussion on the many vital issues that surround the topic of inequality.

References

Atkinson, A., Piketty, T., and E. Saez. 2011. "Top Incomes in the Long Run of History." *Journal of Economic Literature* 49 (1): 3–71.

Krugman, P. 2014. "Why We're in a New Gilded Age." *The New York Review of Books*, May 8.

Piketty, T. 2014. *Capital in the 21st Century*. Cambridge, MA: Harvard University Press.

Piketty, T., and E. Saez. 2003. "Income Inequality in the United States, 1913–1998." *The Quarterly Journal of Economics* 118 (1): 1–41.

Piketty, T., and E. Saez. 2006. "The Evolution of Top Incomes: A Historical and International Perspective." *American Economic Review* 96 (2): 200–205.

Piketty, T., and E. Saez. 2014. "Inequality in the Long Run." *Science* 344 (6186): 838–843.

Solow, R. 2014. "Thomas Piketty Is Right." *The New Republic*, April 22.

Stiglitz, J. 2012. *The Price of Inequality*. New York: Norton.

1 Capitalism, cronyism, and inequality

Randall G. Holcombe

I. Introduction

Inequality in capitalist economies has been an issue in economics since the beginning of capitalism. Capitalism emerged as a distinct economic system in the 1700s.[1] Pre-capitalist societies were marked with substantial inequality of income and wealth, but that inequality was the result of inherited wealth and inherited status. Some people were born into royalty and nobility and were more prosperous because of their inherited status. Princes were more prosperous than commoners not because of their economic productivity but just by the good fortune of their birth. The emergence of a market economy along with the idea, developed around the same time, of political equality, offered the promise of a more equal society in every way. Thus, while inequality would be expected in a class-based society in which some people, by virtue of their birth, are more privileged than others, capitalism brought with it the idea that people should prosper in relation to their productivity.

While differences in productivity may lead to inequality, two distinct arguments have been advanced to reach the conclusion that capitalism inherently leads to inequality, and that this inequality is not simply the result of differences in productivity but is the result of a system that gives advantages to some over others. One view is that capitalism embodies mechanisms that generate increasing inequality, so that over time incomes and wealth become increasingly unequally distributed, unrelated to individual productivity. Another view is that the economic elite are able to influence public policy to give themselves advantages over the masses. One view does not rule out the other: both could be true. After reviewing these two views, this chapter examines a substantial body of literature supporting the view that inequality is exacerbated by cronyism as the elite are able to manipulate public policy for their own benefit.

II. Capitalism causes growing inequality

As capitalism was in its early stages, Malthus (1798) made the dismal projection that population tends to grow faster than the resources available to support that population, so most people are destined to survive at just a subsistence level of existence. Ricardo (1817) further advanced Malthus's ideas on the scarcity of resources, noting that while the inputs of capital and labor can be increased, land is fixed in supply. Capital can increase through investment, and population growth increases the labor supply. As population grows, the demand for food increases. The most fertile land will tend to be the first used for farming, and population growth means that farming must occur on increasingly less fertile land. As less fertile land is brought into production, the owners of more fertile land can charge a rent equal to the difference in the productivity of their land relative to the least fertile land that is being cultivated. Ricardo (1817: ch. 2) notes that rent arises only because the quantity of land is limited and is not of uniform quality. He says, "The rise of rent is always the effect of the increasing wealth of the country, and of the difficulty of providing food for its augmented population."

As population grows, Ricardo argues that rents increase, squeezing profits and leaving workers at a subsistence level of income. The declining profits slow economic growth as a greater share of income goes to landlords, leaving little for investment and eventually leading to a stagnant economy. Ricardo (1817: ch. 6) observes:

> Long indeed before this period [when the economy stagnates], the very low rate of profits will have arrested all accumulation, and almost the whole produce of the country, after paying the labourers, will be the property of the owners of land and the receivers of tithes and taxes.

In Ricardo's view, wages had to be paid to labor to get people to work, and capital had to earn a profit to get people to invest, but land would be just as productive regardless of the rent paid to it, and regardless of whether it earned any rent at all. Rent does not need to be paid to land to get it to be productive, according to Ricardo, so the growing inequality due to the increasing share of national income going to land owners is unrelated to the productivity of those land owners, and accrues to them only because the capitalist system allows ownership of land and allows land owners to collect rents.[2] Ownership of the means of production – in this case, land – is a feature of capitalism that generates growing inequality.[3]

In Ricardo's analysis, growing income inequality is an inherent feature of capitalism, arising directly from the private ownership of land. Ricardo (1817: ch. 1) began his book with a chapter, "On Value," in which he laid out his labor theory of value.

> The value of a commodity, or the quantity of any other commodity for which it will exchange, depends on the relative quantity of labour which is necessary for its production, and not on the greater or less compensation which is paid for that labour.

Ricardo's ideas were extended by Marx (1906), who argued that if the value of a good is equal to the value of the labor embodied in it, the entire sales price of the good should be paid to laborers. Capitalists are able to exploit labor because of a monetary economy in which labor is sold for money and goods are also sold for money. The capitalists receive the money that is paid for goods but only pay part of it to the laborers, keeping the rest for themselves as surplus value. Capitalism allows this exploitation because capitalists own the capital and therefore control the jobs. Capitalists are not producing anything – the laborers are, following Ricardo's theory of value – but they receive their incomes by taking what rightfully belongs to the laborers. Capitalism, by its nature, naturally generates inequality.

More recently, Piketty (2014) drew the same conclusion that the private ownership of the means of production inherently generates increasing inequality. Capital ownership is not equally distributed, Piketty notes, but is heavily concentrated at the top of the income distribution. The top 10% in the income distribution own most of the capital, and those in the bottom 50% own almost none.[4] The incomes of wage earners grow at the same rate as GDP, a growth rate that Piketty labels g. Capital income grows at the rate of return on capital, r, and Piketty notes that $r > g$, so he concludes that the upper end of the income distribution, which receives the capital income growing at r, will see their incomes rising faster than the incomes of most people whose incomes grow at g. Because of the private ownership of capital, the observation that $r > g$ means that capitalism, by its very nature, generates an increasingly unequal distribution of income.[5]

The staunchest defenders of capitalism acknowledge, and even celebrate, the fact that capitalism results in income inequality. Some people are more productive than others, meaning they contribute more to other people's well-being, and they are compensated more because of it. The theories of Ricardo, Marx, and Piketty are different because the marginal productivity theory of income suggests, from a normative angle, that the people with the higher incomes deserve them because they contribute more to everyone else's well-being. Those who earn more income in the analyses of Ricardo, Marx, and Piketty do not receive their higher incomes because they earn them, but rather because they happen to own the means of production.

In one of the most moving sentences in the economics literature, John Stuart Mill (1848: 208) flirts with the idea of communism, saying:

> If, therefore, the choice were to be made between Communism with all its chances, and the present state of society with all its sufferings and injustices; if the institution of private property necessarily carried with it as a consequence, that the produce of labour should be apportioned as we now see it, almost in inverse ratio to the labour – the largest portions to those who have never worked at all, the next largest to those whose work is almost nominal, and so in a descending scale, the remuneration dwindling as the work grows harder and more disagreeable, until the most fatiguing and exhausting bodily labour cannot count with certainty on being able to earn even the necessaries of life; if this or Communism were the

> alternative, all the difficulties, great or small, of Communism would be but as dust in the balance.

Mill's observation squares with the observations of Ricardo, Marx, and Piketty, that the capitalist system produces not only an inequality of income but also an unfairly unequal distribution of income. Ultimately, Mill concludes that the institutions of capitalism can be modified so that these unfairly unequal outcomes can be addressed, but Mill's observation shows the perception of unfairness in the distribution of income in 19th-century capitalism.[6]

III. Institutions and inequality

In contrast to the view that capitalism inherently generates inequality, many observers conclude that inequality is the product of political institutions. The economic and political elite work together to design institutions to provide them with advantages over the masses. Mill's analysis hints at this, because while the preceding quotation shows his observation about the current state of affairs, he believes that institutions can be restructured to preserve the private ownership of property and also produce a fairer distribution of income. Mill (1848: Book II, ch. 1) says:

> The laws and conditions of production of wealth partake of the character of physical truths. There is nothing optional or arbitrary about them. . . . It is not so with the distribution of wealth. This is a matter of human institutions solely. The things once there, mankind, individually or collectively, can do with them as they like.

One can debate the degree to which Mill's analysis is correct. One can conjecture that if mankind collectively decides "From each according to his ability; to each according to his needs" (Marx 1875), people would have little incentive to produce, so the "laws" of production may depend on the laws of distribution. A larger point in Mill's analysis is that the distribution of income is dependent on the institutional framework within which it is produced. As the early institutionalists observed, capitalism is based on a set of institutions that define and protect property rights and specifies what individuals are allowed to do with their property and what they are prohibited from doing with their property. The distribution of income ultimately is determined by those institutions.

Commons (1924, 1934) emphasizes the way institutions affect all economic outcomes, and de Soto (1989, 2000) shows the effects of institutions on economic outcomes by comparing the institutional structures of less developed with more developed economies. Consider the limited liability corporation, which facilitates equity financing by limiting the risk of the owners of businesses. This has facilitated corporate growth and enabled corporate managers to use the corporate governance structure to increase their incomes relative to other workers lower down in the corporate hierarchy.[7] The regulatory state prevents people from using their property in productive activities they might otherwise choose, sometimes through an explicit prohibition on entry (as with New York taxis) and sometimes through regulations that create a barrier to entry and protect the markets of incumbent firms. Antitrust laws and labor laws govern what businesses are allowed to do and conditions under which people can hire out their labor.

Consider another straightforward example: the legal protection of intellectual property. People can copyright software code and patent formulas for medical drugs, giving them a government-granted and enforced monopoly over the use of those ideas. Fashion designs cannot be copyrighted or patented, nor can recipes for preparing food. If someone designs a new software program or a new drug, government gives the designer an exclusive monopoly right to the intellectual property the person has created, but if someone designs a new fashion line or a new recipe, that intellectual property is not patentable or copyrightable under current law and can be copied by anybody who sees it. Institutional design sometimes gives ownership of intellectual property to its creator and sometimes allows anyone to make use of ideas once they are created. These institutional differences affect the income-earning ability of those who do, or do not, have government-assigned and enforced property rights.

Economists are often prone to depict economic activity in equilibrium models that have no explicit institutional content, just assuming that people enter into voluntary agreements to exchange what they own with what their trading partners own. What they own, and the conditions under which they are allowed to use and exchange it, are determined by institutions, whether or not they are explicitly modeled. Ultimately, these institutions determine the degree of income and wealth inequality.

IV. Inequality: elites and masses

Stiglitz (2012: 59), who writes about the negative impacts of inequality, faults the institutional structure that is defined by the elites for their benefit. He says:

> It's one thing to win a "fair" game. It's quite another to be able to write the rules of the game – and to write them in ways that enhance one's prospects of winning. And it's even worse when you can choose the referees.

The importance of regulatory institutions to economic outcomes, noted in the previous section, prompts Stiglitz (2102:59) to go on to say, "The problem is that leaders in these sectors use their political influence to get people appointed to regulatory agencies who are sympathetic to their perspectives." He later says, "It doesn't have to be this way, but powerful interests ensure that it is." Further commenting on the effects of elites on inequality, Stiglitz (2012: 104–105) says:

> When one interest group holds too much power, it succeeds in getting policies that benefit itself, rather than policies that would benefit society as

a whole. When the wealthiest use their political power to benefit excessively the corporations they control, much-needed revenues are diverted into the pockets of a few instead of benefiting society at large.

Inequality is the result of elite control of the public policy process, Stiglitz argues.

Stiglitz, who is viewed as leaning toward the political left, shares that view with David Stockman, writing from the political right.[8] Stockman (2013: 560) says:

> We have a rigged system – a regime of crony capitalism – where the tax code heavily favors debt and capital gains, and the central bank purposefully enables rampant speculation by propping up the price of financial assets and battering down the cost of leveraged finance.

Stockman (2013: 606) goes on to say, "In truth, the historic boundary between the free market and the state has been eradicated, and therefore anything that can be peddled by crony capitalists . . . is fair game." He further argues (2013: 602) that American government "is no longer a system of democratic choice and governance; it is a tyranny of incumbency and money politics." Commenting on the interaction between economic and political institutions, Stockman (2013: 602) says, "the gangs of crony capitalism will fight tooth and nail to preserve their slice of an imperiled pie, thereby disenfranchising even further ordinary taxpayers and citizens who have no voice in the Washington policy auctions."

While Karl Marx explained how capitalism inherently generates income inequality, Marx and Engels (1848: 10–11) also supported the idea that political institutions advanced the interests of the elite at the expense of the masses.

> Each step in the development of the bourgeoisie was accompanied by a corresponding political advance of that class. . . . [T]he bourgeoisie has at last, since the establishment of modern industry and the world market, conquered for itself, in the modern representative state, exclusive political sway. The executive of the modern state is but a committee for managing the common affairs of the whole bourgeoisie.

Marx and Engels make essentially the same argument that was made by Stiglitz and Stockman.

The idea that the elite control public policy for their own benefit is well-established in political science and sociology. Bentley (1908), Truman (1951), and Mills (1956) are developers of the theory, and more recently, Hacker and Pierson (2010: 290) said, "Where the conventional wisdom confidently declares, 'it's the economy,' we find, again and again, it's the politics.'" They further argue (2010: 6), "Step by step and debate by debate, America's public officials have rewritten the rules of American politics and the American economy in ways that have benefited the few at the expense of the many." Gilens (2012: 235, emphasis in original), also noting a bias in public policy remarks:

> *[A]ll* members of Congress, by dint of their congressional salaries alone, are solidly in the top decile of the American income distribution. Perhaps one reason public policy tends to reflect the preferences of the affluent, then, is simply that policy makers who are themselves affluent pursue policies that reflect their personal values and interests.

In an empirical analysis of Senate roll call voting, Bartels (2008: 260, emphasis in original) finds "that senators' roll call votes were quite responsive to the ideological views of their middle- and high-income constituents. In contrast, the views of low-income constituents had *no* discernable impact on the voting behavior of their senators." The idea that political institutions are biased to further the interests of the elite over the masses is well-established in the literature in political science and sociology, as Holcombe (2015) notes.

V. Public choice support for elite theory

Public choice theory has rarely dealt with inequality as a separate subject matter of inquiry, but several strands of public choice theory can be seen as supporting the idea that public policy tends to favor the elite over the masses, therefore supporting the idea that inequality is a result of political institutions designed to support the economic interests of the elite. One reason that public choice theories themselves rarely address inequality is that public choice rests on a foundation of economic theory that is individualistic. This individualistic approach depicts individuals as the unit of analysis, not collectives. In explaining their public choice approach to readers, Buchanan and Tullock (1962: 12) note their individualistic approach and explain that there is no such thing as the public interest beyond all the individual interests of the members of a group.

> In quite similar fashion, we shall also reject any theory of conception of the collectivity which embodies the exploitation of a ruled by a ruling class. . . . Any conception of State activity that divides the social group into the ruling class and the oppressed class, and that regards the political process as simply a means through which this class dominance is established and then preserved, must be rejected as irrelevant for the discussion which follows, quite independently of the question as to whether or not such conceptions may or may not have been useful for other purposes at other times and places.

Buchanan and Tullock explicitly reject the elite theory described in the previous section, for their purposes, while suggesting it may have been useful for other purposes. This section looks at several strands of public choice theory that are consistent with elite theory even though they were not designed to support it, or to examine inequality.

Interest group theory is one of those areas. Olson (1965), one of the contributions that helped define public choice as an area of inquiry, explains how smaller concentrated interests have an advantage in organizing to use the political process for their benefit, whereas larger groups have more difficulty organizing because individual members have an incentive to free ride on the efforts of others. Furthermore, a transfer from a large group to a small group costs each member of the large group a small amount compared to the concentrated gain of members of the small group. Consider the mandate that motor fuels in the United States contain 10% ethanol, for example. The large group of motorists are forced to buy something they otherwise would choose not to at a small cost, which amounts to a sizable transfer to corn farmers and processors who supply the ethanol that is added to the gasoline. The policy gets political support from the smaller and well-connected corn lobby, but almost no pushback from the poorly organized motorists who pay for the transfer from themselves to the ethanol producers. This transfer is effected by institutions, not through the voluntary exchange activity of individuals in a market economy.

It is a small step to see that the well-connected interest groups who gain the rents from public policies such as this are members of the elite who are able to use their political clout to generate public policies that transfer resources from the masses to themselves, just as Stiglitz and Stockman describe. Olson (1982) describes a more dynamic process whereby over time interest groups become more firmly established in the political process, so entrepreneurial efforts of business people are increasingly directed toward capturing rents generated by government rather than engaging in producing goods and services that consumers value. The increasingly entrenched interests shift their entrepreneurial activities from productive to destructive ends, following Baumol (1990, 1993).

This points directly toward the rent-seeking literature pioneered by Tullock (1967, 1975) and Krueger (1974). Rent-seekers attempt to gain by having government enact policies that transfer income from the masses to themselves, either directly or more commonly through regulatory action that forces the masses to pay for the rents generated for the rent-seekers. Not everyone is in a good position to lobby for rents, however. Rent-seekers must have the political connections that allow them to have a good chance to enact policy changes for their benefit, and the masses are not in a good position to do this. The rent-seeking literature did not set out to analyze inequality, or to comment on class divisions in a society, but it is a small step to see that because most people are not in a position to change public policy for their benefit in this way, rent-seekers are a part of the elite.

Similarly, regulatory capture, described by Stigler (1971), fits comfortably within the elite theory described in the previous section, because few people are in a position to capture regulatory agencies. The capture theory says that over time, regulatory agencies tend to adopt policies that favor the regulated industry over the general public interest, but the masses are not in a position to capture regulatory agencies, whereas those regulated industries can easily be viewed as a part of the elite.

While public choice theory was not developed with a class division in mind, and Buchanan and Tullock specifically disavow its applicability (for their purposes), interest group theory, rent-seeking, and regulatory capture are examples of strands of public choice theory that can be used to support elite theory.

VI. The discontinuity in political power

Consistent with the theories of the previous section, Downs (1957) argues that most voters are rationally ignorant because they realize that their one vote will not affect the outcome of an election. Downs' observation applies not only to voting but also to political participation more generally. This is exactly the point Olson (1965) makes when he talks about the problem of free riders in large groups. In both cases, the masses understand that their efforts in the political arena will have a negligible effect on political outcomes, so they do not collect information or participate in politics, except for their own amusement. Just as sports fans invest substantial amounts in supporting their favorite teams when their support will not affect the outcome, some people are interested in politics and engage in the process because they are interested. But when they do, they must realize that their participation will not affect the outcome. Election results and public policies will be the same regardless of whether they participate.

There is a discontinuity in political power that does not exist with economic power. Somebody with twice as much money as someone else has twice the economic power; someone with ten times as much money has ten times the economic power. Economic power varies continuously with income and wealth. Political power is discontinuous as one outcome applies to everyone, because political decisions have binary outcomes – some win while others lose – and because unlike market outcomes, winners can use the force of government to transfer resources from others to themselves.

Consider the market for soft drinks. Some people prefer Coke, others Pepsi. Everyone buys what they prefer, and they can choose not to buy either if that is their preference. If the choice of soft drinks was a public policy, however, one option would be chosen for everyone, so some win while others lose. And if people decide they do not want soft drinks, government policies can be devised to force them to buy the drinks anyway. Substitute ethanol for soft drinks and it is easy to see that this is true. Those who control the power of government are in a position to create policies that impose costs on the masses for their benefit. The members of the elite have this power; the members of the masses do not.

This discontinuity in politics can be understood within another well-established idea in economics: the Coase theorem (Coase 1960). Some people can bargain among themselves to design public policy, while others face high transaction costs and are left out of the bargaining process. The nucleus of the low-transaction cost group is the legislature. The group is small enough that all members know each other, and the logrolling and vote trading that goes on in legislatures is well known. Applying the Coase theorem, legislative activity will maximize the value of legislation to those in the low-transaction cost group. That is, legislators will design legislation to maximize its value to members of the legislature. That does not imply that legislation will be efficient, or will maximize any conception of social welfare. The nature of government allows those in the legislature to design legislation for their benefit by imposing costs on the masses.

In markets, businesses can only gain resources from consumers if consumers voluntarily agree to pay; but in government, those who design public policy can use the force of government to design it for their benefit by imposing costs on others. Those in the low-transaction cost group are the elite. Those in the high-transaction cost group are the masses.

People can buy their way into the low-transaction cost group by offering benefits to policymakers. Lobbyists develop connections, perhaps through previous contact and always by offering something to policymakers in exchange for favorable public policies. Schweizer (2013) describes the process using real-world examples and is good source for understanding how public policy is actually made; that is, what public choice should actually be studying. The economic elite can buy their way into the low-transaction cost group, so that the economic elite support the political elite in exchange for the political elite supporting the economic elite. Benefits to both groups come at the expense of the masses.

In markets, individuals can put in a little more effort, work some overtime, take a second job, or move to a more demanding job and make a little more money. In politics, individuals can put in a little more effort, volunteer for candidates and parties, and contribute a little more money to political campaigns and have no more influence. That is why they remain rationally ignorant, following Downs (1957), or even rationally irrational, as Caplan (2007) explains. There is a discontinuity in political power that does not exist with economic power that is often overlooked by economists, perhaps because their individualistic approach to politics is averse to analyzing people as members of groups.

Applying the Coase theorem, some people are in the low-transaction cost group and can bargain among themselves to produce policies that benefit their group. Others are in the high-transaction cost group and have no choice but to accept the policies the low-transaction cost group imposes on them through the force of government. While this idea has not found its way into the economics literature, at least to any significant degree, it is well-recognized in political science, sociology, and even in popular analysis of public policy. The low-transaction cost group and the high-transaction cost group have variously been referred to as the bourgeoisie and proletariat, the elites and masses, and the 1% and the 99%.

While there is an economic literature to support this idea that the elite are able to control the public policy process for their benefit, there is also some economic analysis that arrives at a different conclusion. Becker (1983) argues that regardless of the objective of public policy, policymakers have every incentive to implement that policy in the most efficient way possible, because doing so leaves the greatest surplus to be divided among the policymakers. Wittman (1989, 1995) offers an even stronger argument that political institutions have developed so that everyone can participate in the bargaining process. Voters may have limited incentives to collect information about candidates and policies, but political parties and interest groups will collect and disseminate information to voters so that they will make informed choices.

A teacher who does not collect much information about candidates or issues might vote based on the recommendations of the National Education Association (NEA), for example. The individual teacher and also all others who vote according to the NEA's recommendations are able to assert their common interests. Similarly, retirees can rely on recommendations from the American Association of Retired Persons (AARP) to further their political interests. These arguments do not take into account that voting for a candidate means voting for the candidate's entire platform, not just individual issues the voter favors, but this argument could be countered by saying that those platforms are influenced by the lobbying of interest groups prior to an election.

Rather than go into the detailed arguments, note that they come down to the application of the Coase theorem to political decision-making. The arguments of Becker (1983) and Wittman (1989, 1995) amount to saying that the Coase theorem applies to politics, and that political institutions allow everyone to participate in the bargaining process, so everyone is in the low-transaction cost group. Elite theory argues that the masses are excluded from the bargaining process that produces public policy, so the elite produce policies that benefit themselves without taking into account the preferences of the masses. Because government forces everyone to abide by its policies, the elite can use the force of government to impose costs on the masses in a way that cannot be done in the market, where resources change hands only when all parties agree.

VII. Inequality, poverty, and public policy

Inequality of income and wealth under capitalism has been a prominent issue since the advent of capitalism. The generally accepted marginal productivity theory of wages concludes that incomes will be unequally distributed in a capitalist economy because of differences in people's marginal productivity. Beyond that, economists have offered two very different explanations for the unfairness of inequality in capitalist economies. Some economists conclude that growing inequality is an inherent feature of capitalism unrelated to individual productivity. Those who own the means of production see their incomes and wealth increase more rapidly than those who do not, and for the last two centuries, most adherents of this view also conclude that the unequal ownership of the means of production has no economic justification. This view criticizes capitalism because it is an inequitable economic system.

A second view is that inequality in capitalist economies is due to the economic and political elite conspiring to control the political system for their benefit, so the rules under which people interact are biased to favor the well-connected few at the expense of the general public. Inequality is a product of the political system. This view, which refers to the system as crony capitalism or corporatism among other names, has adherents throughout the political spectrum, from political left to political right, and there is substantial support for this view in the academic literature in economics, political science, and sociology.

Both of these views point toward normative policy recommendations, but different ones. If the private ownership of the means of production that characterizes capitalism inherently generates increasing inequality, and if capitalism assigns ownership of the means of production inequitably, then there is an equity argument that the capitalist system should be reformed. If government policy creates inequality because government power is controlled by elites who can design policy for their benefit at the expense of the masses, the political system rather than the economic system should be reformed.

The academic literature, discussed in more detail by Holcombe (2015), offers substantial support for this second view – that inequality is generated as a product of the political process – and Nader (2015) notes strong support for this viewpoint throughout the left–right political spectrum. Despite agreement that this is a problem, the political left and right differ on how it should be remedied. The left argues that more government oversight over those with economic power is the solution, whereas the right argues that government interference with the economy is the cause of the problem and the remedy is less government, not more.

Inequality is inevitable in a system that compensates people in proportion to the value they create for others, as the marginal productivity theory of income concludes. Even if people are compensated in proportion to the value they create for others, some will normatively conclude that income redistribution is desirable. Rawls (1971) is an example. The two views discussed here fall into a different category, however, because both argue that inequality arises because of inherently unfair procedures. One view argues that the private ownership of the means of production generates increasing inequality, and that ownership of the means of production is not determined fairly. The other view argues that the elite control the political process and design the rules of the game so that the economic system benefits them at the expense of the masses. In either case, the inequality created by capitalism is unjust. Regardless of whether inequality is the result of some people owning land (Ricardo), or institutions that unfairly give some ownership of capital (Marx, Piketty), or that the rules are slanted to favor some over others (Marx and Engels, Stiglitz, Stockman), inequality under capitalism is unjust. What are the policy alternatives?

Consider first the view that the private ownership of the means of production generates increasing inequality. The obvious remedy is to limit the private ownership of the means of production. The numerous experiments with this remedy in the 20th century and into the 21st century, from the Soviet Union, Cuba, Venezuela, and North Korea, show that this remedy creates disastrous economic consequences. A weaker remedy would be to combine progressive income taxation with income transfer programs targeted to those at the bottom of the income distribution, but those policies lessen economic growth and dampen the incentives for those at the bottom end of the income distribution to engage in productive activities to improve their economic well-being.

The second view, that inequality is due to elite control of the political process so that the system is designed to benefit those at the top and oppress those at the bottom, is widely recognized, but as noted already, there is no agreement on the remedy. The debate about whether more government oversight would be helpful, or whether government is the problem and less government would lower the ability of some to use government power for their benefit, is ultimately a debate about whether government can be designed to prevent those who hold its power from using that power to further their own interests. The evidence from growing government interference in markets, worldwide since the beginning of the 20th century, suggests that more government control over the economy brings with it more cronyism. Olson (1982) and Holcombe (2015) provide explanations for why this is the case, but in any event, this view of widening inequality traces it to the political system rather than to the inherent characteristics of capitalism.

VIII. Conclusion

A common element in both of the views on inequality under capitalism discussed here is that they offer reasons why those at the top end of the income distribution have high incomes and wealth rather than why those at the bottom end have low incomes and wealth. There is a tendency to equate reducing inequality with also reducing poverty, but with little reflection it is easy to see this is not the case. Bringing down the incomes of those at the top of the income distribution will not necessarily bring up the incomes of those at the bottom. If one is really concerned about the well-being of those who are least well-off, the focus should be on how to improve the well-being of the poor, and not on how much the rich have relative to the poor. In this context, the greatest anti-poverty initiative in the history of the world has been capitalism. Support for free markets and limited government, regardless of any resulting inequality, is the best way to improve the well-being of those at the bottom end of the income distribution.

The focus social scientists have placed on inequality under capitalism for more than two centuries has probably been excessive, because it emphasizes people's relative shares of income rather than focusing on the well-being of the most disadvantaged. Setting aside envy, there seems to be little reason to focus on how much those at the top have rather than concentrating on how to improve the lot of those at the bottom. Looked at in this way, an analysis of capitalism and inequality distracts attention from the more important issue.

Capitalism has made more people better off than any other social innovation in the history of mankind, making the issue of inequality under capitalism all but irrelevant to human well-being.

Notes

1 One might debate this, but I use as my authority Heilbroner (1962), who says that capitalism emerges along with markets for factors of production: land, labor, and capital, and that these markets were largely undeveloped until then. Following Heilbroner's analysis, markets have existed for thousands of years, but capitalism is relatively new. Because the analysis in this chapter is not dependent on this claim, there is no reason to defend it by anything more than a footnote.

2 One can debate whether Ricardo is correct on this point. The existence of land rent, and more specifically, differential rents determined by the market, allocates land to its highest-valued use, so land rent facilitates allocating land uses efficiently. The high rental price of land in downtown Manhattan in New York City is why, despite millions of people in the area, the food they eat is grown in far-away locations and shipped to the city rather than grown nearby.

3 This observation led to George (1879) arguing that government should tax the entire rental value of land, which would raise enough revenue that no other tax would be needed.

4 Breaking from Ricardo and Marx, Piketty includes land ownership with capital, and offers justifications for doing so.

5 Piketty's book was translated from French, but one interesting observation in the translation is that Piketty never says that people earn income. They receive income and can get income, but are never credited with earning it.

6 Sturm and De Haan (2015) undertake an empirical analysis and conclude that nations with institutions that are more capitalist do not have higher levels of income inequality, pushing back against the conclusion of Piketty (2014) and others discussed in the following.

7 This was emphasized by Piketty (2014), who is critical of the high income corporate officers are able to earn because of capitalist institutions. See also the classic article by Berle and Means (1932) for their discussion of the separation of ownership and control in capitalist institutions.

8 Holcombe (2014) notes the similarities in the rhetoric of Stiglitz and Stockman. See also Nader (2014) who argues that there is an unstoppable coalition of individuals from the left to the right ends of the political spectrum who are intent on dismantling the corporate state. Nader is probably overly optimistic in his view that this is an unstoppable coalition, because while there are similar views on the problem across the left–right political spectrum, the remedies they propose are very different.

References

Bartels, Larry M. 2008. *Unequal Democracy: The Political Economy of the New Gilded Age*. New York: Russell Sage Foundation; Princeton, NJ: Princeton University Press.

Baumol, William J. 1990. "Entrepreneurship: Productive, Unproductive, and Destructive." *Journal of Political Economy* 98 (5): 893–921, Part 1, October.

Baumol, William J. 1993. *Entrepreneurship, Management, and the Structure of Payoffs*. Cambridge, MA: MIT Press.

Becker, Gary S. 1983. "A Theory of Competition Among Pressure Groups for Political Influence." *Quarterly Journal of Economics* 98: 371–400, August.

Bentley, Arthur F. 1908. *The Process of Government; A Study of Social Pressures*. Chicago: University of Chicago Press.

Berle, Adolf, and Gardiner Means. 1932. *The Modern Corporation and Private Property*. New Brunswick, NJ: Transaction Publishers.

Buchanan, James M., and Gordon Tullock. 1962. *The Calculus of Consent: Logical Foundations of Constitutional Democracy*. Ann Arbor: University of Michigan Press.

Caplan, Bryan. 2007. *The Myth of the Rational Voter*. Princeton, NJ: Princeton University Press.

Coase, Ronald H. 1960. "The Problem of Social Cost." *Journal of Law & Economics* 3: 1–44.

Commons, John R. 1924. *The Legal Foundations of Capitalism*. Madison: University of Wisconsin Press.

Commons, John R. 1934. *Institutional Economics: Its Place in Political Economy*. New York: Macmillan.

de Soto, Hernando. 1989. *The Other Path: The Invisible Revolution in the Third World*. New York: Harper & Row.

de Soto, Hernando. 2000. *The Mystery of Capital: Why Capitalism Triumphs in the West and Fails Everywhere Else*. New York: Basic Books.

Downs, Anthony. 1957. *An Economic Theory of Democracy*. New York: Harper & Row.

George, Henry. 1879. *Progress and Poverty: An Inquiry into the Cause of Industrial Depressions and of Increase of Want with Increase of Wealth: The Remedy*. New York: D. Appleton and Company.

Gilens, Martin. 2012. *Affluence and Influence: Economic Inequality and Political Power in America*. New York: Russell Sage Foundation and Princeton University Press.

Hacker, Jacob S., and Paul Pierson. 2010. *Winner-Take-All Politics: How Washington Made the Rich Richer – and Turned Its Back on the Middle Class*. New York: Simon & Schuster.

Heilbroner, Robert L. 1962. *The Making of Economic Society*. Englewood Cliffs, NJ: Prentice-Hall.

Holcombe, Randall G. 2014. "What Stiglitz and Stockman Have in Common." *Cato Journal* 34 (3): 569–579, Fall.

Holcombe, Randall G. 2015. "Political Capitalism." *Cato Journal* 35 (1): 41–66, Winter.

Krueger, Anne O. 1974. "The Political Economy of the Rent-Seeking Society." *American Economic Review* 64: 291–303, June.

Malthus, Thomas Robert. 1798. *An Essay on the Principle of Population*. London: J. Johnson. Available at wwwleconlib.org/library/Malthus/malPop.html.

Marx, Karl. 1875. "Critique of the Gotha Program." In Karl Marx and Friedrich Engels, eds., *Selected Works*, vol. 3. Moscow: Progress Publishers, pp. 13–30.

Marx, Karl. 1906. *Capital*. Chicago: Charles H. Kerr & Company.

Marx, Karl, and Friedrich Engels. 1948 [1848]. *The Communist Manifesto*. New York: International Publishers.

Mill, John Stuart. 1920 [1848]. *Principles of Political Economy with Some of Their Applications to Social Philosophy*. London: Longmans, Green, and Co.

Mills, C. Wright. 1956. *The Power Elite*. Oxford: Oxford University Press.

Nader, Ralph. 2014. *Unstoppable: The Emerging Left-Right Alliance to Dismantle the Corporate State*. New York: Nation Books.

Olson, Mancur. 1965. *The Logic of Collective Action*. Cambridge, MA: Harvard University Press.

Olson, Mancur. 1982. *The Rise and Decline of Nations*. New Haven: Yale University Press.

Piketty, Thomas. 2014. *Capital in the Twenty-First Century*. Cambridge, MA: Harvard University Press.

Rawls, John. 1971. *A Theory of Justice*. Cambridge, MA: The Belknap Press of Harvard University Press.

Ricardo, David. 1817 [1951]. *On the Principles of Political Economy and Taxation*, 3rd ed. London: John Murray. Available at www.econlib.org/library/Ricardo/ricP.html.

Schweizer, Peter. 2013. *Extortion: How Politicians Extract Your Money, Buy Votes, and Line Their Own Pockets*. Boston: Houghton Mifflin Harcourt.

Stigler, George J. 1971. "The Theory of Economic Regulation." *Bell Journal of Economics and Management Science* 2 (1): 3–21, Spring.

Stiglitz, Joseph E. 2012. *The Price of Inequality: How Today's Divided Society Endangers the Future*. New York: Norton.

Stockman, David A. 2013. *The Great Deformation: The Corruption of Capitalism in America*. New York: Public Affairs Press.

Sturm, Jan-Egbert, and Jakob De Haan. 2015. "Income Inequality, Capitalism, and Ethno-Linguistic Fractionalization." *American Economic Review* 105 (5): 593–597, May.

Truman, David B. 1951. *The Governmental Process*. New York: Alfred A. Knopf.

Tullock, Gordon. 1967. "The Welfare Cost of Tariffs, Monopolies, and Theft." *Western Economic Journal* 5: 224–232, June.

Tullock, Gordon. 1975. "The Transitional Gains Trap." *Bell Journal of Economics* 6: 671–678, Autumn.

Wittman, Donald A. 1989. "Why Democracies Produce Efficient Results." *Journal of Political Economy* 97 (6): 1395–1424, December.

Wittman, Donald A. 1995. *The Myth of Democratic Failure*. Chicago: University of Chicago Press.

2 Globalization and inequality

Does anyone lose from free trade?

Donald J. Boudreaux

I. Introduction

How might free (or *freer*) international trade uniquely affect economic inequality? The qualifier "uniquely" is vital. If free international trade affects inequality only by first affecting some other economic phenomenon – and if this other phenomenon affects inequality even in the absence of trade – then whatever effects on inequality might be ascribed to trade are really effects properly ascribed instead to the other phenomenon.

The most obvious and germane example of one such other phenomenon is economic growth. Economists since Adam Smith have convincingly argued that free international trade is a major source of economic growth.[1] But because trade isn't the sole source of economic growth –and because inequality is affected by economic growth regardless of the causes of that growth – all questions about how trade affects inequality through trade's effect on economic growth are really questions about how inequality is affected by economic growth and not about how inequality is affected by trade as such.

Does growth inevitably promote greater inequality? Does rising inequality matter if growth raises everyone's absolute standard of living? Can government redistribution policies reduce inequality without reducing – or without reducing to unacceptable levels – economic growth? Do actual government policies that are ostensibly meant to reduce inequality affect growth? If so, in what direction? And if such government policies slow economic growth, how much growth is acceptable to sacrifice in exchange for greater equality? As interesting and as important as these questions are, they are readily recognized as being about how inequality is affected by growth (and by government policies of redistribution) and not about how inequality is affected by trade as such. In this chapter, I ignore all such questions.

There is, however, one channel through which trade is believed to uniquely promote inequality. This channel is trade's alleged creation of "winners" and "losers." At the most basic level, the simple fact that trade destroys some particular jobs is proclaimed by nearly everyone to be proof that trade has "losers." And if those who lose come disproportionately from the lower ranks of the income distribution, then trade thereby fuels inequality. A more sophisticated version of this argument is rooted in the Stolper–Samuelson theorem, which identifies trade's impact on factor prices as a potential source of greater inequality. Importantly, both versions of the "trade-creates-winners-and-losers" argument can be described, using the language of economics, as arguments that trade fails to satisfy the Paretian criterion for efficiency.

I argue below that neither version of the "trade-creates-winners-and-losers" argument withstands scrutiny. Central to my argument is the demonstration that, when properly analyzed, trade is revealed in fact to satisfy the Paretian criterion for efficiency, and this demonstration undermines the widespread sense that trade promotes inequality in any way that is policy-relevant.[2]

II. All competitions create "winners" and "losers"

The claim that free trade has losers as well as winners is, unsurprisingly, featured front and center in the arguments made by free-trade opponents and skeptics. Noah Smith's statement is representative: "We've known since the time of David Ricardo that even if free trade makes a country richer overall, many of the people within that country can be left worse off."[3] Another example is from Dani Rodrik: "Economists have long known that trade liberalization causes income redistribution and *absolute* losses for some groups, even as it enlarges a country's overall economic pie. Therefore, trade deals unambiguously enhance national wellbeing only to the extent that winners compensate losers."[4] But the claim that trade has losers is just as frequently and predictably made by free-trade *proponents*. To pick just one among countless examples: the Cato Institute's Brink Lindsey – whose credentials as a knowledgeable, principled, and eloquent free trader are beyond question – describes as a "hard truth" the claim that "International trade creates losers as well as winners."[5]

The conventional economic case for free trade rests on the demonstration that the value of the winners' gains from expanded trade consistently exceeds the value of the losers' losses. But as even Brink Lindsey says, losers there certainly are. Lindsey's justification for free trade in light of the apparent reality of these losers is representative of those offered by free-trade proponents: "The net result" of freer trade is "higher productivity, and wages and living standards, for the country as a whole."[6] Put into the language of welfare economics, the gains enjoyed by free-trade winners are consistently large enough to allow these winners, in principle, to fully compensate free-trade losers and still enjoy positive gains. In short, free trade is widely believed by economists to be Kaldor–Hicks efficient[7] and, hence justified as a matter of public policy.[8]

Free-trade opponents differ from its proponents in believing that either the size of the total gains from free trade too often falls short of the size of the total losses or, even if the gains from free trade are always larger than the losses, free trade – as Rodrik insists – is unambiguously justified only if its winners actually compensate its losers. Therefore (trade opponents and skeptics argue), because in reality free-trade winners never compensate its losers, free trade in reality is not Pareto efficient and, thus, should enjoy no general presumption of desirability. In other words, trade opponents and skeptics insist that a general presumption in favor of free trade would be justified only if trade were Pareto efficient. Yet because trade, at best, is merely Kaldor–Hicks efficient, economists err in blindly supporting free trade.[9]

And so, we here encounter the most obvious way that trade creates inequalities: while yielding benefits to some, it positively harms others – others who are popularly believed to be overwhelmingly workers in the lower half of the income distribution.[10] The fact that the aggregate size of the winners' gains exceeds the aggregate size of the losers' losses neither eliminates this inequality nor lightens the burdens borne by the flesh-and-blood losers if the "winners" do not actually compensate the "losers."

The argument that trade is not Pareto efficient is mistaken, for two reasons. First, this argument untenably treats international trade and competition differently from domestic trade and competition. Second, this argument assesses the effects of trade over a time period that is illegitimately short. The argument that trade has losers – and, hence, the argument that trade is not Pareto efficient – ignores both the economically relevant past and the economically relevant future.

III. International trade is one among many manifestations of competition

Discussions of the job and wage losses caused by international trade are, almost without exception, conducted as if there is something unique about competition posed by foreign competitors. As Brink Lindsey (2009) correctly explains, however, foreign competition is not unique:

> The problem of displaced workers is real, but it is in no way unique to trade. At the heart of the market economy's dynamism is Schumpeterian "creative destruction" – and it can get a little messy. However, most Americans understand – in the purely domestic context, at least – that the opportunities created by competition more than make up for the turmoil. Nobody sheds many tears for bank tellers put out of work by ATM machines, or receptionists laid off because of voice mail; job churn generated by technological progress is an accepted fact of life. In the end, protectionist arguments rely on a baseless double standard – that, somehow, it's worse to lose your job to a foreigner than to a machine.

All of this is true and relevant. But this passage appears in the same essay in which Lindsey writes that it is a "hard truth" that trade has "losers." This "loser" language – used even by the very finest trade analysts – is mistaken and misleading. Saying that trade has losers, as Lindsey does in the essay quoted here, suggests that stopping trade would eliminate or at least reduce such losses. Yet as Lindsey correctly notes, jobs and businesses in market economies are routinely destroyed even when international trade plays no role.[11] Therefore, even if (contrary to fact) people who lose jobs in market economies are appropriately described as "losers," describing *trade* as producing such "losers" conveys the false impression that trade's role in inflicting such losses is unique. Such a description of trade wrongly suggests that the particular kind of losses that it inflicts can be eliminated if trade is stopped.

This point warrants emphasis. Saying that trade with foreigners creates losers is akin to saying that trade with women creates losers. After all, it's undeniable that when women entrepreneurs introduce new products or devise more efficient means of production that some workers lose jobs and some business owners lose profits. Yet no one would write that it's a "hard truth" that trade with women creates losers. It is obvious that the sex of competitors is utterly without economic relevance. Workers who lose jobs to innovations introduced by entrepreneurs who happen to be female are properly regarded as losing jobs simply to market competition, with nothing uniquely determined by the competitors' sex. No analytical insight or improved perspective would be gained, and much confusion (and political mischief) would be sown, by singling out competition coming from women as a unique source of gains and losses.

For the same reason, competition coming from producers who happen to be foreign is also no unique source of losses. Competition that domestic producers endure from foreign rivals differs in precisely *zero* economically relevant ways from competition that domestic producers endure from each other.

This reality is clearly seen by focusing on the fact that no firm succeeds in making sales in a free market unless it persuades consumers to buy its outputs. It is ultimately the choice of the consumer that determines which firms sell fewer and which firms sell more outputs. And the number of different reasons that motivate consumers to change the ways they spend their money is practically uncountable. Just as only one of these reasons is greater availability of goods produced by women-owned firms, only one of these reasons is greater availability of goods produced by foreign-located firms.

Consumer Frank who chooses today to buy fewer shirts than he bought yesterday from Harry the Haberdasher causes Harry's sales to fall regardless of the particular reason for Frank's choice. Perhaps Frank retired and no longer needs as many shirts as before. Perhaps Frank's tastes have changed so that now he wears only t-shirts (which Harry doesn't sell). Perhaps Frank has taken up sewing as a hobby and now makes more of his own shirts. Perhaps Frank starts buying more of his shirts from Charlene the Shirt Maker, who last month opened a competing shop across the street from Harry's. Or perhaps Frank buys more of his shirts online directly from a tailor in Hong Kong.

In each of these examples, Harry suffers lost sales, but only the last example involves international trade. From Harry's perspective, each dollar of lost sales is a dollar of lost sales regardless of where that dollar is now instead spent. Harry suffers just as much when Frank shifts his patronage from Harry's shop to Charlene's shop across the street as when Frank shifts his patronage from Harry's shop to the tailor shop in Hong Kong. Therefore, to talk about the costs of *international* trade – or about the losers from *international* trade – is to use language that sneaks into the discussion the illegitimate suggestion that international trade uniquely imposes costs or uniquely causes losses. Talking of the losses *from trade* suggests that if international trade is restricted, such losses would be fewer and incurred less frequently. But such a suggestion would be incorrect.

Recognizing that trade is merely one manifestation of competition reveals the flaw in using trade's apparent failure to satisfy the Pareto-efficiency criterion as a justification for restricting trade. If trade with foreigners fails to satisfy the Pareto criterion, then trade with women fails to satisfy this criterion. And if restrictions on trade with foreigners are thereby justified, then restrictions on trade with women are equally justified. In both cases, one can identify apparent losers who are not actually compensated by the winners. Until and unless one is prepared to argue that economic competition itself is not Pareto efficient, singling out international trade as the one manifestation of competition that does not satisfy the Pareto criterion is inexcusably arbitrary and unjustifiably fuels demands for government to restrict international trade in order to protect its "losers."

Yet the case against condemning trade for its failure to satisfy the Paretian criterion is stronger still. As I argue in the next section, trade *does* satisfy the Paretian criterion.

IV. An appropriate time period: the relevant past

There's no denying that today's changes in trade patterns destroy some workers' jobs *today* and reduce some people's incomes *today*. It is these trade-induced losses that are believed to render trade in violation of Pareto's criterion for efficiency. Yet this conclusion about trade is faulty.

If the economy as it is today had sprung randomly yet fully formed into existence last night, then the destroyed jobs and lowered incomes suffered today by domestic producers because of today's greater import penetration might legitimately be called "losses." But today's economic arrangements are the product of a long series of nonrandom and interconnected past events. These past events include a wide array of consumption and production opportunities made possible by international trade. Many of the jobs that are destroyed today by trade were themselves, in the past, created by trade. And much of the real income that workers today do not wish to lose to trade would not exist were it not for trade. Viewing today's economic arrangements and economic changes as part of a stream of economic arrangements and changes that play out over time reveals that what appear today to be "losers" from trade are, in fact, not only not losers from trade but are actually *winners* from trade.

Consider, for example, workers in a Boeing plant that manufactures 787 wide-body jets, the fuselages of which are made of aluminum. The United States imports more than $1 billion worth of aluminum each month.[12] Regardless of whether Boeing itself uses imported or American-made aluminum to produce its airplanes, aluminum imports into America ensure that the prices that Boeing pays for aluminum are lower than they would be in the absence of these imports. Boeing's costs of production, in turn, are kept lower by this international trade in aluminum, allowing Boeing to produce and sell more planes – and thereby to employ more workers.

The jobs of some of Boeing's workers were thus created by international trade. If intensified competition today from Airbus or Bombardier causes Boeing to lose enough sales that it lays off some workers, in what way are these laid-off workers appropriately described as trade's *losers*? The very jobs that they are now losing, and would prefer not to lose, were created and sustained by trade. These jobs would not have existed in the absence of trade. So, to count workers who today lose such jobs as trade's "losers" is to lose sight of the economically relevant past. It is to chalk up an effect (that is, today's job losses) on trade's debit side while failing to chalk up on trade's credit side a series of effects that are economically inseparable from the effect that is chalked up on the debit side.

Suppose that worker Smith today, at the age of 21, has two employment options, 1 and 2. Option 1 is a single job with guaranteed lifetime employment and a stream of lifetime income with a certain net present value today of $1 million. Option 2 is quite different. Option 2 is the exposure to an array of several different job prospects over time, none of which comes with any guarantees. With option 2, Smith can at any time be fired from his current job. And he is constantly confronted with the chance of keeping that job (or of getting a new job) only if he agrees to take a cut in pay. But the expected net present value today of option 2 is $2 million. Which option will Smith choose?

If Smith is very risk averse, he might choose option 1. But surely no one would be surprised if instead Smith chooses option 2. And if Smith does choose option 2, he is – in making this choice – willingly incurring the risk of losing jobs and income in the future. Smith voluntarily incurs this risk in exchange for the opportunity to earn income higher than he would be guaranteed to earn with option 1. In effect, in choosing option 2, Smith purchases the chance of earning a larger stream of lifetime income by agreeing to subject himself to the possibility of temporary – or even permanent – job loss, the final result of which might be a stream of lifetime income that in the end is less than Smith would have earned had he instead chosen option 1. The price that Smith pays for the opportunity to earn a lifetime stream of income higher than is offered by the option with more security is exposure to greater job and income insecurity.

In short, the downside of option 2 is internalized on Smith no less than is the upside. Indeed, Smith's choice of option 2 is no different in essence from the cost that Smith incurs in any other exchange that he makes in the market. Smith is compensated for these losses by the expected gains that he achieves by actively engaging in the competitive marketplace. *All* market exchanges have attendant costs. Yet those who incur these costs are not thereby classified as "losers" from exchange. The parallel between simple market exchanges and the job creation and destruction caused by international trade is instructive.

Consider a different example, this one of a more realistic market exchange: Smith buys a new Chevy Malibu for $20,000. Of course, Smith would prefer to get the new car without having to pay for it. But if he voluntarily gives to the Chevy dealer $20,000 in exchange for the car, we conclude correctly that Smith gains from this transaction. The car dealer, of course, also gains even though he would prefer to get the $20,000 without having to give up a car in exchange. We do not conclude that Smith's turning over $20,000 to the car dealer is evidence that in the new-car market Smith is a "loser." Nor do we conclude that the car dealer's turning over the car to Smith is evidence that in the new-car market the car dealer is a "loser." We recognize that this exchange satisfies the Pareto criterion for Smith and the car dealer: while both Smith and the car dealer each incur a *cost* in this exchange, both Smith and the car dealer are made better off as a result. Each of their "losses" is more than fully compensated by each of their gains.

Let's alter the car-buying example just a bit: suppose now that Smith buys the new Chevy Malibu by taking out a car loan. Smith gets the car today and is required to pay nothing for it until one month from today. If we begin our analysis one month from today, when Smith's first monthly loan payment is due, it appears that financial markets harm Smith. In the credit market Smith appears to be a loser. We see the burden he endures in paying his creditor, while we miss the associated benefit that Smith enjoys – a *net* benefit that Smith would not enjoy had he no access to credit markets.

Again, from a Paretian perspective, the fact that Smith incurs a *cost* to acquire a new car is, correctly, never interpreted as the competitive price system inflicting on Smith a *loss*. Smith's payment to the Chevy dealership is not a Paretian loss. Likewise, from a Paretian perspective, the fact that Smith is obliged to submit a payment to a creditor today who loaned him the funds to buy a car last month is, again correctly, never interpreted as financial markets inflicting on Smith a *loss*. Smith's loan payments are not Paretian losses. In the case of Smith buying a car using borrowed funds, everyone gains – the Chevy dealer, the creditor, and Smith – with no one losing. This purchase is clearly a Pareto-efficient move.

The same is true for international trade. When evaluated over the appropriate length of time, job and income losses suffered today by workers and other producers are seen to be the prices paid for those jobs in the first place, as well as for the high purchasing power of the incomes earned at those, and other, jobs. While worker Smith would prefer to get the higher stream of lifetime income without having to pay for it (in the form of sacrificing valuable job and income security), he nevertheless – like consumer Smith who willingly agrees to pay to acquire a new car – prefers having the opportunity to earn the higher stream of lifetime income over having greater job security. In the case of acquiring the new car, as well as in the case of acquiring access to a chance to earn a higher stream of lifetime, Smith's obligation to pay for the superior options inflicts on him no losses. In neither of these cases is it legitimate to conclude that Smith "loses" because he pays the price for the better option.

Costs are not losses. Each of these economic activities satisfies the Pareto criterion for efficiency.

Furthermore, it is widely and correctly recognized that if government relieves Smith of the necessity of paying these costs of acquiring a new car, then, while Smith today might receive additional benefits that he did not bargain for – namely, a car that he doesn't pay for – economic harm is thereby inflicted not only on Smith in the future but also on nearly everyone else in the economy. Sellers who fear that they will be unable to collect payments for the goods and services that they sell will stop selling goods and services. Creditors who fear that they will be unable to collect from debtors to whom they extend credit will stop extending credit. For the same reasons, government efforts to protect workers and other producers from today's downside consequences of trade – consequences wrongly called "losses" – will over time only reduce these producers' and others' access to beneficial exchange opportunities with foreigners. Highly ironically, government restrictions justified by imaginary Paretian losses end up unleashing not only very real Paretian losses but also losses over time in many cases on the very people the restrictions are meant to protect.

V. An appropriate time period: the relevant future

The most likely response to the argument that today's trade-induced "losses" are really nothing more than internalized costs of trade is that workers do not actually make such trade-offs. Workers, if they don't simply seize whatever are the best jobs open to them at the moment, neither estimate with any precision the chance of each available job to be destroyed in the future by international trade nor weigh any such estimates against differences in the wages offered by these various jobs.

I disagree with this response. I believe that workers generally make current choices in the labor market with eyes to the future and, hence, many workers *do* make such estimates, albeit not as consciously or as precisely as theorists can imagine. (No one in reality ever does *anything* as consciously and as precisely as theorists can imagine!) While exceptions surely exist, nearly every worker in the developed world confronts when young various broad career options. Attend college or not? Major in nursing, in education, or in accounting? Pursue an MBA, an MD, or a JD? Accept this job offer or that job offer? Although the relevant variables for making such decisions are many, it is unrealistic to suppose that job security is not among these variables.[13]

It is also unrealistic to imagine that individuals have no or only inaccurate information to rely upon when assessing the security of different jobs. At one extreme, young men and women who enlist in the military know the terms of enlistment and can be confident that the option to reenlist will be available in the future. At the other extreme, first-time entrepreneurs who launch new firms selling never-before-available goods or services understand that the probability of failure is high. In between is a wide spectrum of different jobs and career paths, nearly every one of which is accompanied by some public knowledge about its pay, amenities, prestige, difficulty, and security.

This public knowledge doesn't have to be perfect in order for workers with different preferences for job security to sort themselves more or less accurately into different jobs with different degrees of security. People with a very high demand for job security will, at the margin, choose government jobs over private-sector jobs. They will tend to choose jobs in large, long-established firms over jobs in small upstart firms funded with venture capital. They are more likely to move, in search of work, away from geographical locations that are in economic decline to geographical locations that are growing and seem likely to continue to grow. People with different preferences for job security choose differently.

Just as importantly, employers have incentives to discover if and how strongly workers want job security. All other things equal, employers who offer greater job security can pay their workers lower wages than are paid by employers who offer less job security. Workers who do not value additional job security enough to accept lower wages will work in jobs that pay more but offer less security, while workers who have higher demands for job security will be attracted to jobs that offer greater security but with lower wages. This sorting process makes all workers better off even though a result is greater inequality in monetary incomes.

Employers have every incentive to supply additional units of such security as long as the costs of supplying additional units of job security fall short of the benefits employers receive in return in the form of lower wage bills. Therefore, the greater are workers' demands for job security, the greater are the reductions in wages and fringe benefits that workers are willing to accept in exchange for increased job security – and the greater are employers' abilities and willingness to supply such security.

Given that labor markets are generally competitive, we can reasonably presume that the market today supplies something close to optimal levels of job security for different workers. The amount of such security wasn't greater earlier than it is now because the cuts in wages and fringe benefits that workers would have to accept in exchange for greater security are judged by workers to be too great. But it cannot be denied that different jobs supply different degrees of job security. Nor can it be denied that many jobs, perhaps most, supply at least *some* degree of job security, even if such security does not appear as a formal term in employment contracts. (Clerks in a McDonald's restaurant are not laid off after one day of lower-than-expected sales volume.) If nothing else, workers form plausibly correct expectations about just how secure each job is, and wages adjust up or down to reflect these expectations.

Insofar as workers not only can bargain for greater job security (and can choose among jobs offering different degrees of job security) but also can form plausibly correct expectations about just how secure each job is, the loss of jobs to competition is not a "loss" imposed on workers. Such job losses were – or should have been – expected with some probability higher than zero. In each of the many cases in which a worker chooses a higher-paying but less-secure job over a lower-paying but more-secure alternative, each such worker has already been paid to endure the risk of job loss. But even in those cases in which a worker makes no such explicit choice, the risks of job loss enter workers' expectations. And these expectations are reflected in the prevailing pattern of wage rates. *Ceteris paribus*, the greater the likelihood of a job being destroyed, the higher the wage. The resulting differential in wages compensates workers in relatively insecure jobs for bearing relatively high risks of job loss.

Put differently, because by the very nature of a market economy no producer is guaranteed a continuing market for his or her services (beyond what he or she contracts for), the loss by workers and other producers of jobs and incomes when competitive forces turn against them is not an economically relevant loss. A foundational rule of a market economy is that production is a means to promote consumption. It's not the reverse. Production is justified only if, to the extent, and as long as it is judged to support consumption, with this judgment rendered continuously by consumers in the market spending – and withholding the spending of – their own money.

Choosing to enter the market as a producer is to choose to play by this rule.[14] The gain that you anticipate is a greater ability to consume over time. Among the conditions that you agree to in exchange for this (very high) probability of increased consumption opportunities is to adjust yourself to the demands of consumers rather than insisting that consumers adjust themselves to your demands as a producer. Having actually to adjust yourself as a producer to the demands of consumers, therefore, is part of the bargain. The necessity of making such adjustments is a cost, but it is not a loss. To agree to make such adjustments is simply to agree to pay part of the necessary price for the opportunity to enjoy maximum possible consumption opportunities over time. Paying this price – that is, making such adjustments if and when they are called for – is no more a loss than it is a "loss" to pay the price you pay to buy an automobile that you wish to drive or to buy a house that you wish to own.

It follows that the way in which trade is most widely regarded, at least by the general public, as promoting inequality is a fallacy. Even without the actual payments of Kaldor–Hicks compensation, international trade, like any other manifestation of market competition, does not create winners at the expense of "losers." Over time, everyone who participates in this "game" wins. Therefore, contrary to Dani Rodrik's (and Paul Krugman's) claim, an unambiguously strong case for a policy of free trade does not require that those whose incomes rise today as a result of trade (the so-called "winners") compensate those whose incomes fall today as a result of trade (the alleged "losers"). In short, when judged over an appropriate span of time, a policy of free trade is Pareto superior to a policy of obstructing trade to protect particular jobs and industries.[15]

VI. Trade-induced changes in factor prices

What about the concern that trade creates larger inequalities in monetary incomes? As with the mistaken claim that trade uniquely creates losers – or that trade uniquely imposes costs on workers and other producers who must adjust to changes in trade patterns – the claim that trade creates larger inequalities in monetary incomes rests on an unjustified distinction between foreign competition and home-grown competition. It is true that expanded trade can create larger differences in monetary incomes. Yet the process through which trade might have this effect is simply a variety of market competition that in principle is no more likely when commerce occurs with foreigners as when it occurs exclusively with fellow citizens.

The standard account of how trade might make incomes more unequal starts with the Stolper–Samuelson theorem.[16] According to this theorem, with freer trade, each country specializes more heavily in supplying to the global economy goods and services the production of which uses relatively intensively that country's abundant factor of production. At the same time, each country increases its imports of – and, hence, reduces its production of – goods and services, the production of which uses relatively intensively that country's more-scarce factor of production.

For example, suppose that the United States has an abundance of high-skilled labor relative to low-skilled labor, while China has an abundance of low-skilled labor relative to high-skilled labor. America will thus have a comparative advantage at supplying goods and services the production of which intensively uses high-skilled labor; China will have a comparative advantage at supplying goods and services, the production of which intensively uses low-skilled labor. Liberalization of trade between the United States and China will result in Americans exporting high-skilled labor-intensive outputs and importing low-skilled labor-intensive outputs. (In China, the pattern of exports and imports will be the opposite.) Because America's expanding industries use low-skilled labor less intensively than do America's shrinking industries, freer trade causes the release from import-competing industries of a greater quantity of America's more-scarce factor of production (low-skilled labor) than is absorbed into the expanding export industries. One result is that the price of low-skilled labor falls not only relative to that of high-skilled labor but also absolutely. Under these assumed conditions, it follows that restricting Americans' freedom to buy imports from China can raise both the relative and absolute incomes of low-skilled workers in America.

It follows also, under these assumed conditions, that freer trade increases income inequality in America: freer trade raises the relative (and absolute) pay of high-skilled workers as it lowers that of low-skilled workers. Because high-skilled workers have already (that is, before trade is liberalized) earned higher wages than do low-skilled workers, freer trade further increases this inequality in pay.

Rivers of ink have been spilled in efforts to spell out clearly the precise conditions under which the Stolper–Samuelson theorem holds.[17] I here am not concerned with these nuances. Instead, I argue that increased demand for an economy's abundant factors of production (relative to the demand for an economy's more-scarce factors of production) can arise from purely domestic changes in the patterns of competition. That is, the very same forces that raise the relative demands for an economy's abundant factors of production when competition intensifies across international borders are just as likely to raise the relative demands for an economy's abundant factors when competition intensifies internally.

Consider an entrepreneur whose actions are confined exclusively to the domestic market. Let this entrepreneur have a creative idea for a new product to produce and sell domestically – say, a battery-powered and app-controlled mousetrap. To build this better mousetrap, suppose that the entrepreneur chooses a production method that uses intensively the economy's abundant factor of production. As production in this economy shifts in the direction of using the abundant factor more intensively, the very same forces identified by Stopler and Samuelson work to raise the pay of the abundant factor relative to the pay of the more-scarce factor. If this economy is one in which the abundant factor is high-skilled labor (or some other relatively highly paid factor) and the more-scarce factor is low-skilled labor, this purely domestic innovation of a better mousetrap will further raise the wages of high-skilled labor relative to the wages of low-skilled labor. Monetary incomes will thus become more unequal.

Furthermore, as additional entrepreneurial innovations occur in this economy, the production processes to which they give rise are more likely than not to use intensively this economy's relatively abundant factor of production. The reason for this outcome is precisely the same as the reason a country whose international trade expands is likely to export more goods or services, the production of which use intensively that country's relatively abundant factor. Compared to the relatively more-scarce factor, the relatively abundant factor – being relatively inexpensive – is more attractive for use in production.

The upshot is that *any* changes in the pattern of trade, specialization, and production[18] that increase the demand for a country's abundant factor relative to the demand for its more-scarce factor is likely to raise the pay of the abundant factor relative to that of the more-scarce factor. And so, any country in which freer trade would – through such changes in relative factor prices – result in greater income inequality is a country in which *any* market-driven change in the pattern of production would result in greater income inequality. Put differently, the source of changes in relative factor prices is market competition. Because there is nothing unique about market competition that arises as a consequence of lowered trade barriers, it is highly misleading to single-out for observation and criticism changes in factor prices caused by international trade.

Understanding this fact is to understand the pointlessness of the recent debate in the literature over just how much of the measured increase in *intra*-country income inequality is due to international trade and how much of it is due to innovation or to other nontrade factors.[19] While increased economic growth might (and likely does) promote greater income inequality – and while increased international trade almost certainly helps to fuel such growth – any changes in relative factor prices are simply the consequences of market competition. To return to an earlier hypothetical example, debating how much of the increase in intra-country income inequality is caused by foreign competition and how much is caused by domestic competition makes no more analytical sense than debating how much of this inequality is caused by competition from women compared to how much is caused by competition from men.

In summary here, to blame increased income inequality on free trade is, really, to blame increased income inequality on market competition. It follows that if objections to income inequality justify government-imposed restrictions on the new source(s) of competition from abroad, these objections also justify such restrictions on new source(s) of competition that arise domestically. Yet because very few economists stand ready to give government officials the discretionary power to decrease economic inequality by tempering the forces of economic competition (as opposed, say, to using redistributive fiscal policies), there is no legitimate economic case for giving government officials the discretionary power to decrease economic inequality by tempering the forces of economic competition that happen to come from abroad.

VII. Trade-induced changes in skills

There is yet one more objection to using the increased inequality as identified by the Stolper–Samuelson theorem as a justification for trade restrictions – namely, in reality workers' skill sets are not fixed. It is undeniable that a low-skilled worker in a factory that confronts newly intensified competition will be at great risk of having his or her income fall. It's also undeniable that, as explained by Stolper–Samuelson, if that worker is in a country (such as the United States) where low-skilled workers are a relatively more-scarce input, the result might well be to reduce that worker's income both absolutely and relative to the wages of workers with more skills and, thus, to increase income inequality in that country. But the prevailing distribution of skills in the workforce is determined neither randomly nor exogenously. Instead, that distribution of skills is determined by, and reflects, the relative returns to different skill levels. Therefore, if those relative returns change, the distribution of skills in the workforce will change in response.

If a relatively abundant factor today in the American economy is high-skilled labor, and a more-scarce factor is low-skilled labor, the reason is that over time it paid an increasing proportion of workers to become more skilled (or, in some cases, it paid employers to assist their workers to become more skilled). Had the relative returns to workers of becoming high-skilled been lower, a smaller portion of the American workforce would today be high-skilled and, hence, a larger portion of the workforce would be low-skilled. Therefore, when the relative returns to different skill levels change, so do the proportions of these different skill levels in the workforce. This change isn't instantaneous, of course, but it makes no sense to deny or to ignore such a change.

When a country with a relative abundance of high-skilled labor begins to trade more freely, income inequality, as predicted by Stolper–Samuelson, might at first increase as the wages of low-skilled workers fall relative to those of high-skilled workers. But falling relative and absolute wages of low-skilled labor – or, put differently, rising relative and absolute wages of high-skilled labor – incite more workers than previously to enhance their skills. So one longer-run benefit of freer trade in an economy in which the relatively scarce factor is low-skilled labor is intensified incentives for workers to improve their skills.

Speculating on what the ultimate equilibrium outcome of endogenous, trade-induced changes in a nation's factor endowments might be is beyond the scope of this chapter. I mention these endogenous changes only to draw attention to the pitfalls of assessing trade policy as if that policy itself has no effects on factor endowments. Failure to consider the factor-endowment changes *induced* by trade – as opposed to looking only at how trade is induced by differences in factor endowments – fuels poor understanding of trade. A likely result is poor trade policy.

An example – one of countless – of this poor understanding of trade occurs in a 2017 letter in the *Wall Street Journal* by Craig Cantoni. Cantoni, a self-described "free marketer," complains that recent increases in globalization have created in the United States "not blue-collar jobs, but white-collar jobs in research, engineering and marketing."[20] On its face, this complaint is odd. Why would someone *complain* that the new jobs created by globalization are disproportionately higher-skilled, white-collar jobs? Why would someone *complain* of the creation of a disproportionate number of jobs, each of which, on average, pays more than did the typical job that was destroyed? This complaint makes sense only if it is realized that the complainer (in this case, Craig Cantoni) implicitly assumes that the array of skills in the economy is exogenous to trade. If the economy has in it a certain number (or proportion) of workers of different skill levels, and if this distribution of skills is exogenous to trade, then trade that disproportionately destroys jobs for blue-collar workers leaves such workers permanently worse off. Not only are today's blue-collar workers assumed, perhaps with some realism, to be stuck with their current skill sets, the number (or proportion) of workers who will in the future be stuck with such skill sets is also assumed to be unchanging.

Yet, if and to the extent that workers in countries with relative abundances of high-skilled labor respond to the trade-induced rising pay of high-skilled workers by improving their skills, worker pay in those countries will, over time, rise further. In addition, it is not at all clear that this increased spread in wage rates results in greater economic inequality. Even according to criteria used by Progressives who decry economic inequality, the trade-induced increase in the proportion of workers earning wages at the higher end of the wage distribution might result in decreased inequality. Suppose that before trade liberalization Ruritania had six high-skilled workers, each earning $40 per hour, and four low-skilled workers, each earning $12 per hour. Suppose that following trade liberalization and the resulting improvement in worker skills that it induces, Ruritania has nine high-skilled workers, each earning $50 per hour, and one low-skilled worker, earning $8 per hour. A strong argument can be made that, in this case, trade liberalization *decreased* economic inequality in the country with a relative abundance of high-skilled labor. Indeed, in this hypothetical example, Ruritania's Gini coefficient falls from 0.233 to 0.083 – indicating that the post-liberalization distribution of income is more equal than was the pre-liberalization distribution.

VIII. Conclusion

Changes in the pattern of international trade invariably change relative and absolute incomes. Under certain plausible real-world conditions, these changes might not only cause measured economic inequality to rise but also cause the absolute incomes of some people to fall. Those who experience these income changes are routinely classified as trade's "winners" and "losers." And economists interpret these results of trade as proof that, while the changes brought about by trade nearly always satisfy the Kaldor–Hicks criterion for efficiency, they do not satisfy the more stringent Paretian criterion for efficiency.

This manner of talking about and assessing the consequences of international trade is highly misleading. When international trade is put into proper institutional context, it is revealed to be simply one particular manifestation of market competition, no more or less likely to create winners or losers, or more or less likely to increase or decrease economic inequality, than is any other manifestation of competition. And when international trade is put into proper temporal context, it – again, like market competition generally – is revealed to create over time only winners and no losers. This conclusion is only strengthened when account is taken of workers' self-interested responses to trade-induced changes in relative wage rates.

Notes

1 By encouraging greater specialization, trade promotes economic growth by better enabling each worker and each firm to specialize in the performance of those tasks at which each has a comparative advantage. In one of the most famous and most remarkable findings of economics, David Ricardo demonstrated that specialization according to comparative advantage causes total economic output to increase. (See David Ricardo, *On the Principles of Political Economy and Taxation* [1817].) And the larger the number of people in the economy, the greater are opportunities for deeper specialization. Trade also promotes economic growth through the incentives it gives to entrepreneurs to innovate both in the creation of new consumer outputs and in better, less-costly ways to produce outputs.

2 Named after Vilfredo Pareto, the Italian economist who first proposed this criterion for efficiency, an economic change is said to be "Pareto-improving" if that change makes at least one person better off without making anyone worse off. When all possible Pareto-improving changes have been made, the result is "Pareto-efficiency" – an allocation of resources that cannot be changed without making at least one person worse off.

3 Noah Smith, "Free Trade Is No Longer a No-Brainer," *Bloomberg View*, October 7, 2015. Available at www.bloomberg.com/view/articles/2015-10-07/free-trade-is-no-longer-a-no-brainer-for-economists

4 Dani Rodrik, "Too Late to Compensate Free Trade's Losers," *Project Syndicate*, April 11, 2017. Available at www.project-syndicate.org/commentary/free-trade-losers-compensation-too-late-by-dani-rodrik-2017-04. Here's one more example, this one from the

self-described socialist Sen. Bernie Sanders (I-VT): "Congress is now debating fast-track legislation that will pave the way for the disastrous Trans-Pacific Partnership (TPP) unfettered free trade agreement. At a time when our middle class is disappearing and the gap between the very rich and everyone else is growing wider, this anti-worker legislation must be defeated." *Huffpost*, "The TPP Must Be Defeated," May 21, 2016. Available at www.huffingtonpost.com/rep-bernie-sanders/the-tpp-must-be-defeated_b_7352166.html

5 Brink Lindsey, "Book Review: *Free Trade Under Fire*," *National Review*, April 22, 2009. Available at www.cato.org/publications/commentary/book-review-free-trade-under-fire

6 Lindsey (2009).

7 Named after British economists Nicholas Kaldor and John Hicks, the Kaldor–Hicks criterion for efficiency is less strict than the Pareto criterion. An economic change is Kaldor–Hicks-efficient if those who gain from the change can in principle fully compensate those who lose from the change and still be better off than before the change. In practice, this criterion for efficiency identifies as efficiency-enhancing any economic change that produces gains that are larger, when measured in monetary terms, than are the costs of that change.

8 See, for example, Paul Krugman, Maurice Obstfeld, and Marc Melitz, *International Economics: Theory and Policy*, 9th ed. (Boston: Addison-Wesley, 2012), p. 66: "It is always better to allow trade and compensate those who are hurt by it than to prohibit the trade. All modern industrial countries provide some sort of 'safety net' of income support programs (such as unemployment benefits and subsidized retraining and relocation programs) that can cushion the losses of groups hurt by trade. Economists would argue that if this cushion is felt to be inadequate, more support rather than less trade is the answer. . . . Most economists, while acknowledging the effects of international trade on income distribution, believe that it is more important to stress the overall potential gains from trade than the possible losses to some groups in a country."

9 In tension with, if not in outright contradiction of, his own textbook, *ibid.*, Paul Krugman recently offered an argument similar to that of Rodrik. In a March 9, 2016, blog post ("A Protectionist Moment?") at *The Conscience of a Liberal*, Krugman wrote that "the conventional case for trade liberalization relies on the assertion that the government could redistribute income to ensure that everyone wins – but we now have an ideology utterly opposed to such redistribution in full control of one party, and with blocking power against anything but a minor move in that direction by the other. So, the elite case for ever-freer trade is largely a scam, which voters probably sense even if they don't know exactly what form it's taking." Available at https://krugman.blogs.nytimes.com/2016/03/09/a-protectionist-moment/

10 Here again is Sen. Bernie Sanders: "I voted against NAFTA, CAFTA, PNTR with China. I think they have been a disaster for the American worker. A lot of corporations that shut down here move abroad. Working people understand that after NAFTA, CAFTA, PNTR with China we have lost millions of decent paying jobs. Since 2001, 60,000 factories in America have been shut down. We're in a race to the bottom, where our wages are going down. Is all of that attributable to trade? No. Is a lot of it? Yes. TPP was written by corporate America and the pharmaceutical industry and Wall Street. That's what this trade agreement is about. I do not want American workers to be competing against people in Vietnam who make 56 cents an hour for a minimum wage." *On the Issues*, "Bernie Sanders on Free Trade," October 2015. Available at www.ontheissues.org/2016/Bernie_Sanders_Free_Trade.html

11 Lindsey, of course, is not unique in pointing out this important reality. Here, for example, are Krugman, Obstfeld, and Melitz (2012: 66): "Income distribution effects are not specific to international trade. Every change in a nation's economy, including technological progress, shifting consumer preferences, exhaustion of old resources and

discovery of new ones, and so on, affects income distribution. Why should an apparel worker, who suffers an unemployment spell due to increased import competition, be treated differently from an unemployed printing machine operator (whose newspaper employer shuts down due to competition from Internet news providers) or an unemployed construction worker laid off due to a housing slump?"

12 Available at www.tradingeconomics.com/united-states/imports-of-bauxite-aluminum

13 A May 2017 poll conducted in the United States by Yahoo! Finance found that workers do indeed assess the job-security aspects of different employment options. See Rick Newman, "Labor Shortages? Blame Corporate America," June 13, 2017. Available at https://finance.yahoo.com/news/labor-shortages-blame-corporate-america-173604463.html

14 It is possible to exit the market nexus. Opportunities for self-sufficient existence are readily available. For a sum of money within reach of any ordinary American, an individual (or a family) can purchase a plot of land in a rural or wooded area of North America and transform it into a self-sufficient homestead. Life on such a farm, disconnected from the commercial market, would be extremely difficult, dangerous, and poverty-ridden. But such an existence would have the advantage of shielding its denizens from changes in the patterns of global (and domestic) trade. The fact that almost no one today chooses such an "independent" existence is powerful evidence that the expected benefits of escaping the vicissitudes of the market are much lower than the costs of doing so – the costs, of course, being the sacrifice of the tremendously high standard of living available to everyone in modern society who participates in the market.

15 Here is James Buchanan: "The members of the group may be observed to agree on changes in the rules that produce results that, when classified by the orthodox Pareto criterion, are clearly 'nonoptimal'; in other words, 'optimal rules,' *defined as those that cannot be changed by general agreement*, may generate results that may be classified as non-optimal." James M. Buchanan, "The Relevance of Pareto Optimality," *Journal of Conflict Resolution* 6 (December 1962): 341–354. (The quotation appears on page 348; original emphasis.) Buchanan argues here that rules rather than particular results are the relevant "variables" over which assessments of Pareto optimality are most useful. Everyone can agree that Rule A is superior to Rule B while recognizing that a particular set of results that emerge under Rule A might appear to the observing economist to be Pareto suboptimal – that is, to create "losers" who are uncompensated by "winners." And especially because, as a practical matter, it is always rules rather than specific outcomes that are chosen in the political process, it is inappropriate to seize upon instances of Pareto-inferior *results* as proof that the rule or policy regime that generates those results is itself suboptimal. The application of this insight to trade is straightforward. Under a policy of free trade, of course some people lose jobs or income whenever patterns of international trade change. But this reality does not imply that there exists an alternative trade policy under which there will be fewer such Pareto suboptimal results or one in which the expected welfare gains over time of each individual are higher than they are under a policy of free trade.

16 Wolfgang F. Stolper and Paul A. Samuelson, "Protection and Real Wages," *Review of Economic Studies* 9 (November 1941): 58–73.

17 See, for example, Lloyd Metzler (1949) and Ronald Jones and Jose Scheinkman (1977).

18 Arnold Kling (2016) emphasizes that economic stability and growth depend crucially upon getting "correct" the intricate details of the patterns of specialization and trade.

19 See, for example, Elhanan Helpman, "Globalization and Wage Inequality," *Journal of the British Academy* 5 (2017): 125–162; François Bourguignon, *The Globalization of Inequality* (Princeton, NJ: Princeton University Press, 2015).

20 Craig Cantoni, Letter to the Editor, *Wall Street Journal*, June 22, 2017. Available at www.wsj.com/articles/exporting-jobs-and-training-modern-workers-1498080555

References

Bourguignon, F. 2015. *The globalization of inequality*. Princeton, NJ: Princeton University Press.

Buchanan, J. M. 1962. "The Relevance of Pareto Optimality." *Journal of Conflict Resolution* 6 (4): 341–354.

Cantoni, C. 2017. "Exporting Jobs and Training Modern Workers." *Wall Street Journal*, June 22. Available at www.wsj.com/articles/exporting-jobs-and-training-modern-workers-1498080555

Helpman, E. 2017. "Globalization and Wage Inequality." *Journal of the British Academy* 5: 125–162.

Jones, R. W., and J. A. Scheinkman. 1977. "The Relevance of the Two-Sector Production Model in Trade Theory." *Journal of Political Economy* 85 (5): 909–935.

Kling, A. 2016. *Specialization and Trade: A Re-Introduction to Economics*. Washington, DC: Cato Institute.

Krugman, P. 2016. "A Protectionist Moment?" *The Conscience of a Liberal*, March 9 [blog post]. Available at https://krugman.blogs.nytimes.com/2016/03/09/a-protectionist-moment/

Krugman, P., Obstfeld, M., and M. Melitz. 2012. *International Economics: Theory and Policy*, 9th ed. Boston: Addison-Wesley.

Lindsey, B. 2009. "Free Trade Under Fire [Review of the Book]." *National Review*, April 22. Available at www.cato.org/publications/commentary/book-review-free-trade-under-fire

Metzler, L. A. 1949. "Tariffs, the Terms of Trade, and the Distribution of National Income." *Journal of Political Economy* 57 (1): 1–29.

Newman, R. 2017. "Labor Shortages? Blame Corporate America." *Yahoo Finance*, June 13. Available at https://finance.yahoo.com/news/labor-shortages-blame-corporate-america-173604463.html.

Ricardo, D. 1817. *On the Principles of Political Economy and Taxation*. London: John Murray.

Rodrik, D. 2017. "Too Late to Compensate Free Trade's Losers." *Project Syndicate*, April 11. Available at www.project-syndicate.org/commentary/free-trade-losers-compensation-too-late-by-dani-rodrik-2017-04.

Sanders, B. 2016. "The TPP Must Be Defeated." *Huffpost (Senator?)*, May 21. Available at www.huffingtonpost.com/rep-bernie-sanders/the-tpp-must-be-defeated_b_7352166.html

Smith, N. 2015. "Free Trade Is No Longer a No-Brainer." *Bloomberg*, October 7. Available at www.bloomberg.com/view/articles/2015-10-07/free-trade-is-no-longer-a-no-brainer-for-economists

Stolper, W. F., and P. A. Samuelson. 1941. "Protection and Real Wages." *Review of Economic Studies* 9 (1): 58–73.

3 The institutional justice of the market process

Entrepreneurship, increasing returns, and income distribution

Peter J. Boettke, Rosolino A. Candela, and Kaitlyn Woltz

I. Introduction

Critics of economics have long claimed that economists are deaf to the cries of the poor. This, however, is not an accurate portrayal of the situation. In keeping with the spirit of economics as a science that focuses on the means that best serve to achieve certain ends, economists have long debated the best ways to reduce poverty. They have, therefore, always been sensitive to the plight of the poor and have always paid due attention to the closely related problems of poverty and inequality.

The classical political economists working in the methodological tradition of David Hume and Adam Smith emphasized how an institutional framework of private property, freedom of contract, and mutual consent channels competitive behavior away from negative-sum games in the distribution of wealth into positive-sum games that generate an ever-growing pie of wealth to distribute. This expansion of wealth is based upon the discovery of pure profit by entrepreneurs alert to opportunities to trade and to innovate.[1] The entrepreneurial market process in turn creates generalized increasing returns and reinforces the scope for peaceful social cooperation under the division of labor (Boettke and Candela 2017). In short, classical political economy, by demonstrating the effectiveness of a "system of natural liberty" (Smith 1776 [1981]) to generate peace and prosperity, illustrates the complementarity of individual liberty, economic prosperity, and peace.

This does not imply, however, that classical political economists, as well as early neoclassical economists, such as Carl Menger, did not emphasize the *justice* of the market process. "The economic policy of classical political economy," Menger writes,

> was precisely dedicated to the most immediate and urgent needs of the time in which it came into being, a time full of unjust class privileges and detrimental restrictions on the poor and weak, full of irrational and self-interested over-regulation. Smith and his disciples recognized the needs of *Social-Politik* in their time very precisely when they first pressed for the

> abolition of the harmful restrictions on workers and when they opposed the state interventions in the economy detrimental to the poor.
>
> (emphasis original, Menger 1891 [2016]: 482)

The justice of the market process, according to classical political economists, is based on institutions that foist neither legal discrimination nor dominion upon individuals but instead afford each individual equal opportunity before the law to realize their full potential in cooperation with others.

It is important to note here, however, that economists from Smith to Menger were not advocating a public policy conclusion per se; rather, their public policy conclusions were a by-product of a particular understanding of economic science. The pursuit of profit opportunities in the marketplace generates patterns of income distribution that disproportionately accrue to successful entrepreneurs. These same market processes, however, also generate a *tendency*, not only to attract entry by competing entrepreneurs but also to erode monopoly power and drive profits down to zero. "Uncertainty and entrepreneurship," Machovec states, "were central to the classicals' understanding of the market process – a centrality that is irreconcilable with the equilibrium vision that succeeded it" (1995: 158).[2]

We argue in this chapter that the transformation in the vision of economics from one in terms of processes to one in terms of equilibrium yielded public policy implications regarding the role of government and distributive justice. Although classical political economists had made a case regarding the *institutional justice* of the market process, this argument became overshadowed in the late 19th and early 20th centuries by early neoclassical economists who defended the market in terms of the equilibrium pricing of factor payments. Justice according to the early neoclassical economists was defined in terms of market outcomes that approximate the marginal valuation of the productive contribution of each factor of production. The persistence of this equilibrium paradigm today, among both proponents and critics of the market, has led to the notion that there is an inherent trade-off between income equality and economic prosperity. By squeezing from our analysis of the market not only the notion of uncertainty and entrepreneurship, but more importantly our understanding regarding the institutional context in which capital is accumulated and maintained *through time*, we also exclude from our analysis the inherent tendency by which payments to factors of production are equalized across markets by entrepreneurial arbitrage opportunities. In other words, without including institutions and entrepreneurship into our analysis, we fail to understand how it might be possible for the market process to generate a tendency toward greater income equality and greater economic prosperity simultaneously.

Absent an understanding of the institutional framework generating this dynamic pattern of equalization, the appearance of income inequality at a given point in time will justify government intervention as a *deus ex machina* for distributive justice. However, such intervention itself will only redirect the market process toward the pursuit of profit opportunities in the form of regulatory capture (Stigler 1971) and in the seeking of monopoly privileges among special interest groups (Tullock 1967), perpetuating income inequality against the desires of those who wish to use government intervention to eliminate income inequality. Ultimately, our policy conclusions regarding distributive justice cannot be divested from our understanding of what is regarded as economic science. This chapter proceeds as follows. In Section II, we outline the justice of the market process as discussed primarily by Buchanan and Kirzner. In Section III, we juxtapose more recent critiques regarding the distributive justice of the market by Piketty with those made by Tullock, Stiglitz and Zingales. Section IV concludes.

II. The demand for justice in the market process

II.I The emergence of the allocation paradigm

Despite the fact that socialism failed to achieve its stated goals of income equality and advanced industrial production over the course of the 20th century, critics of the market continue to see these goals as substitutes, and not complements, to the market process. "It is because capitalism is seen by millions as being built on injustice as one of its essential and defining characteristics," Israel Kirzner writes, "that the system is despised and even hated in much of the world" (1989 [2016]: 5). The fact that the outcomes of income distribution through the market mechanism have been considered unjust has also generated wide support for income redistribution, namely, through progressive income taxation and transfer payments. Like many public policy conclusions, the justification for income redistribution among economists is based upon the way in which economists conceptualize the market as a mechanism of income distribution.

In *The World in a Model*, Mary Morgan shows how economists build models "to depict some particular phenomenon or to figure out some puzzle or problem about a set of relations in the economic world" (2012: 387). She focuses on modeling as a method of inquiry that economists think about and use to contextualize historical phenomena. Morgan focuses on two meanings of the term modeling. The first relates to the formalization of an economic argument, including forming, shaping, and outlining an argument. Through formalization, the second meaning of modeling relates to making historical data subject to rules of conduct or manipulation (2012: 20).

Such model formation can be understood as a process of idealization, or the formation of "ideal types"[3] in the Weberian sense; it is "a process of picking out the relations of interest, and isolating them from the frictions and disturbances which interfere with their workings in the real world to give form to simpler, and 'ideal', world models" (Morgan 2012: 21). Like maps, models rely on omission as they cannot represent every detail but are to be understood as articulate artifacts – compressed accounts of things in the world expressed in an appropriately specialized form and language. As such, economic narratives "*are built into the identity of the model from the start*" (emphasis original, Morgan 2012: 362). Morgan's point is important for our analysis because alternative models of income distribution generated by the market will highlight not only different historical narratives about income distribution but also alternative policy conclusions regarding the state's role in generating a more equal distribution of income.

The narrative that markets generate an unjust distribution of income follows from the emergence of an *allocation paradigm* in economic modeling beginning in the late 19th century. "The main assumption of the allocation paradigm," Coyne writes, "is that the outcome of exchange is an equilibrium where all gains from exchange are exhausted" (2010: 16). Viewed in terms of this paradigm, the market is always in a state of static equilibrium, where each individual has perfect information regarding the endowments of all the other market participants, and therefore of the underlying distribution of income, which is predetermined by given institutional, technological, and resource constraints. "But this way of perceiving the society's economic problem as an allocation problem implies, in turn, that the problem of distribution is *a problem of sharing out a given pie*" (emphasis original, Kirzner 1988b: 177), which, by logical construction, is also known to a "distributor" who wishes to redistribute income.

Though classical political economists were able to demonstrate the complementarity of peace, prosperity, and individual liberty with a market economy, as James Buchanan has highlighted, their demonstration implied nothing directly about the *distributive justice* of the market (1991: 245). Unfortunately, however, the analytical response that their neoclassical successors delivered failed to directly confront claims of market injustice, specifically because it delivered an argument of market justice in terms of equilibrium.

The allocation paradigm that emerged amongst the early neoclassical economists, including John Bates Clark (1899) and Phillip Wicksteed (1894),[4] was based upon an application of Euler's theorem to the distribution of income, which states that under the assumption of constant returns to scale, the separate marginal value products of each factor of production exhaust the total value of output. The exhaustion of payments from total output to factors of production had both positive and normative implications. Positively speaking, Euler's theorem illustrated mathematically that the share of total output accrued to owners of capital is derived from its marginal contribution to output. Normatively speaking, this implies that the redistribution of income is unjustified, because the income paid to capitalists is not a result of exploitation or theft of labor income.

However, the marginal revolution in economics introduced, as Thomas Kuhn would put it, a change in basic economic paradigms – one that causes "scientists to see the world of their research-engagement differently." Such a change, in fact, is so far-reaching that "in so far as their only recourse to that world is through what they see and do, we may want to say that after a revolution scientists are responding to a different world" (Kuhn 1962 [1996]: 111).

This point is especially relevant when it comes to the response of the early neoclassical economists to Marxist accusations of exploitation and injustice in the marketplace, for this response failed to address these points in terms of how Marxists had understood the market, namely, in terms of the market as a rivalrous process – a paradigm that they shared with the classical political economists.[5]

Marxists regarded exploitation as a positive aspect of the capitalism system. By abolishing private property, and subsuming production for direct use under a single, rational plan, Marxists argued that market rivalry between capitalists would be abolished, and with it the exploitive extraction of surplus value. Moreover, Marxists condemned market rivalry for its monopolistic tendencies. This monopolistic tendency, according to Marx, ultimately results in capitalist production becoming centralized under larger enterprises that would subsume production under the conscious guidance of fewer and fewer producers. The end result of the rivalrous process can be conceived of a bilateral monopoly, in which one immense firm is a single seller of goods and the single "buyer" of labor.

The allocation paradigm that emerged after the marginal revolution, however, failed to confront these criticisms head on. Instead, it dismissed the critiques of the market made by Marxists only by assuming such critiques away. As the allocation paradigm became increasingly dominant among early neoclassical economists, particularly after its explication by Francis Edgeworth (1881) and later Frank Knight (1921), its preoccupation with static equilibrium meant that it could not offer a coherent defense of the Marxist claim that markets give capitalists increasing monopoly power. Rather than employ equilibrium analysis as a method of contrast to illustrate the functional significance of institutions, specifically by engendering alternative patterns of income distribution under conditions of uncertainty, competitive equilibrium instead became a normative benchmark among early neoclassicals by which to assess the competitive outcome of income distribution (Boettke 1997).

Ironically, the neglect of market rivalry and entrepreneurship as a part of economic science by its early neoclassical defenders would yield the same normative implications regarding the justice of the market process as those held by their early Marxist critics. Because neoclassical economists take the model of perfect competition as their point of theoretical departure, defining entrepreneurial profits out of existence, the presence of firms selling goods above opportunity costs not only implies monopoly power, but even worse, the presence of "unearned" rents to capitalists.

Let us be clear, however, that our intent has not been to provide a wholesale critique and dismissal of the marginal revolution, or of the neoclassical theory of marginal productivity that followed. Rather, we simply wish to point out that by justifying the distribution of income in terms of market *outcomes*, early neoclassicals were able to provide a mathematically valid explanation for the justice of income distribution through the market mechanism. However, by constructing a case for the distributive justice of the market in terms of the productive contributions of land, labor, and capital to output *after the production process has been concluded*, it would be more precise to say that the early neoclassicals demonstrated that the incomes paid through the market mechanism were *not unjust*. By defining their argument in terms of equilibrium, they could not provide an argument for the justice of *residual payments*, or the profits earned by the entrepreneur under conditions of uncertainty.

In a most recent article, Israel Kirzner has made this point quite clearly by critically analyzing what he refers to as "Friedman's universal ethic" (2019: 90), justifying income distribution under capitalism. As Kirzner argues, "Friedman, like most mainstream micro-economic theorists, see the economics of the market, basically, from the ex post perspective" (2019: 97), after a productive process has been concluded, and in which all payments to factors of production have exhausted the value of total output. In *Capitalism and Freedom* (1962 [2002]: 161–162), Friedman states that the "ethical principle that would directly justify the distribution of income in a free market society is, 'To each according to what he and the instruments he owns produces'." Friedman does not neglect that there is a role for the state to enforce private property rights under the rule of law, which we also discuss further in Section III.

However, for Friedman, like his early neoclassical predecessors, distributive justice was assessed strictly in terms of productive contribution, and therefore irrelevant to explaining why entrepreneurial profits emerge, and why they might be just or unjust *before a production process has been concluded*. The main reason, Kirzner explains, is that distributive justice in terms of productive *outcomes* "has no relevance for any kind of 'production' into which nothing is deliberately contributed. Discovery is exactly this kind of 'production': it does not, by definition, result from any consciously planned deployment of resource services" (2019: 95–96). Before factors of production can earn their relative contributions to the value of total output, these productive factors must be discovered in the first place, after which they are allocated to their most valued uses in production. This production process does not occur automatically; it must be catalyzed by entrepreneurs, who earn profits for creating value for consumers by allocating resources to their most valued uses and bear losses for misallocating resources to less valued consumer uses.

The implication here is that payments to land, labor, and capital are not earned by virtue of their ownership. As Ludwig von Mises has argued:

> *Ownership of the means of production is not a privilege, but a social liability.* Capitalists and landowners are compelled to employ their property for the best possible satisfaction of the consumers. If they are slow and inept in the performance of their duties, they are penalized by losses. If they do not learn the lesson and do not reform their conduct of affairs, they lose their wealth. No investment is safe forever. He who does not use his property in serving the consumers in the most efficient way is doomed to failure. There is no room left for people who would like to enjoy their fortunes in idleness and thoughtlessness. The proprietor must aim to invest his funds in such a way that principal and yield are at least not impaired.
>
> (emphasis added, 1949 [2007]: 311–312)

Rather, such payments are a *by-product* of entrepreneurs discovering their productive contributions to output in the first place, and deploying them to productive uses in such a way that creates additional economic wealth. Increases in the productive contributions of land, labor, and capital owe their value to their discovery by entrepreneurs.

However, neoclassical theory has remained relatively silent on the *ex ante* process by which entrepreneurs discover the productive contributions of resources to output, and how such competitive behavior unintendedly generates a pattern of income distribution, which is not fixed and given. However, by defending the justice of the market in terms of static *equilibrium* under constant returns, early neoclassical economists remained silent in their defense of distributive justice in terms of *rivalry* under *increasing returns*, where economic profits are omnipresent. As Buchanan and Yoon argue, "Euler's theorem simply did 'too much work' in the whole explanatory enterprise to be jettisoned" (1999: 516), leading to the neglect of how markets work to generate such an outcome in the first place. By deemphasizing the role of entrepreneurship and how alternative institutional arrangements incentivize different forms of entrepreneurship, mainstream economic theory has had little explanatory power regarding whether one pattern of income distribution is just or unjust. The neglect of an institutional analysis of the entrepreneurial market process left a gap in the analysis of distributive justice, which would be later filled by a discovery paradigm that emerged in the post–World War II era.

II.II. The resurgence of the discovery paradigm

Our discussion thus far has highlighted and emphasized the fact that the emergence of an allocation paradigm in economic science during the late 19th and early 20th centuries has had public policy implications regarding income redistribution, which remain among economists to this day. During this same period, however, the

> truth is that there was, among most economists (Austrian, Marshallian, or Walrasian) in the early twentieth century, a superficial, shared understanding of markets that submerged important distinctions that would become apparent only much later. In this shared understanding, there coexisted elements of appreciation for dynamic market processes and elements of appreciation for the degree of balance – the degree of equilibrium held to be achieved by markets.
>
> (Kirzner 1988a: 2)

This shared understanding would bifurcate during the middle and latter half of the 20th century not only into the dominant allocation paradigm that we have discussed thus far but also into a discovery paradigm that came to be refined and articulated by economists of the Austrian School, such as Ludwig von Mises, F.A. Hayek, and Israel Kirzner, economists of a "neglected branch" of the Chicago School (Boettke and Candela 2014), including Armen Alchian,

James Buchanan, Ronald Coase, and Harold Demsetz, and more recently, Edmund Phelps (2013) and Deidre McCloskey (2006, 2010, 2016).

These economists, working in the tradition of Adam Smith, have concentrated primarily on exchange behavior in an open-ended world of uncertainty and "the various institutional arrangements that arise from this form of activity" (Buchanan 1964: 214). Like the classical political economists, they understood that in an institutional context of private property, freedom of contract, and the rule of law, the entrepreneurial actions of individuals are coordinated and guided by relative price changes. Analytical attention is not restricted to the world of static equilibrium but to the dynamic evolution toward equilibrium, wherein entrepreneurs discover the marginal contribution of each factor of production and are rewarded with residual profits for doing so.

The main assumption of the discovery paradigm is that knowledge regarding the marginal value products of the factors of production is not assumed to be given. Rather, it must be *learned* through a process of entrepreneurial discovery. "The problem of economic organization," Alchian and Demsetz argued, "the economical means of metering productivity and rewards, *is not confronted directly in the classical analysis of production and distribution.*[6] Instead, that analysis tends to assume sufficiently economic or zero cost means, as if productivity automatically created its reward" (emphasis added, 1972: 778). In a world of uncertainty, however, not only the total output but also the separate marginal products of land, labor, and capital cannot be perfectly identified. Moreover, the marginal value products of land, labor, and capital do not exhaust the sum of total output. Rather, there exist *generalized increasing returns* to total output that result as a by-product of entrepreneurial discovery.

Generalized increasing returns do not refer simply to the increasing returns to scale that sometimes characterize production within firms. Rather, generalized increasing returns refer to the returns that result from broadening the *scope of production and exchange*, i.e., by broadening the extent to which individuals can engage in specialization in the market. For example, as Randall Holcombe notes:

> Henry Ford could not have succeeded in mass-producing automobiles until there was a substantial market, including infrastructure such as roads, gasoline stations, and repair facilities. Bill Gates could not have made his fortune had not Steve Jobs seen the opportunity to build and sell personal computers, and Steve Jobs could not have built a personal computer had not Gordon Moore invented the microprocessor.
>
> (Holcombe 1998: 50–51)

According to our account, generalized increasing returns occur concurrently and continuously with specialization among owners of land, labor, and capital (Buchanan and Yoon 1999: 514). The extent of productive specialization and social cooperation under the division of the labor is institutionally contingent. What determines the extent of the market is the security of private property and freedom of contract under the rule of law. Without the rule of law, however, there will exist generalized increasing returns to entrepreneurial activity in the form of rent-seeking, cronyism, and regulatory capture. The opportunity to transfer existing wealth through political discretion attracts unproductive entrepreneurship, resulting in the destruction of economic wealth that would have otherwise been distributed via the price mechanism.

How does our account of generalized increasing returns relate to an account of the *institutional justice* of income distribution in the market process? According to Israel Kirzner, a market society under private property and the rule of law is characterized most distinctively "*by freedom of entrepreneurial entry*" (emphasis original, 1985: 29). The institutional justice of the market process, and the pattern of income distribution that it engenders, is based upon the fact that it allows and protects the possibility for the discovery of wealth *where it did not previously exist in the minds of other individuals.*

The institutional justice of the market process that arises from such generalized increasing returns is based on the fact that entrepreneurial discoveries feed on each other, giving each individual the possibility and opportunity to *discover* what is due to them in terms of overall well-being. The complementarity of peace, prosperity, and individual liberty in a market economy does not simply manifest itself in a greater availability of consumption, but as a greater range of options available to individuals in the way they are able to participate as producers under the division of labor. Contrary to the objections that specialization under capitalism is unjust and fosters routine and monotonous work that is alienating and exploitative to the worker, Edmund Phelps argues that

> an increasing general level of wages is *liberating* (emphasis added): it enables persons confined to the lower reaches of the available wages – unskilled workers, in the usual terminology – to move from work they previously could not afford to reject to work that is more desirable. A person working in the "domestic economy" as a homemaker or as paid help in other people's homes could afford to move to a job that is not so isolating; someone working in the underground sector could afford to take a job in the legitimate economy with its greater respectability and lesser dependency; someone could afford to leave a job in the business economy for one with initiatives, responsibilities, and interactions that make it more rewarding. Thus higher wages also result in what may be called *economic inclusion.*
>
> (emphasis original, 2013: 47)

Rather than being limited in their choice of work by class, social status, or legal discrimination, greater freedom of entry and exit, due to greater social mobility, is *liberating* to workers and allows them to work with greater dignity. The most important consequence of generalized increasing returns is not just increases in productivity that afford individual's higher income. Rather, "it has been the opportunities it has offered to men and women to extend and develop and improve their capacities" (Friedman 1962 [2002]: 169).

Generalized increasing returns harness the creative powers of individuals who would otherwise be excluded from specialization under the division of labor due to legal impediments that are unjust, such as regulatory restrictions, licensing, or other monopoly privileges that bar entry. As private property becomes more secure under the rule of law, individuals become freer to enter and exit contractual relationships with other prospective employers. Individuals become free to pursue an entrepreneurial project of their own by forming a new firm, introducing new products, or initiating a new technique of production.

III. Income inequality and institutions: rent-seeking versus profit-seeking

Economists in the post–World War II era have done extensive research on the consequences of long-term economic growth for the distribution of income (Solow 1956; Kaldor 1957; Stiglitz 1969; Katz and Murphy 1992). Since the financial crisis of 2008 and the ensuing recession, however, the subject of income inequality has generated a great deal of interest, among both economists in favor of income redistribution, such as Thomas Piketty and Joseph Stiglitz, and economists skeptical of income redistribution, such as Gordon Tullock and Luigi Zingales. Much of the current debate has turned on the nature of capital and how returns on both physical and human capital are earned.

In his widely acclaimed book *Capital in the Twenty-First Century* (2014), Thomas Piketty argues that capitalism contains within it tendencies that lead to growing inequalities over time. The main argument Piketty puts forth is that the rate of return on capital tends to be higher than an economy's growth rate. As a result, wealth accumulated in the past grows faster than output and wages. He offers the reader a simple model to illustrate why the accumulation of capital causes ever-increasing inequality.[7]

Though indeed Piketty's model is disciplined by *syntactic clarity*, yielding a logically valid argument, it comes at the expense of *semantic clarity*, based upon logically unsound assumptions (Boettke 2012: 314). Revisiting the discussion by Morgan mentioned earlier, the logical unsoundness of Piketty's argument is based on his underlying assumption about capital. As Morgan states:

> Any scientist's ability to reason in a chosen style is thus clearly dependent on the contingent history of that discipline, and whether that method is accepted within it. . . . Once accepted by a group of scientists, a style of reasoning comes to seem natural to them, so natural that they do not question it.
>
> (Morgan 2012: 17)

This observation made by Morgan has great relevance for Piketty's adoption of an aggregative concept of capital, which can be traced back to Knight's

"Crusonia Plant" model of capital as an ever-growing homogenous mass (1944). The Knightian capital theory differs markedly from the Austrian capital theory, where capital is viewed as something that is heterogeneous and multi-specific (Lachmann 1956 [1978]). In fact, as several prominent capital theorists working in the Austrian tradition have noted, if capital was homogenous in use and capable of perpetual and automatic growth, there would be no economic problem of capital maintenance or of allocating capital to its most valued uses (Hayek 1936). Moreover, monetary calculation would also become unnecessary because, for example, there would be no need to rationally calculate the least costly way to build a railroad, as there would be no difference between platinum and iron (Mises 1920 [1975]).

Returning to Piketty's argument, those economists following the Austrian tradition of Mises and Hayek would counter Piketty by stating what Holcombe captures best in his review of *Capital in the Twenty-First Century*:

> β measures the aggregate monetary value of wealth (including land), whereas in fact capital is a heterogeneous collection of producer goods that, combined with labor, produce output. Capital and monetary wealth are two different things. This obscures the fact that owners of capital must first make decisions about what type of capital to invest in, and then decide how that capital can be best employed to earn a positive return.
>
> (Holcombe 2014: 552)

What Holcombe is suggesting here is a fundamental distinction that Mises draws in *Human Action* between "capital goods" and "capital" (1949 [2007]: 259). Individuals may choose to increase the amount of capital goods by engaging in more roundabout production. However, the processes of capital investment, allocation, and maintenance are not independent and cannot be separated from one another. Precisely because the structure of capital is heterogeneous in use, multi-specific, and complementary, though not perfectly so, to alternative capital combinations for the demands of entrepreneurs (Lachmann 1956: 12), the monetary value of capital has economic relevance only within a context of private property rights.

Without monetary exchange in the means of the production, it will be impossible to calculate the relative returns of investing in particular capital goods across competing consumer demands (Mises 1949 [2007]: 262). Yet Piketty argues that the higher rate of return on capital is not attributed to the derived demand of heterogeneous capital goods. Piketty makes it appear that a return on capital is a passive activity devoid of any active entrepreneurial discovery or monetary calculation of heterogeneous capital goods for that matter.

For Piketty, the capitalist earns a return on capital simply by virtue of his ownership, rather than the fact that capital has value only because it derives a stream of income from its being employed productively toward its highest-valued uses. Therefore, the recurring theme in Piketty's book is that inequality of income and wealth is generated by inherited wealth, which requires "public institutions and policies that would counter the effects of this implacable logic: for instance, a progressive global tax on capital" (2014: 35).

The question here is not whether less inequality is a desirable goal. As George Stigler has written elsewhere, economists since Adam Smith "have always been opposed to inequality of income" (1949: 1) as a policy objective. The question, rather, is whether the most effective means to reduce income inequality is by taxing the rich and redistributing income to the poor or by eliminating legal barriers that impede the discovery of profit opportunities and generate productivity gains among the least advantaged in society, the latter being proposed by Adam Smith. Building on this point, Friedman states that there "is a clear justification for social action of a very different kind than taxation to affect the distribution of income," namely, by adjusting

> the rules of the game so as to eliminate these sources of inequality. For example, special monopoly privileges granted by government, tariffs, and other legal enactments benefiting particular groups, are a source of inequality. The removal of these, the liberal will welcome.
>
> (Friedman 1962 [2002]: 176)

There is also a more important distinction to be made between the justification and the motivation behind income redistribution. Though liberals may agree with egalitarians that the reduction of income inequality is a justifiable goal, this does not necessarily mean that existing income transfer programs are actually motivated by this goal. The "poor do indeed receive substantial amounts of money in the United States," Tullock argues, "but nowhere near the total amount transferred. The bulk of the transfer goes to the politically influential and well organized" (Tullock 1997: 3).

According to the U.S. Census Bureau, total outlays by the U.S. federal government were just over $3.8 trillion, of which roughly $2.4 were allocated toward transfer payments between individuals (U.S. Census Bureau 2012: 313). Therefore, roughly two-thirds of the U.S. federal spending has gone to income redistribution. Of the $2.4 trillion spent toward transfer payments, however, roughly $623 billion went to "income security," or transfer payments to the poor, needy, and disabled, roughly 26% of the total amount of all transfer payments (U.S. Census Bureau 2012: 312).

Though an appalling figure from the standpoint of an individual who desires policies that benefit the least well-off in society, this is a logical outcome of democratic politics, which incentivizes public policy officials to concentrate benefits on well-organized and well-informed special interest groups and disperse the cost of such income redistribution on the masses of the ill-informed citizenry. Tullock's discussion on rent-seeking and wealth transfers relates directly to our account of generalized increasing returns. Both highlight how the institutional framework directs entrepreneurial activity. An institutional environment that grants ever greater political discretion over the distribution of income will generate generalized increasing returns to cronyism, rent-seeking, and the accumulation of wealth via income transfers, at the expense of the least advantaged in society.

Similar to Tullock's analysis, both Joseph Stiglitz and Luigi Zingales, although on opposite sides of the political spectrum, have been fervent critics of the crony capitalist environment in the United States and its contribution to increasing income inequality. Tullock is not alone in attributing increasing income inequality to rent-seeking. Stiglitz most recently has written that rent-seeking has not only undermined income equality but also a just distribution of income. As he states, "rent seeking is pervasive in the American economy, and that it actually impairs overall economic efficiency. The large gaps between private rewards and social returns that characterize a rent-seeking economy mean that incentives that individuals face often misdirect their actions" (Stiglitz 2012: 133–134), such as

> selling to government products at above market prices (noncompetitive procurement). The drug companies and military contractors excel in this form of rent seeking. Open government subsidies (as in agriculture) or hidden subsidies (trade restrictions that reduce competition or subsidies hidden in the tax system) are other ways of getting rents from the public.
> (Stiglitz 2012: 50)

Income redistribution has been most unjust precisely because it creates incentives whereby individuals earn monopoly rents through the use of government force, diminishing the extent to which individuals can create new wealth by taking advantage of new productive opportunities that would have been afforded to them via the generalized increasing returns to peaceful cooperation and productive entrepreneurship under the division of labor.

In a recent book, *A Capitalism for the People* (2012), Luigi Zingales argues that the rules of the economic game have shifted such that the United States is much less of the land of opportunity than it was when he moved here from Italy. Instead, as the United States has more and more sought to mimic the European social democracies, a regulatory environment that has produced a *different* sort of capitalist system, one in which regulatory capture becomes increasingly pervasive in a regulatory environment that grows increasingly complex. As Zingales argues:

> [F]or markets to work their magic, the playing field must be kept level and open to new entrants. When these conditions fail, free markets degenerate into inefficient monopolies – and when these monopolies extend their power to the political arena, we enter the realm of crony capitalism.
> (2012: 47)

Rent-seeking, cronyism, and the distributive injustice that emerges from the capitalist system that Zingales discusses are a by-product of the expansion of regulation that concentrates benefits on the politically connected, the costs of which are dispersed on the masses of rationally ignorant voters (Holcombe 2013). The point here is not to argue that all income inequality is driven by the unintended consequences of the redistribution of the income by government, namely, to special interest groups. Rather, it is to suggest that such public policy measures, despite the best intentions of policymakers, redirect entrepreneurial incentives toward the unjust accrual of monopoly rents, thereby perpetuating income inequality, precisely because such efforts will be corrupted by the influence of interest-group politics, however well-intended income redistribution may be.

IV. Conclusion

As Adam Smith once wrote, the "difference of natural talents in different men, is, in reality, much less than we are aware of" and the "difference between the most dissimilar characters, between a philosopher and a common street porter, for example, seems to arise not so much from nature, as from habit, custom, and education" (Smith 1776 [1981]: 28–29). Though the source of exchange and specialization is the differences in skills and physical endowments between individuals, these differences are much more a by-product, rather than a cause of specialization itself, from which the distribution of income emerges.

Questions of distributive justice in the marketplace are about what distribution of income is due to each individual. However, if the source of growing income inequality is not due mainly to any natural inequalities in skills, talents, or physical talents, and if our goal is to promote the conditions by which individuals do not earn income in a zero-sum or negative sum-manner, the question to ask then is the following: what set of institutional arrangements generates a pattern of income distribution that is consistent with affording individuals the greatest scope of possibilities for specialization under the division of labor?

As our predecessors in classical political economy had taught us, questions of distributive justice are institutional in nature, and therefore require an institutional solution. The institutional framework of a market economy not only generates peace, prosperity, individual liberty and distributive justice by unleashing the possibility for generalized increasing returns to exchange and production. Questions regarding distributive justice that are answered in terms of equilibrium analysis assume away ex ante the process by which income is generated and distributed, and whether or not the equilibrium outcome in the distribution of income from comparative institutional arrangements is just or unjust.

In an open-ended world of uncertainty, where marginal products of factors of production must be discovered, an institutional environment that erects legal barriers, stifles productive entrepreneurship, and provides monopoly privileges will generate generalized increasing returns to unproductive entrepreneurship. This perverse redirection of generalized increasing returns to capturing political discretion generates a pattern of income redistribution that is unjustified, not only because income is redistributed by rent-seeking at the expense of the least advantaged in society, but also because it crowds out the possibility for the least advantaged individuals in society to climb the economic and social ladder, thereby perpetuating income inequality.

Notes

1 It is important to mention here that although we used the term "classical political economists" broadly, we acknowledge exceptions to the broad characterization we make. Nevertheless, as Machovec writes, unlike "Ricardo, the vast majority of the classical economists, including those of the UK, reasoned about the market by addressing one or more aspects of the competitive process" (Machovec 1995: 98). Moreover, "Ricardo reasoned purely in equilibrium terms. . . . Ricardo therefore is the odd man out. His narrow treatment of the market was uncharacteristic of his era, more neoclassical than classical, but consistent with his desire to focus exclusively on comparative statics" (Machovec 1995: 96–97). See also Holcombe (1998).

2 As Stigler notes, in "their explanations of the workings of a competitive economy the most striking deficiency of the classical economists was their failure to work out the theory of the effects of competition on the distribution of income" (1957: 5). Thus, the classical economists were not able to provide a logically satisfactory theory of income distribution to complement their theory of competition and the market process and thus failed to deliver a convincing argument regarding the distributive justice to critics of the market process (Buchanan 1991: 244).

3 According to Caldwell (2004: 90), "The ideal type selects out from an infinite reality the characteristic features that are of interest to the *investigator*. An ideal type is not a description of objective facts but, rather, what Weber calls. . . 'a purely ideal *limiting* concept with which the real situation or action is *compared*.'"

4 To say that both Clark and Wicksteed were exclusively equilibrium theorists who had no understanding or appreciation of the market as a dynamic process of adjustment would be misleading. For example, Wicksteed's *The Common Sense of Political Economy* (1910 [1933]) is much closer to classical political economy in emphasizing the process by which market prices guide individuals and coordinating the plans of buyers and sellers toward equilibrium (see also Kirzner 1999 [2015]). Our point here is that in their defense of the justice of income distribution, Clark and Wicksteed had defended the distributive justice of the market in terms of equilibrium, which had defined away a defense of entrepreneurial profits.

5 As Don Lavoie states in *Rivalry and Central Planning*, "it is a great merit of Marxian – and Austrian – analysis that capitalism is understood to be always in disequilibrium" (1985: 35). Schumpeter as well writes that "what [Marx] aimed at analyzing was not a state of equilibrium which according to him capitalist society can never attain, but on the contrary a process of incessant change in the economic structure" (1942 [1947]: 28). This is evidenced by Marx, in which he writes the following: "They [purchase and sale] will of course always attempt to equalize one another, but in the place of the earlier immediate equality there now stands the constant movement of equalization which evidently presupposes constant nonequivalence" (1939 [1973]: 147–148). See also Lavoie (1983) on Marx's disequilibrium theory of money.

6 To put this into context, we interpret Alchian and Demsetz's use of the term "classical analysis" to refer not to the way in which classical economists, such as Smith, Hume, or even Mill, analyzed production and distribution. Rather, they are addressing how the neoclassical approach typically treated its analysis of production and distribution, which is, as they mention in the quote, in a framework of zero transaction costs.

7 Though a comprehensive discussion of Piketty's argument is beyond the scope of this chapter, let us briefly explain Piketty's argument. Although Piketty keeps the mathematical

sophistication of his argument to a minimum, the historical phenomena that he describes about the convergence and divergence of income distribution are nonetheless modeled by isolating a few key variables of interest into mathematical relationships. Piketty identifies three mathematical relationships that form his economic model: (i) the first fundamental law of capitalism (FFC); (ii) the second fundamental law of capitalism (SFC); and (iii) the central contradiction of capitalism (CCC).

The FFC, which represents an accounting identity, postulates that the share of income going to capital, α, is equal to the return on capital, r, multiplied by the capital/income ratio, β, i.e., $\alpha = r \times \beta$ (Piketty 2014: 52). The SFC postulates that the capital/income ratio (β) will tend to equal the ratio of saving (s) to economic growth (g), i.e., $\beta = s/g$. Unlike the FFC, the SFC represents a long-run tendency (Piketty 2014: 166). From these two equations, Piketty derives the CCC, which postulates that in the long run, particularly as capital markets grow more perfectly competitive, the rate of return on capital exceeds the growth rate of the economy, or $r > g$. What logically follows from the CCC is that inherited wealth grows faster than output and wages (Piketty 2014: 571).

Piketty's main policy conclusions, such as the implementation of a global progressive tax on capital coupled with a highly progressive income tax to remedy income inequality, are derived from the CCC. Yet, such normative conclusions are based on the modeling of certain key economic variables, the interaction of which deductively yields the CCC.

References

Alchian, Armen A., and Harold Demsetz. 1972. "Production, Information Costs, and Economic Organization." *The American Economic Review* 62 (5): 777–795.

Boettke, Peter J. 1997. "Where Did Economics Go Wrong? Modern Economics as a Flight from Reality." *Critical Review* 11 (1): 11–64.

Boettke, Peter J. 2012. *Living Economics: Yesterday, Today, and Tomorrow*. Oakland: The Independent Institute.

Boettke, Peter J., and Rosolino A. Candela. 2014. "Alchian, Buchanan, and Coase: A Neglected Branch of Chicago Price Theory." *Man and the Economy: The Journal of the Coase Society* 1 (2): 189–208.

Boettke, Peter J., and Rosolino A. Candela. 2017. "The Liberty of Progress: Increasing Returns, Institutions, and Entrepreneurship." *Social Philosophy and Policy* 35 (2): 136–163.

Buchanan, James M. 1964. "What Should Economists Do?" *Southern Economic Journal* 30 (3): 213–222.

Buchanan, James M. 1991. "The Potential and the Limits of Socially Organized Humankind." In James Buchanan, ed., *The Economics and the Ethics of Constitutional Order*. Ann Arbor: University of Michigan Press.

Buchanan, James M., and Yong J. Yoon. 1999. "Generalized Increasing Returns, Euler's Theorem, and Competitive Equilibrium." *History of Political Economy* 13 (3): 511–523.

Caldwell, Bruce. 2004. *Hayek's Challenge: An Intellectual Biography of F.A. Hayek*. Chicago: University of Chicago Press.

Clark, John Bates. 1899. *The Distribution of Wealth: A Theory of Wages, Interest and Profits*. New York: Macmillan.

Coyne, Christopher J. 2010. "Economics as the Study of Coordination and Exchange." In Peter J. Boettke, ed., *Handbook on Contemporary Austrian Economics*. Northampton, MA: Edward Elgar.

Edgeworth, F. Y. 1881. *Mathematical Psychics: An Essay on the Application of Mathematics to the Moral Sciences*. C. Kegan Paul & Co.

Friedman, Milton. 1962 [2002]. *Capitalism and Freedom, Fortieth Anniversary Edition*. Chicago: University of Chicago Press.

Hayek, F. A. 1936. "The Mythology of Capital." *The Quarterly Journal of Economics* 50 (2): 199–228.

Holcombe, Randall G. 1998. "Entrepreneurship and Economic Growth." *The Quarterly Journal of Austrian Economics* 1 (2): 45–62.

Holcombe, Randall G. 2013. "Crony Capitalism: By-Product of Big Government." *The Independent Review: A Journal of Political Economy* 17 (4): 541–559.

Holcombe, Randall G. 2014. "Thomas Piketty: Capital in the Twenty-First Century." *Public Choice* 160: 551–557.

Kaldor, Nicholas. 1957. "A Model of Economic Growth." *The Economic Journal* 67 (268): 591–624.

Katz, Lawrence F., and Kevin M. Murphy. 1992. "Changes in Relative Wages, 1963–1987: Supply and Demand Factors." *The Quarterly Journal of Economics* 107 (1): 35–78.

Kirzner, Israel M. 1985. *Discovery and the Capitalist Process*. Chicago: University of Chicago Press.

Kirzner, Israel M. 1988a. "The Economic Calculation Debate: Lessons for Austrians." *The Review of Austrian Economics* 2 (1): 1–18.

Kirzner, Israel M. 1988b. "Some Ethical Implications for Capitalism of the Socialist Calculation Debate." *Social Philosophy & Policy* 6 (1): 165–182.

Kirzner, Israel M. 1989 [2016]. "Discovery, Capitalism, and Distributive Justice." In Peter J. Boettke and Frédéric Sautet, eds., *The Collected Works of Israel M. Kirzner*. Indianapolis: Liberty Fund.

Kirzner, Israel M. 1999 [2015]. "Phillip Wicksteed: The British Austrian." In Peter J. Boettke and Frédéric Sautet, eds., *The Collected Works of Israel M. Kirzner: Austrian Subjectivism and the Emergence of Entrepreneurship Theory*. Indianapolis: Liberty Fund.

Kirzner, Israel M. 2019. "The Ethics of Pure Entrepreneurship: An Austrian Economics Perspective." *The Review of Austrian Economics* 32 (2): 89–99.

Knight, Frank H. 1921. *Risk, Uncertainty, and Profit*. Boston: Houghton Mifflin Company.

Knight, Frank H. 1944. "Diminishing Returns from Investment." *Journal of Political Economy* 52 (1): 26–47.

Kuhn, Thomas S. 1962 [1996]. *The Structure of Scientific Revolutions*, 3rd ed. Chicago: University of Chicago Press.

Lavoie, Don. 1983. "Some Strengths in Marx's Disequilibrium Theory of Money." *Cambridge Journal of Economics* 7 (1): 55–58.

Lavoie, Don. 1985. *Rivalry and Central Planning: The Socialist Calculation Debate Reconsidered*. Cambridge: Cambridge University Press.

Lachmann, Ludwig M. 1956 [1978]. *Capital and Its Structure*. Kansas City: Sheed Andrews and McMeel.

Machovec, Frank M. 1995. *Perfect Competition and the Transformation of Economics*. New York: Routledge.

McCloskey, Deidre N. 2006. *The Bourgeois Virtues: Ethics for an Age of Commerce*. Chicago: University of Chicago Press.

McCloskey, Deidre N. 2010. *Bourgeois Dignity: Why Economics Can't Explain the Modern World*. Chicago: University of Chicago Press.

McCloskey, Deidre N. 2016. *Bourgeois Equality: How Ideas, Not Capital or Institutions, Enriched the World*. Chicago: University of Chicago Press.

Marx, Karl. 1939 [1973]. *Grundrisse*. New York: Random House.

Menger, Carl. 1891 [2016]. "The Social Theories of Classical Political Economy and Modern Economic Policy." Translated by Erwin Dekker and Stefan Kolev. *Econ Journal Watch* 13 (3): 467–489.

Mises, Ludwig. 1920 [1975]. "Economic Calculation in the Socialist Commonwealth." In F. A. Hayek, ed., *Collectivist Economic Planning*. Clifton: August M. Kelley.

Mises, Ludwig. 1949 [2007]. *Human Action: A Treatise on Economics*. Indianapolis: Liberty Fund.

Morgan, Mary S. 2012. *The World in a Model: How Economists Work and Think*. New York: Cambridge University Press.

Phelps, Edmund. 2013. *Mass Flourishing: How Grassroots Innovation Created Jobs, Challenge, and Change*. Princeton, NJ: Princeton University Press.

Piketty, Thomas. 2014. *Capital in the Twenty-First Century*. Cambridge, MA: Harvard University Press.

Schumpeter, Joseph A. 1942 [1947]. *Capitalism, Socialism and Democracy*, 2nd ed. New York: Harper & Brothers.

Smith, Adam. 1776 [1981]. *An Inquiry into the Nature and Causes of the Wealth of Nations*. Indianapolis: Liberty Fund.

Solow, Robert. 1956. "A Contribution to the Theory of Economic Growth." *The Quarterly Journal of Economics* 70 (1): 65–94.

Stigler, George J. 1949. *Five Lectures on Economic Problems*. London: Longman, Green, and CO.

Stigler, George J. 1957. "Perfect Competition, Historically Contemplated." *Journal of Political Economy* 65 (1): 1–17.

Stiglitz, Joseph E. 1969. "Distribution of Income and Wealth Among Individuals." *Econometrica* 37 (3): 382–397.

Stigler, George J. 1971. "The Theory of Economic Regulation." *The Bell Journal of Economics and Management Science* 2 (1): 3–21.

Stiglitz, Joseph E. 2012. *The Price of Inequality: How Today's Divided Society Endangers Our Future*. New York: Norton.

Tullock, Gordon. 1967. "The Welfare Costs of Tariffs, Monopolies, and Theft." *Western Economic Journal* 5 (3): 224–232.

Tullock, Gordon. 1997. *The Economics of Income Redistribution*, 2nd ed. New York: Springer.

U.S. Census Bureau. 2012. *Statistical Abstract of the United States: 2012*, 131st ed. Available at https://www2.census.gov/library/publications/2011/compendia/statab/131ed/2012-statab.pdf

Wicksteed, Philip. 1894. *An Essay on the Co-Ordination of the Laws of Distribution*, 1932 ed., Reprint No. 12. London: London School of Economics.

Wicksteed, Phillip. 1910 [1933]. *The Common Sense of Political Economy*. London: Routledge & Kegan Paul.

Zingales, Luigi. 2012. *A Capitalism for the People: Recapturing the Lost Genius of American Prosperity*. New York: Basic Books.

4 Growth, inequality, and unfairness

Comparing the progressive and classical liberal perspectives

Steven Horwitz

I. Introduction

Contemporary discussions of inequality are full of challenges, from different people using words differently, to the finer points of knowing and interpreting economic data, to the relative roles of ethical and social scientific perspectives in how we understand the issues in play. Many such discussions also move back and forth between concerns about inequality per se and poverty. An implicit assumption made by many intellectuals troubled by rising inequality is that it is linked with an increase in poverty, or at least a stagnation of middle-class and working-class incomes or material well-being. That is, they are implicitly arguing that recent increases in inequality do not meet the test of Rawls' (1971) "difference principle" because they do not work to the benefit of the least well-off.

This perspective, which I will refer to as the "Progressive" view, is not the only way to see these issues. Rawls' presentation of the difference principle in *The Theory of Justice* is, at least in theory, institutionally neutral: his claim that justice requires inequality to benefit the least well-off does not involve an empirical claim about the set of economic institutions and policies that will lead to this result. The Progressive view is that broadly free market economies, including the U.S. economy, do not meet the Rawlsian test, which leads its adherents to believe that greater government intervention is necessary.

By contrast, what we might call the "Classical Liberal" view argues that not only would free market economies meet the difference principle in theory, but that even imperfectly free economies like that of the United States actually do meet it in practice. For this group, accepting the Rawlsian conception of justice embodied in the difference principle does not require a larger role for government. In fact, Classical Liberals argue that this criterion will be better achieved with a smaller role for government, because a significant amount of existing government intervention actually *worsens* the well-being of the least well-off.

The debate between the Progressives and Classical Liberals, then, is largely an empirical one: has the increase in inequality worsened or improved the material well-being of the least well-off?[1] In this chapter, I present evidence that suggests that the Classical Liberals have it right. The standards of living of both the average American household and the poorest American households have risen significantly in the last 40 or 50 years, even as inequality might have grown. This evidence suggests that the U.S. economy has met the requirements of the difference principle, and therefore the growth in inequality is consistent with a Rawlsian conception of justice.

I also take this argument a step further by exploring the relationship between these two perspectives on inequality and larger concerns about "fairness." Recent research indicates that people are more concerned with the fairness of distributions than their equality, per se. That is, people are willing to accept more inequality if they think it was produced by a fair process.

Even though recent increases in inequality have, in the aggregate, benefited the least well-off, not all individual increases in inequality have done so. Building on Geloso and Horwitz (2017), I distinguish between desirable and undesirable forms of growing inequality and argue that most of the causes of rising inequality that do not meet the Rawlsian test are the ones that would be characterized as "unfair." That is, they result from different groups of people getting different treatment under the law, with some getting access to special privileges, while others being denied the opportunity to pursue the economic activities they wish to. This differential treatment gets enshrined in the law through a variety of successful rent-seeking and rent-protecting activities whose effects are clearly regressive. So at least *some* portion of the growth in inequality might be harming the least well-off, and those concerned about both inequality and poverty need to make the distinctions in question. If so, rather than indulging in the Progressive policy preferences for things like increasing the progressivity of the tax system or increasing spending on government anti-poverty programs, this Classical Liberal perspective suggests the alternative of removing the problematic policies already in place.

In short, my argument in this chapter is that the Classical Liberal view that rising inequality has benefited the least well-off is empirically correct. Moreover, not only does this increase in inequality meet the Rawlsian criterion for fairness, but it also meets a more general conception of fairness by improving the lives of the poor through processes that treat people as equals as opposed to a variety of poverty-inducing causes of inequality that involve special privileges for some. In the end, the Classical Liberal approach of treating people as equals under the law will produce inequality, but that inequality will work to the benefit of the least well-off and satisfy people's concerns about fairness, while attempts to favor some groups over others (what people may well perceive as "unfair") will lead to greater inequality that harm the poor.

II. Multiple meanings of equality

Any examination of inequality will have to contend with the multiple meanings of equality and inequality that are invoked in discussions of those topics. The simplest distinction we can make is between equality of *outcomes* and equality *before the law*. What is meant by "equality of outcomes" as a goal for social policy is generally clear: people should have roughly equal material resources to pursue the lives they wish to live. Supporting such a view of equality does not require that people are the same along other dimensions. It only requires that none have significantly more material resources at their disposal than anyone else. The assumption, which is sometimes implicit, in arguments for equality of (material) outcomes is that inequality of outcomes leads to other problematic consequences because those with greater resources are able exercise some form of dominance or power over those who have less. Such arguments also often assume that movements away from equality of material outcomes work, or at least *have worked* in the recent past, to the disadvantage of the least well-off. That is, they assume that increasing inequality causes increasing poverty and that movements toward equality of outcomes will reduce poverty.[2]

The Progressives who wish to use public policy to create more equality in material outcomes must address a number of questions before that desire can be translated into concrete policies. For example, what is the relevant economic unit whose material outcomes should be made equal? Should it be those of individuals, or households, or families? This question matters because households and families are buffers between the market and the material resources received by individuals. If individuals are the relevant units who should be equal, policymakers need to consider how households and families redistribute resources or bargain over household production in ways that undermine equality at the individual level.

Similarly, if we are to make households or families the relevant unit of equality, how do we deal with the variation in household composition or the shifting structure of families? For example, the increase in the divorce rate over the last few decades has contributed to measured inequality by frequently turning one "rich" household into two poorer ones. Thus, if we measure household inequality, we find that it has risen; but if we measure individual inequality, we find that it has not. Divorce is also more common among the poor, which means it more often turns one somewhat poor household into two very poor ones.[3] Such considerations make it evident that equalizing material outcomes is not as simple as it might seem.

A second consideration, and one that I will explore in depth in what follows, is how we measure "material outcomes." Are we talking about equality of wealth, of income, of total compensation, or of consumption?[4] In what follows, I will argue that what people are able to consume is a much better indicator of how well-off they are and is, therefore, what we should focus on if we are concerned with issues of inequality and poverty. The whole point of acquiring financial wealth and earning an income is, presumably, to be able to purchase the goods and services that we believe will enable us to live better lives. Our ability to purchase food, clothing, and shelter, or the ability to keep ourselves warm in the winter and cool in the summer, or to buy life-saving or life-enhancing medical products and services, are the kinds of things that ultimately matter for our well-being. Increased income, via increased earning power or redistribution, might be one way to equalize consumption possibilities, but so might a reduction in the costs of basic goods and services. It follows that if our concern with equality of material outcomes is to be centered on consumption, there might be many ways available to ensure greater equality.

The Classical Liberal conception of equality before the law, by contrast, does not face similar conceptual ambiguities and, in fact, requires far less of policymakers. Respecting the rule of law and what Hayek (1960: 151–54) has called the "generality principle" only requires that governments treat all citizens equally: the law cannot identify particular persons or classes of persons for differential treatment and cannot take the form of privileges that some have and others do not. In addition, the law must apply to everyone, including those who make the law. In a society in which equality means this sort of equality before the law, everyone has equal moral and political status in terms of his or her treatment by other people and by the state.

Of course, there is no assurance that material outcomes will be equal in a Classical Liberal society. In fact, it is almost certain that societies characterized by equality before the law will be ones with a notable degree of material *inequality*. Once we acknowledge that individuals are different in their skills, abilities, and knowledge, it should be clear that treating them equally before the law will not produce equality of outcomes. As Hayek (1960: 87) argued:

> From the fact that people are very different it follows that, if we treat them equally, the result must be inequality in their actual position, and that the only way to place them in an equal position would be to treat them differently. Equality before the law and material equality are therefore not only different but are in conflict with each other; and we can achieve either the one or the other, but not both at the same time.

For Hayek, the argument for equality before the law is premised not on the similarity of humans but on our differences. By recognizing our equal freedom under the law, he argues, we enable each of us to contribute our distinct skills and knowledge to the larger whole. Because we are different, we must give each other the maximum space to exercise our unique abilities and thereby bring value to others.[5]

Conversely, the Progressive desire to achieve equality in material outcomes means that we will have to treat people very differently and unequally. In the simplest case, if we wish to tax the rich to equalize incomes, we will have to tax some people at higher rates than others and provide some people with public resources that others do not get. One can also imagine policies such as minimum or maximum wage laws that prohibit people of certain skill levels from engaging in labor contracts of their choosing. Finding a way to eliminate the differences that produce inequality of outcomes will be necessary if one wants equality of outcomes. Doing so will require that governments treat those with skills or abilities that produce greater incomes or wealth differently from those who lack those skills or abilities.[6]

From Hayek's argument it follows that the desire to achieve any particular pattern of household incomes must necessarily involve restricting people's freedoms and treating them differentially under the law. Free people will produce outcomes that do not conform to the desires of social planners, including those making the choices in question.[7] Consider the way in which many people who object to high levels of inequality gladly turn over large portions of their incomes to purchase Apple products, making their corporate leadership and stockholders very rich in the process. Isn't the only way to prevent that sort of inequality to restrict our freedom to purchase the products we prefer? That liberty upsets attempts to impose patterns means that either we must give up on patterned outcomes in the name of liberty or give up liberty in the name of patterned outcomes. This is another way to put the point that Hayek made almost 60 years ago.

The distinction between equality of material outcomes and equality before the law, however, does not capture all of the relevant distinctions in modern debates over inequality. The Apple example noted previously can help us see why. Given that a good number of people who think income inequality is a big problem seem to be comfortable with the idea that their choices to purchase Apple products has made a lot of people very rich, perhaps the concern many have with inequality is not a concern about inequality of material outcomes in and of themselves. In the next two sections, I will explore two other concerns that might be at the bottom of complaints about inequality and begin to look at some empirical data to help us understand if those concerns are valid.

III. Inequality or unfairness?

The Progressive and Classical Liberal perspectives on inequality seem to suggest different views over what constitutes "fairness." When Progressives talk about income inequality, their conception of fairness seems to be bound up with some notion of equality of outcomes, or at least equality of starting points and resources provided by society, if not strict equality of outcomes. Fairness, in their intellectual arguments, is about patterns of resource allocation, whether at the starting point or in terms of material outcomes. By contrast, Classical Liberal discussions of fairness focus not on outcomes but on the *processes* by which resources change hands. This is consistent with their emphasis on equality before the law. What makes something fair is that the rules of the game are fair and agreed upon and that all the choices made under those rules conformed to them. As long as people earn and spend their money in ways that conform to the rules of the game, the fact that those decentralized choices produce patterns of income that are unequal is not deemed to be "unfair." In fact, such an outcome is fair, in precisely the same way that a very lopsided score in a baseball game is fair if all played by the rules.

That said, it's not clear in practice that the Progressives disagree with the process view of fairness. The Apple example suggests that even critics of inequality are not as enthusiastic about criticizing very high incomes if those incomes seem to meet some ethical criterion that matters to them other than equality. If the concern that manifests itself as a complaint about inequality is not about inequality per se, what might it be about? I offer two alternatives. First, in this section, I explore in more depth the relationship between inequality and "fairness." In the next section, I do the same for the relationship between inequality and poverty. What bothers Progressives about inequality might not be inequality per se but the belief that inequality is linked with unfairness and the worsening of poverty.

Consider the example of inequality critics who buy Apple products, thereby enhancing the incomes of many very rich people. The users of Apple products often feel that those products are not only extraordinarily functional but that they are also aesthetically pleasing. Apple has significant brand loyalty from many of its customers. Perhaps even those customers critical of inequality understand that Apple is providing them with something in return or that the exchanges they make with Apple are "fair" in a way that is not true, in their view, of other kinds of market interactions. It is okay that Steve Jobs and everyone else got very rich making Apple products because what we get for our money is such a good product that it overrides any concern about how it might contribute to inequality. If Progressive critics of inequality are thinking this way, it suggests that inequality per se is not the problem and that some other ethical concern is.

If high incomes are acceptable when the exchanges that produced them are deemed to be ethically acceptable, then we need to know more about what might constitute "ethically acceptable" in this regard. In a recent study, Starmans et al. (2017) showed, using a variety of evidence from laboratory studies and various forms of cross-cultural research, that what bothers people is not inequality per se but the perception of unfairness. Many prior studies of inequality made use of small group situations where it was easy for concerns about inequality and unfairness to be confounded. Later work has enabled researchers to untangle the two and see more clearly that what humans care about is the perception of fairness. We are willing to accept unequal outcomes if we believe the process that produced them was fair. We will not be happy with equal outcomes if we believe those outcomes were achieved by processes that were not fair.

If Starmans et al. are correct, it suggests that the next set of questions to be answered will be about what sorts of things are considered fair and unfair. Without delving into the complex psychological and philosophical literature on those questions, I want to suggest that there are three sorts of arguments about fairness that might be directly relevant to concerns about inequality. The first two of those are more abstract, while the third is more empirical.

As the opening section suggested, there are alternative views of what constitutes the form of equality we might wish to achieve. If equality of outcomes is not valued more than fairness, then perhaps one way of reconceiving the argument for equality before the law is to frame it as a way of treating everyone *fairly*. To the extent that equality before the law means that no person or group has specific privileges or that no person or group has specific restrictions on their freedoms, then everyone is being treated equally and, perhaps, fairly. Perhaps the Classical Liberal version of fairness is one that Progressives can agree to, at least in principle if not in all applications.

One form of unfairness that people routinely object to is when some persons or groups are thought to have privileges, in the form of unearned advantages, that others do not. As Hayek (1960: 154) notes, the word "privilege" suggests this notion of unfairness, as it comes from the Latin "privus" for private and "lex" or "leg," meaning "the law." The word means "private law" in the sense that some rules apply to some people and other rules to other people. Rules that apply selectively are recognized as unfair by humans from our earliest ages. If the equality of outcomes that Progressives generally desire requires the creation of such privileges, then, perhaps, many of the means to the end of equality of outcomes will be seen as unfair. One way to better align the discussion of economic inequality with our concern about fairness is to focus on the processes by which either equality will be achieved politically or inequality emerges economically and ask which processes seem more fair.

The other way to approach the debate over inequality in terms of fairness is to think through the economic processes by which unequal outcomes emerge. For the moment, assume we have an unhampered market in which people are free to buy and sell as they please. The first lesson of economics is that such exchanges are mutually beneficial, at least at the moment of exchange. More generally, exchange is value creating for both parties. For the buyer, the subjective value associated with a want being satisfied is the gain, while for the seller, the gain is the profit made on the purchase. Consumers give up money for want-satisfaction and producers give up goods and services for money profits. Both parties give something up and get something in return.

If the mutually beneficial nature of market exchange is thought to be fair, then perhaps the outcomes such exchanges produce will be seen as fair as well, even if they produce rising inequality. When Progressives buy Apple products, they presumably think the incomes earned by Apple employees and stockholders are ethically acceptable because the company has created value for them as consumers. They can see the mutually beneficial nature of the exchange as they hold the Apple products in their hand and use them happily. Here too, if the fact that genuine market exchanges create value for both parties can be understood in terms of "fairness," then perhaps we can get around the more simplistic versions of the debates over inequality.

There are several obvious barriers to be overcome for Progressive critics of inequality to see the value creation of market exchange as being presumptively fair. One barrier will be over how "voluntary" market exchanges are, especially in the labor market. Concerns about power will come into play and any attempt to cast market exchanges as presumptively fair will have to have an answer for why workers are not exploited. Those answers are available from a Classical Liberal perspective and may well require recourse to the empirical evidence on the way in which competitive markets have driven up wages over the long run of economic history.

A second barrier will be making the case for value creation in more abstract sorts of exchanges, especially those involving the financial sector. It is easy to see the value creation, and therefore the fairness, when you can hold an iPhone in your hand. It is less easy when we are talking about the seven- or eight-figure salaries of hedge fund managers who move around the abstractions we call money or wealth. Understanding how those activities, at least in a genuine market context, are value creating for customers and society at large will be important if market exchanges and the pattern of incomes and wealth they produce are to be seen as presumptively fair. Those concerns noted, the evidence that the debate over inequality might really be a debate over fairness suggests that it is well worth asking how people understand fairness in the context of the economy and what that means for the competing judgments Progressives and Classical Liberals make about inequality and various policies surrounding it.

IV. Inequality, poverty, mobility, and fairness

In addition to being crosscut by issues of fairness and unfairness, the debates over inequality are often confounded with debates over poverty. Many Progressive critics of inequality seem to assume that rising inequality comes at the expense of the poor, and that the fight against inequality is simultaneously a fight against increasing poverty. This claim, which is usually implicit, has both an ethical and an empirical component to it. The ethical claim can be understood as a Rawlsian concern that any inequalities are only justified if they work to the benefit of the least well-off. This ethical claim can also be understood as a worry that the processes producing inequality are unfair in the sense discussed previously.

However, this ethical claim is intertwined with an empirical one: is it true that rising inequality is associated with rising poverty? If so, then there really is no confounding of rising inequality and poverty – they move in step. If not, then we need to separate the two topics and ask whether rising inequality that is associated with improvements in well-being for the least well-off is really a matter for concern and whether it is rightfully seen as "unfair." Finally, we can also analyze the relationship between rising inequality and income mobility. Has rising inequality made it substantively more difficult for poor people to eventually get richer? This too might enter our judgments of fairness both as noted in the previous section and in Rawlsian terms. Like the relationship between inequality and poverty, there is much empirical data here. The remainder of this section explores these questions.

IV.I. Inequality and poverty

For the sake of argument, I will assume that both the Progressives and the Classical Liberals accept the Rawlsian difference principle as their standard of justice.

I will also accept the claim that measured income inequality has been rising over the past few decades, acknowledging that there is substantial debate over this claim. To the degree that Progressives are concerned because they believe that this increase in inequality is causing greater poverty, they are making an empirical claim that can be challenged. And given the difference principle, that empirical claim has consequences for our moral judgments. Furthermore, it is at least possible that these questions are also bound up with the notions of fairness that may well be more morally salient than is inequality per se.

Theorists often distinguish between absolute and relative poverty, with the former referring to the income or consumption of the poor regardless of what others in the same society are able to earn or buy. Relative poverty, by contrast, measures poverty in comparison to the income or consumption of the other members of that society. If poverty is understood only in relative terms, then indeed the poor will always be with us. However, the Rawlsian concern is with the absolute condition of the least well-off. Growing inequality is acceptable if the least well-off are better in absolute terms. It has to be understood that way, or rising inequality could *never* satisfy the Rawlsian criterion because, virtually by definition, rising inequality means the poor are worse off in relative terms. In what follows, therefore, I focus on absolute measures of poverty.

The decline in absolute poverty is quite obvious with a long enough time frame. If we go back 300 years or more, nearly all humans lived in what could rightly be called absolute poverty. Even those who lived relatively well for the time were quite poor compared to not just the typical Westerner today but even the poorest in the West. One need only consider the access to medicines, consumption opportunities, and life expectancy of North Americans who live below the poverty line in comparison to what was available to an 18th-century king to see this point. The preindustrial world could rightly be called one of a mostly even distribution of misery. Critics of rising inequality would likely have no truck with this point. Their claim is about the much more recent history of the last 40 or 50 years. Are the poor and the middle class substantially worse off today than they were in, say, the 1970s? That is a different question.

The inequality critics can point to some data that support their concern about poverty. It is true, for example, that the share of total income earned by the bottom 20% of income earners has fallen since the 1970s and that the top 20%, and especially the top 5% and 1%, have seen their share of total income rise substantially. However, a declining share of total income does not mean that the bottom 20% are worse off in absolute terms. If the total pool of income has grown sufficiently, then a smaller *share* of the larger pool might be a larger absolute amount of income. In fact, this is what has happened. The real incomes of the poorest 20% have grown, though only slightly, since the 1970s. Even if we look at real wages across the income distribution, the evidence since the 1970s is that there has been growth, but only a very little. So the absolute value of the poor's share of total income and the real wage series do not support the claim that the poor have been made worse off in absolute terms, but not by much. This would be a very thin reed to grab onto in order to satisfy the Rawlsian difference principle.

The evidence on stagnant real wages depends greatly upon the measure of inflation that is used to convert nominal wages to real wages. The most widely used data on real wages use the Consumer Price Index (CPI) to make this conversion. Economists have long argued that the CPI overstates the actual degree of price inflation faced by most households. If we are overstating inflation, then we are reducing nominal wages too much, which in turn understates real wage growth. In a recent paper, Sacerdote (2017) applied three alternatives to the standard CPI to adjust the nominal wage series since 1975: (1) he used the Personal Consumption Expenditure measure used by the Fed; (2) he adjusted the CPI downward by 20%, in line with the conclusions of the Boskin Commission's results on CPI biases; and (3) he applied the widely recognized adjustments recommended by Hamilton (1998) and Costa (2001). All three adjustments show higher real wage growth than the unadjusted CPI, with the Hamilton/Costa adjustments showing positive real wage growth in each ten-year period from 1975 to 2015. With the appropriate adjustments in our measure of inflation, the real wage series shows clearly positive growth since the 1970s, though nothing spectacular.

Wages and income are not the only ways to measure poverty, however. What we ultimately care about is what people are able to consume with the incomes they earn. The last 40 years have seen a remarkable expansion of the kinds of goods and services available to all consumers as well as a decline in the real costs of most consumption items that has made these goods and services more easily obtainable by the poor. If we measure absolute poverty by the consumption of poor households, we see a more dramatic reduction in absolute poverty than we do by wages and incomes.

We can start this analysis by recognizing that one way to measure the real cost of goods and services is by the number of work hours it takes the average person to purchase them. Note that this is not a "labor theory of value." Rather, it is an attempt to reduce nominal prices down to a common real measure, much like the CPI does for wages. For example, if in one year a 3-lb chicken costs $2.00 and the average manufacturing wage is $6 per hour, we know that it takes 20 minutes of work to purchase that chicken. If a decade later, the chicken still costs $2.00 but the average wage is now $10 per hour, the labor time needed to purchase that chicken has now fallen to 12 minutes, or a decline of 40%. Notice too that we do not have to make inflation adjustments here because we are comparing two nominal values by the same metric: work time necessary to purchase the good. Table 4.1 shows how the work time needed to purchase most goods and services has fallen over the last 50 plus years. It should not surprise us to find that those items are more widely found in the typical American household, including, and perhaps particularly, among the poor.

Horwitz (2015a) provides a more detailed discussion of the data and further sources, but the general result is that the costs of many major household items (such as kitchen appliances, TVs, automobile tires, etc.) have fallen

Table 4.1 Retail prices and the time cost of household appliances: 1959 versus 1973 versus 2013 (Perry 2013)

Household Appliances	*Retail Price 1959*	*Hours of Work @ $2.09*	*Retail Price 1973*	*Hours of Work @ $3.95*	*Retail Price 2013*	*Hours of Work @ 19.30*
Washing machine	$210	100.5	$285	72.2	$450	23.3
Clothes dryer (gas)	$170	81.3	$185	46.8	$450	23.3
Dishwasher	$190	90.9	$310	78.5	$400	20.7
Refrigerator	$350	167.5	$370	93.7	$432	22.4
Freezer	$320	153.1	$240	60.8	$330	17.1
Stove (gas)	$190	90.9	$290	73.4	$550	28.5
Coffee pot	$23	11	$37	9.4	$70	3.6
Blender	$22	10.5	$40	10.1	$40	2.1
Toaster	$14	6.7	$25	6.3	$37	1.9
Vacuum cleaner	$95	45.5	$90	22.8	$130	6.7
Color TV	$267	127.8	$400	101.3	$400	20.7
Total	$1,851	885.6	$2,272	575.2	$3,289	170.4

dramatically since the 1970s, on the order of 70% on average. These trends are evident across the entire period from the mid-70s until the present as well as within any subperiod. The decline in costs shows up as significant increases in the percentage of households that possess such goods, as seen in Table 4.2. By 2005, American households below the poverty line were more likely to have a clothes dryer, dishwasher, refrigerator, stove, color TV, and air conditioner than was the average American household in 1971. In addition, substantial percentages of poor households in 2005 had VCRs, cell phones, and microwaves, which were essentially unavailable to even the richest households in 1971.

Even if we look over a shorter period (Table 4.3), we see that the gap between the percentage of poor and rich (not average) households with these various items narrows for almost all of them. The only item where the poor–rich gap expanded (by 6 percentage points), that is, where consumption inequality was greater, was in landline phones, but that is only because the gap with respect to cell phones declined by an even greater amount (almost 10 percentage points). Sacerdote (2017) finds similar results with respect to consumption of households below median household income and households below the 25th percentile of income extending until 2014.

But even this analysis leaves out full consideration of two other factors. First, as I already hinted at, we should account for the fact that there now exist goods and services obtainable with relative ease by the poor which did not even exist 40 years ago. It's one thing to point out the decline in the cost and increase in ownership of long-standing consumer durables. It is another thing altogether to consider the innovations of the last few decades and the rapidity of their increased affordability for the masses.[8] Medical innovations such as

Table 4.2 Percentage of households with various consumer items, 1984–2005 (Horwitz 2015a)

% Households with:	*Poor 1984*	*Poor 1994*	*Poor 2003*	*Poor 2005*	*All 1971*	*All 2005*
Washing machine	58.2	71.7	67.0	68.7	**71.3**	**84.0**
Clothes dryer	35.6	50.2	58.5	61.2	**44.5**	**81.2**
Dishwasher	13.6	19.6	33.9	36.7	**18.8**	**64.0**
Refrigerator	95.8	97.9	98.2	98.5	**83.3**	**99.3**
Freezer	29.2	28.6	25.4	25.1	**32.2**	**36.6**
Stove	95.2	97.7	97.1	97.0	**87.0**	**98.8**
Microwave	12.5	60.0	88.7	91.2	**1.0**	**96.4**
Color TV	70.3	92.5	96.8	97.4	**43.3**	**98.9**
VCR	3.4	59.7	75.4	83.6	**0.0**	**92.2**
Personal computer	2.9	7.4	36.0	42.4	**0.0**	**67.1**
Telephone	71.0	76.7	87.3	79.8	**93.0**	**90.6**
Air conditioner	42.5	49.6	77.7	78.8	**31.8**	**85.7**
Cellular Telephone			34.7	48.3	**0.0**	**71.3**
One or more cars	64.1	71.8	72.8 (2001)		**79.5**	

Table 4.3 Percentages of poor and rich households with various consumer items, 2003 and 2005 (Horwitz 2015a)

% Households with:	*Poor 2003*	*Rich 2003*	*2003 Gap*	*Poor 2005*	*Rich 2005*	*2005 Gap*	*Gap Change*
Washing machine	67.0	94.8	**27.8**	68.7	95.2	**26.5**	*−1.3*
Clothes dryer	58.5	93.6	**35.1**	61.2	94.3	**33.1**	*−2.0*
Dishwasher	33.9	86.1	**52.2**	36.7	88.4	**51.7**	*−0.5*
Refrigerator	98.2	99.6	**1.4**	98.5	99.8	**1.3**	*−0.1*
Freezer	25.4	44	**18.6**	25.1	43.7	**18.6**	*0.0*
Stove	97.1	99.6	**2.5**	97.0	99.7	**2.7**	*0.2*
Microwave	88.7	98.6	**9.9**	91.2	98.8	**7.6**	*−2.3*
Color TV	96.8	99.5	**2.7**	97.4	99.5	**2.1**	*−0.6*
VCR	75.4	97.7	**22.3**	83.6	98.5	**14.9**	*−7.4*
Personal computer	36.0	87.9	**51.9**	42.4	92.7	**50.3**	*−1.6*
Telephone	87.3	98.6	**11.3**	79.8	97.1	**17.3**	*6.0*
Air conditioner	77.7	90.3	**12.6**	78.8	89.1	**10.3**	*−2.3*
Cellular telephone	34.7	88.6	**53.9**	48.3	92.4	**44.1**	*−9.8*

beta-blockers and MRIs, along with smartphones and 3D printing and a whole bunch of other technology, are available to even the poorest of households. All of this would have seemed like magic to even the wealthy of a generation or two ago. Along with increased ownership of existing goods and services, we should include the ability of the poor to afford new items as part of the case for a decline in absolute poverty.

The second excluded factor is quality improvements. Even the goods that have been part of households for a generation or two are far different today than they were in the past. Appliances are far more energy efficient and offer features that they did not in the past. The typical TV in the 1970s was a 19″ low-definition screen, without a remote control or internet connectivity or any of the other features we take for granted today. Even as we compare the prices of color TVs over time, what we are buying is far from the same good. One need only consider the advances in automobile technology, from safety to mileage to convenience, to see this point. These changes are the ones that are not captured by the CPI or similar measures of inflation, yet they certainly represent an increase in real well-being that is on top of changes in ownership rates.

The evidence on ownership is very clear that the poor are better off in absolute terms than they were 40 years ago, and there is evidence that they are also better in relative terms as well, having narrowed the ownership gap with the rich in recent years. Over both the long run of economic history and more recently, we have moved from a society in which there was a small group of haves and a large group of have-nots to one in which there is a large group of haves and a small group of have more and betters. If there is rising inequality, it has come alongside a very clear increase in the material well-being of the least well-off. As such, it would seem to satisfy the Rawlsian criterion for moral justification.[9]

IV.II. Inequality and income mobility

One other concern we might have about the relationship between inequality and poverty is the question of income mobility. Even if the absolute condition of the poor has improved significantly over the last 40 years, we might be interested in knowing whether those who start off poor stay poor or whether they have a reasonable chance of moving up the income ladder. If households in the bottom 20% are highly unlikely to move out of that quintile over time, we might legitimately weigh that against the gains in absolute living standards. As it turns out, this is not a major worry. Both intragenerational and intergenerational mobility have been thoroughly studied over the last few decades.[10] The consensus view is that while mobility has declined somewhat since the 1970s, there is still a great deal of movement among the quintiles. One recent study indicated that 44% of households in the lowest quintile in 2001 had moved up at least one quintile by 2007. Earlier studies showed somewhat higher mobility, and mobility will, of course, be greater the longer period of time we examine. We would also expect mobility to drop as societies get richer, if our comparison uses the same statistical groupings. As wealth increases, the size of each quintile expands, making it more difficult to jump out of a given quintile with a specific increase in income. A $10,000 raise might be enough to move out of the middle class to the upper middle class in one year, but not enough a decade later. That would appear to be a decline in mobility as measured by quintiles, even though the absolute amount is the same. Acknowledging this statistical fact means that mobility is probably higher than the data suggest.

A similar story holds for cross-generational mobility. Isaacs (2007) reports that those born into the top 20% of households in 1969 had real incomes in 2000 that were about the same as what their parents had in 1969. Of those born into the lowest quintile of households, 82% had incomes in 2000 that were higher than what their parents had in 1969. The group of children born into the lowest quintile had a median income that was double that of their parents. That half of the children of the 1969 poor had incomes more than double that of their parents reflects opportunities for upward mobility across generations, and it should be kept in mind that there were still members of that group who were below the median but still earning above what their parents did in 1969.

It is tempting to conclude from this discussion that rising inequality is not worth worrying about. However, this argument has made a tacit assumption that is worth bringing to the surface. The discussion of fairness and the mutual benefit of market exchange can help us to understand why rising inequality might be associated with reductions in poverty: the gains of the top 20% or top 1% have come from providing precisely the sorts of goods and services that have fallen in real cost, or that did not exist a generation ago, and that have thereby enriched the lives of the masses. The investments in capital made by those same high earners have improved the productivity of labor and increased real wages. The churn of the market ensures that no fortune is assured, as producers must continue to innovate, cut costs, and please consumers. This helps us to understand the degree to which mobility is alive and well. However, this all assumes that incomes are earned in this sort of competitive marketplace. Given the large role played by government regulation and intervention in modern Western economies, how do we account for people who earn high incomes, or are denied the ability to earn any income, as a result of poor public policies? Do the recipients of bailouts, for example, provide the mutual benefit that Apple does? What if the redistributive state is contributing to rising inequality? Is this a matter of concern? Should it be? Can this type of growth in inequality pass the Rawlsian test? Is it perceived as fair? The final sections take up these questions.

V. Socially beneficial and socially harmful causes of inequality

Building on the analysis in Geloso and Horwitz (2017), we can distinguish causes of inequality that are socially beneficial (or at least neutral) and those that are socially harmful. The first category includes the kinds of market processes discussed previously. If inequality arises as the unintended consequence of market exchanges that are mutually beneficial ways of taking advantage of differences in abilities in a world of equality before the law, then it is socially beneficial and we should see it as justifiable, especially if it benefits the least well-off, as it in fact has. Creating value for others is socially beneficial even if it produces unintended inequality. Other nonproblematic causes of inequality might include demographic changes, such as the way in which divorce creates two poorer households out of one richer one, and structural changes to the economy, which have created greater heterogeneity in people's work-leisure tradeoffs.

In contrast, we can identify a number of possible causes of increased income inequality that are problematic as they prevent people from engaging in mutually beneficial exchanges, and thereby enrich those who already have wealth and power *at the expense of* those who do not.[11] For example, consider agricultural policies in a variety of countries. Such policies distort prices in ways that harm the poor and help the better off. Policies that restrict imports and/or subsidize domestic producers raise prices of agricultural staples, disproportionately harming poorer households in the domestic economy. If we take a global perspective, these policies increase global inequality by shutting out access to the domestic market to foreign producers. As such producers tend to be smaller-scale and less well-off, the closing off of those opportunities impoverishes them while enriching producers in the economy imposing the import restrictions.

Because access to politically dispensed favors is easier for those who already have wealth, the beneficiaries of such policies tend to be larger-scale farmers with political clout. This is an example of the more general phenomenon of government largess providing benefits to a small number of concentrated interests while dispersing the costs across larger groups. Each household might only feel the pinch of a few extra dollars to pay the higher prices of agricultural products, but each of those small costs adds up to a significant benefit for those who obtain the subsidies or import protections. Such policies have highly regressive effects and widen income inequality.[12]

A variety of labor market policies work in similar ways. The literature on the effects of minimum wage laws is vast and, despite perceptions to the contrary, there is a clear consensus that such laws cause greater unemployment, especially among low-skilled workers and new entrants to the labor market. The size of that effect remains a matter of significant debate, but the consensus is that the effect exists. The history of minimum wage laws as a tool used by higher-skilled incumbents to intentionally block the entry of lower-skilled, lower-wage competition is widely known. Such laws are regressive as they reduce the income earning potential of lower-paid workers and allow higher-paid workers to maintain artificially high wages. This exacerbates income inequality but by a transfer of resources up the income ladder rather than by enriching all in the process.

Similarly, occupational licensure laws raise the costs of entry for poorer workers who have to spend often substantial resources to obtain the politically required license. Here too, incumbent practitioners use their wealth and political influence to get laws passed that protect their wages and thereby reduce the income prospects of the relatively poor. These laws also contribute to income inequality in socially undesirable ways by redistributing rather than creating wealth. The percentage of occupations requiring a license has grown dramatically over the last several decades, with approximately 30% of U.S. jobs now requiring a license, up from around 5% in the 1950s. Kleiner and Krueger

(2010) estimate that licensing increases wages by about 15% and, when combined with union membership, that wage premium averages 24%.[13] This evidence suggests that such laws might be a contributing factor to growth in income inequality over the same period. Implementing the various proposals to increase the minimum wage would exacerbate these effects.

Another socially harmful cause of rising inequality is the variety of regulations on small businesses that constrain entrepreneurship among those with fewer resources. Zoning regulations frequently make it prohibitively expensive for individuals or very small firms to open new businesses, especially ones out of their homes. For people with fewer resources, and especially for people with small children where a home-based business would allow them to take advantage of economies of scope in work and childcare, these restrictions limit their opportunities to earn higher income. A similar story can be told about street vendors. The rise of food trucks in recent years has generated a response by brick-and-mortar restaurants to try to make it more difficult for such trucks, and other street vendors, to operate. Those regulations also fit the pattern of well-resourced incumbents using regulatory intervention to protect or enhance their own incomes while reducing those of smaller, less well-resourced competitors. As one example, consider the cost of getting a business license in a major U.S. city like Chicago:

> A recent US Chamber of Commerce study found that Chicago not only averaged 32 days to approve a permit for a professional services business, it charged $900 for doing so. The state of Illinois then charged an additional $500, plus an annual fee of $250, to organize as a Limited Liability Company. Although those are both well above the national averages, the Chamber of Commerce report shows that almost every major city imposes some sort of significant permit-related burden on new business start-ups.
>
> (Horwitz 2015b: 13)

Such regulations protect the profits of existing firms and prevent upward mobility among the poor, thereby contributing to income inequality in socially undesirable ways.

Of course, the most well-known example of battles between incumbents and new businesses in recent years has been the one between licensed taxicab companies and ride-sharing innovators like Uber and Lyft. Uber and Lyft have proven to be very effective competition for cab companies by offering ride services at both lower cost and greater convenience, as well as better customer service. In response, the cab companies, who are often the beneficiary of various forms of monopoly protection, have gone to local governments to try to either ban the ride-sharing firms or to at least increase the regulatory burden on them to the point where they will simply leave town. This strategy has been successful in a number of cities. The result, however, is not just to further enrich the entrenched cab companies and their drivers at the expense of the Uber and Lyft drivers, who are themselves often trying to work their way up the income ladder. Those drivers can make up to $70,000–$90,000 driving full time in major cities.[14] Laws that shut out Uber and Lyft deny those opportunities to the relatively poor. In so doing, such laws also raise costs for poorer consumers who do not own cars and need transportation by preventing beneficial price competition. The restrictions on Uber and Lyft (and similar regulations on Airbnb and other platform economy firms) exacerbate inequality both on the income side and the expenditure side. They redistribute income upward by limiting earning opportunities and raising prices for the relatively poor.[15]

VI. Socially harmful causes of inequality are also unfair

Distinguishing between causes of inequality that are beneficial/neutral or harmful enables us to return to the opening discussion of the distinction between inequality and unfairness. If what people really object to is unfairness not inequality per se, then the distinction I have developed can be seen in a new light. I would argue that all of the harmful causes of inequality discussed in the previous section amount to a form of privilege for powerful incumbents that enable them to play by a different set of rules than less well-resourced (potential) competitors. When cab companies can provide ride service but individuals using their own cars to connect with customers through the internet cannot, those cab companies and their drivers have the right to engage in an activity that other similarly situated people do not. When one set of rules applies to some people but not others, and when one group clearly benefits from it, this is a textbook case of what is meant by "privilege." In the cases we have examined, these privileges serve to enhance the incomes of the relatively rich at the expense of the relatively poor. That is, such privileges exacerbate income inequality.[16]

This point about privilege has long been recognized in the literature on rent-seeking. Lobbying governments to protect your wages or profits, or to reduce those of your competition, is a way of acquiring a privilege that enables you to earn a return above opportunity cost, which is what comprises the "rent" in rent-seeking. We see the same idea at work in the various bailouts during the Great Recession that angered so many all across the political spectrum. The bailouts of financial institutions in the spring and summer of 2008 were particularly extreme because not only were the bailouts themselves a privilege, not all firms that appeared to be in similar trouble got similar help. Those bailouts were a privilege and were provided with what seemed to be a degree of capriciousness.

Seeing these inequality-enhancing policies as a form of privilege can help shed light on what people are really objecting to when they are critical of increasing inequality. If the idea that unfairness is a bigger problem than inequality is correct, then perhaps much of the concern with rising inequality from at least some Progressives is really a concern about the game of the market becoming increasingly unfair, thanks to an increased role for privileges that increase inequality. To the degree that the public is largely comfortable with the high incomes earned by entrepreneurs who provide them with valuable goods and services, but chafe when banks, investment houses, government-sponsored enterprises, and auto companies are given bailouts and subsidies, then perhaps people can distinguish among the causes of inequality and are largely objecting to those they find to be unfair. The same could be said of the regulatory interventions such as occupational licensure and zoning laws, along with the other ones discussed in the prior section. Do people find these to be problematic and, if so, is it because they are perceived to be unfair? Seeing these debates as being about fairness rather than equality enables us to see some consistency in positions people hold that might otherwise appear to lack it. It is not a contradiction to protest rising inequality while happily paying out for your Apple computer and objecting to bailouts of financial institutions if the real problem is unfairness. This vantage point also lets us cut across the Progressive versus Classical Liberal divide to find common ground in their objections to privilege-driven incomes.

I do not mean to suggest that seeing the real problem as an unfair privilege rather than inequality in and of itself is the position that most people actually hold. I do, however, mean to suggest that those of us who understand that not all causes of (rising) income inequality are problematic, and that some of them are quite desirable in that they also involve a reduction in absolute poverty or other benefits to other people, should make these distinctions when we write and talk about these issues. The old distinction of equality of material outcomes versus equality before the law may not be helpful if humans have evolved to respond more strongly to questions of fairness than ones of equality or inequality. Hayek's point that equality of outcomes requires that we treat people unequally remains true but can be reframed by noting that treating people unequally is unfair. This will play out in two ways.

First, we can talk, as I have here, about the different causes of inequality in terms of their social desirability and link that to questions of fairness. It is a possible path by which we might reduce Progressive objections to socially desirable causes of inequality and shift the focus to those causes that are more clearly problematic that both Progressives and Classical Liberals share. If we can make the argument that market-driven or demographically driven increases in inequality are fair and at least neutral, we can then turn to talk about why the other causes of the increase are not. Second, it gives us a way to talk about why the conventional responses to rising inequality are themselves problematic. As discussed earlier, progressive taxation and various forms of redistribution violate the idea of treating everyone as equal before the law. To that extent, they are forms of privilege for those who are taxed less or receive the benefits of redistribution. They are not substantively different in that way from the bailouts and subsidies so often criticized. In addition, if fairness is what matters most, we can offer the elimination of the policies generating the harmful increases in inequality as a way to increase fairness and as an alternative to the traditional tax and spend solutions. Shifting the debate toward fairness opens up new ways to both conceptualize the issues at stake and make the case for the appropriate policy recommendations, and to do so in ways that cross existing ideological and philosophical divides.

VII. Conclusion

The objections that many people have to rising inequality are not all without merit. Given the evidence that humans are more inclined to respond negatively to perceived unfairness rather than inequality in and of itself, and given that the socially harmful causes of inequality arise from violations of Hayek's generality principle through the creation of privileges, we should be linking unfairness, privilege, and problematic increases in inequality. At the very least, we should be asking critical questions of the Progressives who often appear to object to all increases in inequality to see whether we can tease out what the real objections are. It may well turn out that the problem is not inequality per se, but a correct perception of unfairness in the way in which an increasing amount of economic activity is driven by politically acquired privileges that rig the game in favor of those who have already won. Challenging such policies and privileges might be a way to cross partisan and ideological lines to move toward economic policies that continue the long-term reduction in absolute poverty that markets have brought and to help us avoid adopting policies that would further entrench privilege at the expense of the most vulnerable.

Notes

1 As I note below as well, I am assuming for the sake of argument that there has been an increase in inequality as traditionally measured. Part of the later argument is to challenge the claim that the increase in question is as large or as significant as many believe.
2 There have been a number of recent books making this Progressive argument. Three of the best-known examples are Stiglitz (2012), Piketty (2014), and Reich (2015).
3 See the discussion in Roberts (2013). See also Lundberg et al. (2016) for a discussion of some of the demographic changes in households and the ways they might affect inequality. Burkhauser et al. (2012) provide some data on the difference between "households" and "tax-units" that further complicate these questions.
4 On the question of wages versus total compensation, see Feldstein (2008). On consumption inequality being less than income inequality, see Meyer and Sullivan (2011, 2013). For an overview of the consumption inequality issue, see Attanasio and Pistaferri (2016).
5 In the words of Rabbi Lord Sacks (2003): "It is through exchange that difference becomes a blessing, not a curse."
6 The *reductio ad absurdum* of this point is best made in Kurt Vonnegut's 1961 short story *Harrison Bergeron.*
7 Hayek's argument can be seen as a precursor to Nozick's (1974) critique of Rawls.
8 Cox and Alm (1999) attempted to document a variety of items that were available in the late 1990s that did not exist earlier in the century. It is amusing to read that list now, because so many of those things are simply part and parcel of life in the West, and missing from the list is a huge set of technological and medical innovations that have become part of our lives in the succeeding 20 years.
9 My focus has been on Western economies, but the data on the reduction of absolute poverty on a global scale is also quite clear. Inequality has grown if you look at the data

at a country level, but when you examine it at an individual level, global inequality has fallen, thanks mostly to the rise of the middle class in India and China.

10 Again, see Horwitz (2015a) for a brief summary of this literature. See also Winship (2015) for a more detailed examination of the data in the context of the possible decline of "equality of opportunity."

11 Lindsey and Teles (2017) offer a book-length version of this general argument.

12 The regressive effects of government regulation, at all levels of government, has seen recent attention in public policy research by Thomas (2012) and Horwitz (2015b).

13 See Kleiner and Krueger (2010).

14 See McFarland (2014).

15 Alcohol and other "sin" taxes also have similar regressive effects and are therefore socially harmful causes of greater inequality.

16 See the similar argument from a philosophical perspective in Skoble (2018).

References

Attanasio, Orazio P., and Luigi Pistaferri. 2016. "Consumption Inequality." *Journal of Economic Perspectives* 30 (2): 1–27.

Burkhauser, Richard V., Jeff Larrimore, and Kosali I. Simon. 2012. "A Second Opinion on the Economic Health of the American Middle Class." *National Tax Journal* 65 (1): 7–32.

Costa, Dora L. 2001. "Estimating Real Income in the United States from 1888 to 1994: Correcting CPI Bias Using Engel Curves." *Journal of Political Economy* 109: 1288–1310.

Cox, W. Michael, and Richard Alm. 1999. *Myths of Rich and Poor: Why We're Better Off Than We Think*. New York: Basic Books.

Feldstein, Martin. 2008. "Did Wages Reflect Growth in Productivity?" *Journal of Policy Modeling* 30 (4): 591–594.

Geloso, Vincent, and Steven Horwitz. 2017. "Inequality: First, Do No Harm." *The Independent Review* 22: 121–134.

Hamilton, Bruce W. 1998. *The True Cost of Living: 1974–1991*. Working Papers in Economics. Baltimore: The Johns Hopkins University Department of Economics, January.

Hayek, F. A. 1960. *The Constitution of Liberty*. Chicago: University of Chicago Press.

Horwitz, Steven. 2015a. "Inequality, Mobility, and Being Poor in America." *Social Philosophy and Policy* 31 (2): 70–91.

Horwitz, Steven. 2015b. *Breaking Down the Barriers: Three Ways State and Local Governments Can Get out of the Way and Improve the Lives of the Poor*. Mercatus Research, Mercatus Center at George Mason University. Available at http://mercatus.org/publication/breaking-down-barriers-three-ways-state-and-local-governments-can-improve-lives-poor.

Isaacs, Julia B. 2007. *Economic Mobility of Families Across Generations*. Brookings Institution Economic Mobility Project. Available at www.brookings.edu/wp-content/uploads/2016/06/11_generations_isaacs.pdf.

Kleiner, Morris M., and Alan B. Krueger. 2010. "The Prevalence and Effects of Occupational Licensing." *British Journal of Industrial Relations* 48: 676–687.

Lindsey, Brink, and Steven M. Teles. 2017. *The Captured Economy*. New York: Oxford University Press.

Lundberg, Shelly, Robert A. Pollak, and Jenna Stearns. 2016. "Family Inequality: Diverging Patterns in Marriage, Cohabitation, and Childbearing." *Journal of Economic Perspectives* 30 (2): 79–102.

McFarland, Matt. 2014. "Uber's Remarkable Growth Could End the Era of Poorly Paid Cab Drivers." *Washington Post*, May 27. Available at www.washingtonpost.com/blogs/innovations/wp/2014/05/27/ubers-remarkable-growth-could-end-the-era-of-poorly-paid-cab-drivers/.

Meyer, Bruce, and James X. Sullivan. 2011. *The Material Well-Being of the Poor and the Middle Class Since 1980*. American Enterprise Institute Working Paper No. 44. Washington, DC: American Enterprise Institute.

Meyer, Bruce, and James X. Sullivan. 2013. "Consumption and Income Inequality and the Great Recession." *American Economic Review* 103 (3): 178–183.

Nozick, Robert. 1974. *Anarchy, State, and Utopia*. New York: Basic Books.

Perry, Mark. 2013. *When It Comes to the Affordability of Common Household Goods, the Rich and the Poor Are Both Getting Richer*. Available at www.aei-ideas.org/2013/10/when-it-comes-to-the-affordability-of-common-household-goods-the-rich-and-the-poor-are-both-getting-richer/.

Piketty, Thomas. 2014. *Capital in the Twenty-First Century*. Cambridge, MA: Harvard University Press.

Rawls, John. 1971. *A Theory of Justice*. Cambridge, MA: Harvard University Press.

Reich, Robert B. 2015. *Saving Capitalism: For the Many, Not the Few*. New York: Alfred Knopf.

Roberts, Russ. 2013. "Inequality in Two Graphs." *Café Hayek*. Available at https://cafehayek.com/2013/11/inequality-in-two-graphs.html.

Sacerdote, Bruce. 2017. *Fifty Years of Growth in American Consumption, Income, and Wages*. NBER Working Paper 23292. Available at www.nber.org/papers/w23292.

Sacks, Jonathan. 2003. *The Dignity of Difference*. London: Bloomsbury Academic.

Skoble, Aeon J. 2018. "Social Justice, Egalitarianism, and Rights." In Christopher Coyne, Michael Munger, and Robert Whaples, eds., *Egalitarianism: Fair and Equal?* Oakland, CA: The Independent Institute.

Starmans, Christina, Sheskin, Mark, and Paul Bloom. 2017. "Why People Prefer Unequal Societies." *Nature Human Behavior* 1, April 7, online. Doi:10.1038/s41562-017-0082.

Stiglitz, Joseph. 2012. *The Price of Inequality: How Today's Divided Society Endangers Our Future*. New York: Norton.

Thomas, Diana. 2012. *Regressive Effects of Regulation*. Working Paper 12–35. Mercatus Center at George Mason University. Available at www.mercatus.org/system/files/Regressive Effects_Thomas_v1-0.pdf.

Vonnegut, Kurt. 1961 [1968]. *Harrison Bergeron* (Reprinted in *Welcome to the Monkey House*). New York: Dell.

Winship, Scott. 2015. "Has Rising Income Inequality Worsened Inequality of Opportunity?" *Social Philosophy and Public Policy* 31 (2): 28–47.

5 Government labor policies and the law of unintended consequences

Richard Vedder

I. Introduction

Most income comes from work. The national income accounts of not only the United States but also of most other industrialized nations show that a large majority of income, typically about 60–70%, comes from worker compensation. To be sure, complementary factors of production like capital and natural resources are also important, and technological advances are key to raising labor productivity and incomes. Factors like the mobility of resources and trading in goods and services can positively impact nations as well. Nonetheless, any attempt to seriously change both the magnitude and distribution of incomes must deal very importantly with labor markets. Jobs create prosperity and often reduce poverty and/or increase income equality: poor people typically work less than others.

Therefore, in societies where governments profess to wish to both increase income growth and create a "fairer" or "more equitable" distribution of the fruits of economic progress, much attention is paid to labor market policies. This chapter argues that unfettered markets have some powerful egalitarian properties, and most government policies designed to distort labor market outcomes have unintended consequences, specifically no reduction in poverty or equalization of incomes, and often even worse: the less-advantaged members of society end up worse off.

This chapter first reviews some history of governmental labor market policies, mainly in the United States. It then suggests that high levels of economic freedom are associated with higher prosperity/less poverty. Governmentally imposed constraints and distortions of worker behavior – minimum wage laws, occupational licensing requirements, maximum hours of work regulations, safety rules, laws coercing labor union involvement, public assistance largess and regulations, unemployment insurance, workers compensation, immigration restrictions, mandatory pension (e.g., Social Security) requirements, disability provisions, even high taxes – tend to have unintended consequences. A few of these governmental labor market interventions are examined in some detail.

II. A short history of interventions in labor markets

Before the Industrial Revolution that began in the 18th century, almost all human beings lived in what contemporary Americans would consider poverty. Beginning in that century, the growth in output per person led to what Deidre McCloskey calls "The Great Enrichment," an astronomical rise in the standard of living of people, beginning in Great Britain and spreading ultimately to most of the rest of the world.[1] The creator of the expression "industrial revolution," the Oxford don Arnold Toynbee (1852–1883), said "The essence of the Industrial Revolution is the substitution of competition for the medieval regulations which previously controlled the production and distribution of wealth."[2]

Clearly, many of the "medieval regulations" related to labor. To cite one prominent English example, under the Statute of Apprentices in effect in 17th- and 18th-century England, workers had to serve seven years under a master before they could follow a trade, in addition to all sorts of other local rules, including, for example, a *maximum* (not minimum) wage law on tailors in London.[3] Adam Smith complained bitterly about the practice, citing examples of restrictions on labor:

> In Sheffield, no master cutler can have more than one apprentice at a time. . . . In Norfolk and Norwich, no master weaver can have more than two apprentices under pain of forfeiting five pounds a month to the King.[4]

Yet early in the 19th century, these provisions were repealed. A classical liberal revolution in intellectual thought – a by-product of the Enlightenment – led to a general drift toward an acceptance and support for *laissez-faire* capitalism. The writings of Smith, David Hume, and, on the Continent such French writers as Jean Baptiste Say, Alexis de Tocqueville, and Frederic Bastiat, provided an environment generally supportive of a minimalist government, most vividly illustrated by a move toward tariff elimination and free trade.[5]

The United States was largely "born free" of the spate of medieval regulations that inflicted the Old World. An innovative contractual arrangement, indentured servitude, helped finance the very considerable cost of early workers reaching the New World. In return for passage, workers agreed to work for very low compensation for a period of several years, providing the investor a return for financing the costly migration. America in, say, 1800 or 1850 had *no* restrictions on immigration, few if any rules or regulations on wages, no income or major consumption taxation, no political barriers to movement or labor mobility, with one monumental exception. Slavery, of course, impeded the freedom of millions to move and achieve better economic opportunity.

The American western frontier arguably provided a "safety valve" for American labor – a place one could flee to if one felt exploited, oppressed, or faced with unemployment.[6] This is an extension of the famous frontier thesis of Frederick Jackson Turner.[7] Clearly, the challenges of farming on the frontier fostered a culture of individualism, distrust of collective solutions, a disdain for aristocracy, and a willingness for risk-taking, traits key to the evolution of the American character, powerfully influencing public policy, indicated by America's tepidness, relative to Europe, in moving toward the welfare state.

Nonetheless, there were some calls for public labor market constraints as a consequence of growing industrialization. Whereas in 1820 most free Americans were farmers and worked either as their own bosses or in an enterprise with few employees, by the Civil War already about 10% worked in manufacturing, and railroads were likewise developing that employed large numbers of workers. Inevitably, disputes developed between employers and workers, who were increasingly less well acquainted with one another because of the growing scale of operations. Cries to permit and promote labor unions, to limit hours and employment of child labor, and promote safety legislation started to arise. In 1842, in *Commonwealth v. Hunt*, the Massachusetts Supreme Court ruled that labor unions were not illegal criminal conspiracies. The immediate impact on union membership was negligible – far less than 1% of the labor force was in unions when the Civil War broke out in 1861.

The nation boomed in the postbellum period, with U.S. output surpassing Britain's by the early 1870s, and on a per capita basis by the early years of the 20th century.[8] By any measure, real wages rose, and the number of hours worked declined somewhat with rising prosperity. Still, with more workers in large firms in manufacturing, mining, and transportation, alienation between workers and employers grew, leading to more labor market agitation.

Four periods of progressive activism shaped modern American labor history. The first, the Progressive Era beginning after 1890, saw the first major efforts at using government regulatory powers to control labor markets, coming on the heels of the first independent regulatory agency being created with the Interstate Commerce Act of 1887.

One of the most famous Supreme Court cases grew out of a Progressive Era state labor law. New York enacted a Bakeshop Act of 1895, prohibiting workers from being employed more than 10 hours per day or 60 hours a week. In *Lochner v. New York* (1905), a baker, Joseph Lochner, appealed a conviction under the Bakeshop Act and was successful (albeit in a 5–4 vote) in overturning the law on constitutional grounds of violating due process freedoms guaranteed under the Fourteenth Amendment.[9] Despite *Lochner*, state governments moved aggressively to impose labor legislation, including minimum wage laws, most of which did not survive judicial scrutiny (especially important was the 1923 case *Adkins v. Children's Hospital*). State governments took the lead in passing other labor legislation, such as worker compensation and, in Wisconsin in 1932, unemployment insurance laws. At the federal level, the Clayton Anti-Trust Act of 1914 excluded labor unions from potential anti-trust actions, and President Woodrow Wilson used powers assumed during World War I (including temporarily nationalizing the railroads and creating a pro-union War Labor Board) to promote labor unions, reversing the general hostile-to-neutral stance of governments taken earlier, such as during the Pullman Strike of 1894.[10]

In 1882, reflecting the racial discrimination of the era, the United States excluded Chinese immigrants to the United States. In the first quarter of the 20th century, the federal government began more dramatically retreating from permitting free and unfettered labor migration, culminating in the 1924 Immigration Act, signed by the generally classically liberal-oriented Calvin Coolidge, severely restricting the number of entrants to the United States from other countries, and also discriminating in favor of immigrants from northwestern Europe.

The second, and greatest, revolution in American labor laws began with the New Deal of Franklin D. Roosevelt, although there were some notable precursors during the administration of Herbert Hoover, such as the Norris-LaGuardia Act of 1932, which barred federal court injunctions in labor disputes. Contrary to progressive mythology, the legislation of the 1930s was not always motivated by a concern for the disadvantaged or oppressed. Take the Davis–Bacon Act, a 1931 legislation enacted at a time when many, including President Herbert Hoover, felt high wages would raise purchasing power and reduce unemployment (ignoring the Law of Demand that suggests the quantity of labor demanded should fall as its price, the wage, rises). There was a pronounced anti-black sentiment behind the legislation, because Rep. Robert Bacon was irritated that black Southern laborers had been hired for the construction of a federally funded hospital in his upscale New York district. The Davis–Bacon Act and the 1936 Walsh–Healey Act called for the payment of "prevailing" wages (typically high union scale) to employees on government contracts.[11]

There were lots of important labor legislation passed during the New Deal of the 1930s, but in this abridged account, let me highlight three with profound long-term consequences: the Wagner Act (National Labor Relations Act) of 1935, the Social Security Act of the same year, and the Fair Labor Standards Act of 1938. All were at least partially justified by the High Wage Doctrine prevailing at the time, a belief which I argue was fundamentally wrong.[12]

The Wagner Act created the National Labor Relations Board, providing an environment very favorable to labor unions, including union contracts with a closed shop (workers must belong to the union to become employed). In the first five years under the Wagner Act, union membership nearly doubled, eventually reaching more than one-third of the nonagricultural labor force. Besides its direct effects, the legislation provided unions with political clout for further legislation, expanding the role of government into American life.

The Social Security Act unleashed a federal-state public assistance system of substantial magnitude in addition to taxing employees and employers to finance pensions. The importance of pensions was much less in an era of lower life expectancy than today, so no one foresaw the dramatic future fiscal pressures associated with federal pensions. The extension of Social Security in subsequent legislation is noteworthy, especially the 1956 law, passed under a Republican President, creating the Social Security disability benefit program, which has exploded in magnitude in recent years.

The first federal minimum wage in 1938 was 25 cents per hour. The minimum wage legislation was subsequently expanded in two ways: coverage was expanded to a growing number of workers, and the size of the wage minimum was increased on numerous occasions. Simultaneously, states increasingly imposed minimum wage laws, often with higher minimums than mandated under the federal law.

Several legislative developments of the post-1945 period are noteworthy. The first was actually a modest reversal of federal labor market activism: the Taft–Hartley Act of 1947, passed over President Harry Truman's veto, reduced somewhat the clout of labor unions granted under the Wagner Act, forbidding, for example, secondary boycotts and the closed shop and, most importantly, allowing states to pass right-to-work (RTW) laws prohibiting labor contracts forcing workers to belong to unions. Americans were fed up with the high level of strike activity in the immediate postwar period, and the pro-union political tide of the 1930s began to turn back to a political environment less conducive to unionization.

The third wave of progressive activism was unleashed with Lyndon Johnson's Great Society in 1964 and for several years thereafter. A "war on poverty" was declared in the face of much publicity about American poverty.[13] Although there were several smaller efforts impacting labor markets, such as the Black Lung benefit program of 1969 and the creation of the Occupational Safety and Health Administration in 1970 (under Johnson's successor, Richard Nixon), the major enactments included the Food Stamp Act of 1964, promoting "nutritional assistance" and the creation of Medicare and Medicaid in 1965. It is noteworthy that this latter legislation passed by lopsided majorities (307 to 116 in the House, 70 to 24 in the Senate). Increasingly, health care was viewed as a federal entitlement. One modest move toward *reducing* governmental labor market restrictions came with the 1965 Immigration Act, slightly increasing the number of immigrants and reducing race/ethnic-based limitations. By the early 21st century, immigrant arrivals approached those at the peak in the first decade of the 20th century in absolute numbers, although not relative to population size.

The apogee of movement toward government health care involvement came during the fourth wave of liberal activism in 2010, particularly notable by the passage, by the slimmest of margins (no Republican votes) of the Affordable Care Act (Obamacare), which a divided Supreme Court (6 to 3) found constitutional in *King v. Burwell* (2015). Individuals were mandated to have health insurance – or pay a penalty. Health care was very largely federalized, a dramatic change from, say, 1960, when individuals purchased their own insurance, had employer-provided coverage, or simply had no insurance at all.

III. Equality and markets: some theoretical and empirical observations

The various accelerated governmental interferences in labor markets outlined earlier were usually justified, at least in part, in the interest of promoting income equality and reduced poverty. For example, the Wagner Act was designed to raise wages for mostly relatively unskilled labor who allegedly had weak bargaining power against powerful business enterprises. The Fair Labor Standard Act similarly was perceived as an anti-poverty device – increase low-skilled worker wages from what would otherwise exist. Social Security, and later Medicare, was designed to reduce poverty among the elderly and, later, to aid disabled workers losing the ability to earn an income. Most obviously, burgeoning federal assistance programs like Aid to Families with Dependent Children (AFDC), Medicaid. and food stamps were designed to directly attack poverty by pushing people above the poverty line and improving the quality of their lives.

Inequality largely arises because individuals possess different amounts of human and physical capital. By far the largest cause of inequality arises from differential labor compensation. For example, the Bureau of Economic Analysis reports that in 2018, personal income was $17.569.5 trillion, about 62% of which was labor-derived income, 28% was property-derived income (interest, dividends, and rents), and the remaining 10% was net transfer payments – some $3.0 trillion in payments for Social Security, Medicare, Medicaid, unemployment insurance, etc. minus over $1.3 trillion in Social Security and related taxes.[14]

Differences in work effort, education, cognitive skills, reliability, discipline, and even physical attributes are substantial among workers and lead to wide differences in worker productivity, and thus compensation. Electrical engineers and accountants make more than social workers or artists. Those with extremely great athletic prowess, say Tom Brady or LeBron James, sometimes make 100 times the earnings of more ordinarily endowed workers, as do those with substantial financial acumen or managerial and entrepreneurial abilities. The monopoly power that extremely skilled workers have – there are few if any other basketball players comparable to LeBron James, for example – gives them extraordinary bargaining power that workers with ordinary skills do not have. If a construction worker making $20 an hour threatens to quit unless he or she is given higher pay, the employers will say "quit" and easily hire another comparable worker; the Cleveland Cavaliers and later the Los Angeles Lakers could not do that with LeBron James.

While differences in education, training, and even genetic factors lead to huge differences in wages, causing much inequality, perhaps more important are differentials in *work effort*, particularly with respect to poverty – more contemporary American poverty seems to be related to a lack of hours of work rather than low rates of pay per hour of employment. See Figure 5.1. In 2017, the official poverty rate for those aged 18–64 and not working was an extraordinary 30.7%, while it was only 2.2% for those working full time, year-round.[15]

This hints at what is demonstrated more empirically later: the Law of Unintended Consequences. Suppose the government raises income taxes to fund some social welfare spending designed, in part, to reduce poverty. If higher income taxes reduce after tax wages so that workers reduce the hours they work, the gains from government financed transfer payments to the poor may

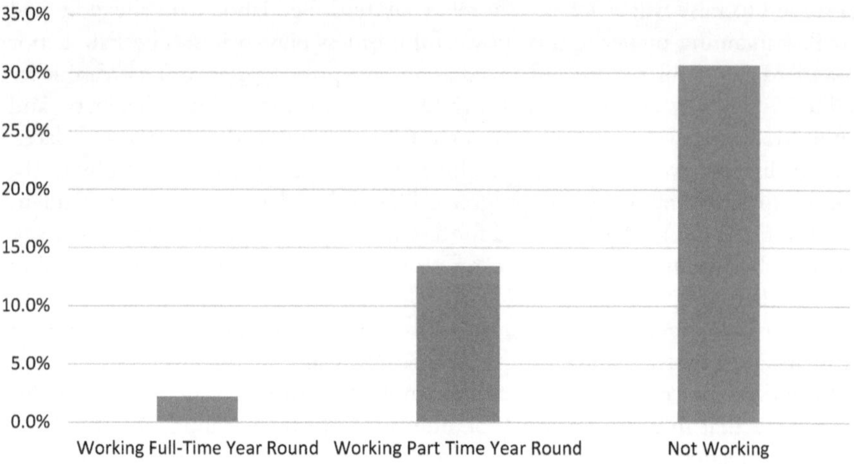

Figure 5.1 Poverty by work status, 2017

Source: U.S. Bureau of the Census

be offset by the loss in worker income resulting from the reduction in after tax wages associated with tax-financed transfer payment spending.

Neoclassical economic theory predicts that markets will eliminate much inequality if trade is allowed to be conducted with low transactions costs, without tariffs, for example, and if resources are allowed to move without government impediments. If workers in some poor country, say Zambia, are paid $1 per hour to make textiles, compared to $15 hourly in the United States, it becomes advantageous for profit-maximizing textile manufacturers to want to relocate their textile mills to Zambia. Similarly, workers in Zambia find it advantageous to move to the United States to acquire the higher living standard available for doing similar type work. Over time, the migration of capital to low labor cost areas and the migration of labor to high-wage areas will work to narrow differences in the ratio of capital to labor in the two different geographic areas and reduce wage differentials: this is the factor price equalization theorem.[16]

A vast literature supports the notion that when the classical liberal conditions assumed by the factor price equalization theorem are approximately achieved, a good deal of convergence in incomes between geographic areas occurs. Consider Figure 5.2. In 1950, South Korea's citizens lived at a barely above-subsistence level, with less than one-tenth the average incomes of Americans. Today, roughly half of that income differential has disappeared, and South Koreans live relatively prosperous lives (using an alternative purchasing power parity measure, even a larger proportion of the differential has disappeared). Meanwhile, in North Korea, similar economically to South Korea in 1950, the

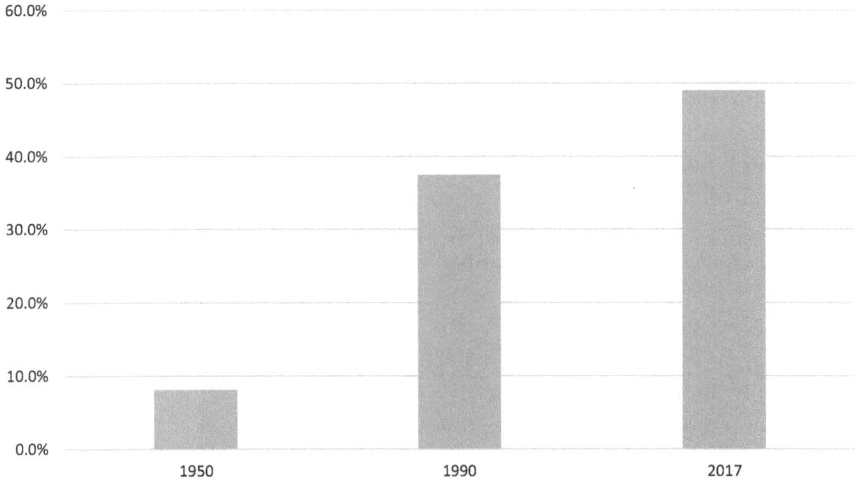

Figure 5.2 South Korean per capita income as percentage of the United States: 1950–2017
Source: Angus Maddison, World Bank

assumptions of the factor price equalization theorem do not hold. There is, for example, no free trade in goods, capital, or labor, and no open markets, property rights, or the rule of law. As a consequence, it has a standard of living probably at best equal to that of its southern neighbor two-thirds of a century earlier.

All this suggests that *classical liberal prescriptions* of free markets, free movement of resources, private property rights, and a rule of law not only lead to more prosperity (higher income, less poverty) but also *promote strong income egalitarian tendencies*: geographic income differentials declining over time. This narrowing of income differentials applies within the United States as well: in 1929, per capita income in Mississippi was but 24% of the level in New York; by 2016, Mississippi's per capita income was roughly 60% that in the Empire State, cutting the differential almost in half.[17]

Moreover, when one evaluates "equality," is it not more appropriate to look at variations in consumption, not income? Human material happiness is presumably determined by spending, not earning: money stuffed into paper assets provide no near-term satisfaction, or certainly far less than comparable sums of money spent taking cruises, buying new cars, or enjoying fancy restaurant meals. So-called "poor" college kids consume far more than they earn (hence they have incurred over $1.5 trillion in college loan debts), presumably because they expect future earnings to absorb the costs of relatively high current consumption – not only for college but also for such luxuries as spring break vacations. An examination of consumer spending habits shows that consumption spending is far less unequally distributed than income.[18]

But there is a more fundamental issue relating to equality. The measurement of inequality involves comparing people within groups, especially nations. But what if the bonds that bring people together as one "people" within a political jurisdiction become frayed, and that common identity becomes less intense? Charles Murray has argued cogently and persuasively that America is "coming apart," that people of different income groups that used to have the same aspirations, the same sense of morality, and who intermingled from time to time (e.g., at school events, concerts, ballgames), increasingly are segregated from one another both physically and mentally.[19] There is, related to that, evidence that intergenerational income mobility is in decline, meaning it may becoming harder to be realizing the American Dream – independent of the issue of the current distribution of income.[20] And critics like Murray believe that government and the welfare state has aggravated this problem, for example, by reducing incentives for poor persons to work hard to get good education and jobs. In a quest for *equality of results* with respect to income, we may have had a reduction in *equality of opportunity* – chances to get ahead. We are getting away from the rough egalitarianism and bountiful opportunity admired by Alexis de Tocqueville and romanticized by the late 19th-century novelist Horatio Alger.[21] We return to this in the following section.[22]

IV. Specific labor market policies and empirical evidence

Let's us turn to some specific government labor market policies and look at the evidence with respect to their economic impact. We specifically will emphasize the impact on poverty and/or income inequality.

IV.I. The minimum wage

One of the oldest governmental interventions in labor markets have been minimum wage laws, in the United States enacted at both the federal and state levels. The initial federal minimum wage, taking effect in October 1938, of 25 cents per hour has increased on many occasions, reaching its current level of $7.25 per hour in July 2009.[23] At this writing, a large majority of states have minimum wages in excess of the federal minimum, reaching $11 or more an hour in several jurisdictions (e.g., Washington State, Massachusetts, D.C.). Some municipalities have even higher minimums, notably, at this writing, a $15 minimum wage in Seattle.

The 1938 legislation had three objectives: to raise wages to stimulate purchasing power and raise aggregate demand, thereby stimulating employment (the High Wage Doctrine), to reduce poverty by lowering the income deficiencies of low-wage workers, and to reduce work hours of full-time workers in the expectation employers then would hire more workers. The latter objective was to be achieved by limiting the work week to 40 hours and requiring employers to pay a sharply higher wage for "overtime" pay. Additional restrictions were placed on teenage labor.[24]

When President Franklin Roosevelt signed the minimum wage bill in June 1938, the national unemployment rate was 20.6% – it has never been that high again.[25] We were very much in a Great Depression, and the primary concern was with the low incomes and poverty associated with low employment. The paramount issue is: has the minimum wage law been an effective device for reducing poverty?

Within a decade of the legislation's passage, George Stigler, a distinguished economist and later Nobel Laureate, argued that the law would have detrimental consequences, posing the question "Does such legislation diminish poverty?" He concluded the answer was no.[26] Subsequent economic analysis of minimum wage laws almost always concluded the impacts are negative or, at best, ineffective. For example, a strongly left-of-center Nobel Laureate, Joseph Stiglitz, once head of President Bill Clinton's Council of Economic Advisers, in a textbook proclaimed, "The minimum wage is not a good way of trying to deal with problems of poverty."[27] Reviews of the literature by the preeminent students of the subject, David Neumark and William Wascher, strongly affirm the Stigler–Stiglitz view, denying claims from some new research that the primary negative effects of minimum wages – reduced employment – in fact did not exist.[28]

Proponents of minimum wages argue they raise the incomes of low-skilled workers, in some cases bringing people above the poverty line. Sometimes they add that raising wages promotes higher morale and worker productivity (the so-called efficiency wage doctrine) and spurs innovation. Yet both economic theory and the evidence reject these arguments.

Labor is subject to the Law of Demand: when something becomes more expensive, people want to buy less of it. At higher wages, employers will employ fewer workers, and some workers currently earning wages will lose their jobs and incomes. Particularly impacted by minimum wage laws are unskilled workers whose limited productivity means they are low paid. Disproportionately, these are very young inexperienced workers (teenagers) and members of some minority groups. At this writing, the unemployment rate for Black Americans was slightly less than twice as high as the rate for whites (6.2% versus 3.3%), and was even higher for teenagers (11.4%).[29] *The much higher unemployment rate for African-Americans did not exist in the era before minimum wage laws*, in an era of massive race discrimination against blacks.[30, 31]

There are other problems with minimum wage laws. When employers like McDonald's are forced to raise wages, it reduces (maybe eliminates) profits, unless counteracted by other measures. Commonly, businesses will raise prices. So a government anti-poverty device (the minimum wage) might lead to a lower standard of living for relatively poor consumers who eat a fair amount of fast food. Moreover, a significant portion of those with minimum wage jobs are second or even third earners in a household. Middle-class teenagers holding minimum wage jobs are typically not in poverty. Therefore, the minimum wage does not even target the poor particularly well.

Because a majority of states have minimum wage laws at above the federal minimum, there is a fair amount of variation in statutory minimums by state.

Do states with higher minimum wages have lower rates of poverty, correcting for other factors that might also impact the presence of poor persons? Using the 2015 state poverty rate data, I used ordinary least squares regression analysis to look at the relationship between the minimum wage and poverty rates and found – *nothing* (see Table 5.1).[32] While the overall model was a good predictor of differences in poverty in the 50 states (explaining about 80% of the variation), and certain factors (such as the overall prosperity of the states as denoted by household income, the degree of unemployment, or the proportion of the population that were immigrants) were statistically significant explanatory factors, the minimum wage was not statistically significantly associated with poverty. While with a high minimum wage some individuals are pushed above the poverty line by higher wage-related income, others are pushed *below* it by unemployment. A recent National Bureau of Economic Research study of a sharp rise in the minimum wage in 2016 in Seattle concluded that the higher minimum wage

> reduced hours worked in a low-wage job by around 9 percent, while hourly wages . . . increased by around 3 percent. Consequently, total payroll fell. . . . [T]he minimum wage ordinance lowered low-wage . . . earnings by an average of $125 per month.[33]

This is consistent with the view that minimum wages are horrible anti-poverty devices.

I altered the model reported in Table 5.1 in many different ways – adding the District of Columbia, removing the noncontiguous states (Alaska and Hawaii), looking at other variables (e.g., the employment–population ratio, state and local tax burden, etc.). In no case did I observe a statistically significant negative relationship between the minimum wage and the poverty rate.[34] I even looked at the overall income distribution, as measured by the Gini coefficient, rather

Table 5.1 Fifty States: poverty rate regression-dependent variable: poverty rate 2015

Dependent Mean	12.86600	R-Square		0.8106
Coeff Var	10.97521	Adj R-Sq		0.7842
Variable	*Parameter Estimate*	*Standard Error*	*t Value*	*Pr > |t|*
Intercept	26.22725	3.46844	7.56	<.0001
Minimum wage 2015	−0.09308	0.35434	−0.26	0.7941
Foreign born 2015	0.13024	0.04236	3.07	0.0037
Union membership 2015	−0.12143	0.06362	−1.91	0.0630
Median household income 2015	−0.00026996	0.00003168	−8.52	<.0001
Right to work 2015	−0.68402	0.60021	−1.14	0.2607
Unemployed 2015	0.62006	0.23550	2.63	0.0117

Source: Author's calculations from data from the Bureau of the Census, Bureau of Labor Statistics

than the poverty rate, as the dependent variable. Again, I *never* obtained a statistically significant negative relationship, suggesting that the minimum wage was an effective device to reduce income inequality.

To conclude, the evidence supports a conclusion another distinguished (Nobel Laureate) liberal economist, James Tobin, made over 50 years ago:

> People who lack the capacity to earn a decent living need to be helped, but they will not be helped by minimum-wage laws, trade-union pressures or other devices to compel employers to pay them more than their work is worth. The more likely outcome . . . is that the intended beneficiaries are not employed at all.[35]

IV.II. Public assistance programs and the law of unintended consequences

As indicated earlier, both the New Deal programs of the 1930s and the Great Society extensions of the 1960s enormously expanded governmental assistance to persons who were disadvantaged: Social Security, disability payments, food stamps, housing subsidies, Medicaid, etc. The purpose of these programs was explicitly and almost exclusively to reduce poverty in America. Indeed, Lyndon Johnson in 1964 declared a War on Poverty, involving a massive expansion of federal assistance to lower-income persons. In the year of Johnson's declaration, the official U.S. poverty rate was 19%. The rate declined sharply with the expansion of federal assistance, reaching a low of 11.1% by 1973. But, despite continued growth in governmental assistance programs, poverty not only stopped falling, but it started rising and has *never* reached the 1973 low: the 2015 rate of 12.3%, in a period of relative prosperity, is over 10% higher than what it was 42 years earlier when overall affluence was lower.

What happened? The expanded welfare system had two unintended consequences that greatly increased poverty. First, it reduced incentives to work – to earn income. Why work when the government pays you, in effect, to *not* work? Even while poverty rates were falling in the 1960s at the very beginning of the Great Society programs, economists were observing significant disincentive effects of public assistance.[36] Recall that poor people are very seldom fully employed. As work income increases, public assistance payments fall, imposing high marginal "tax" rates (loss of income) associated with work. Second, as Charles Murray so vividly argued in his book, *Losing Ground*, on the welfare system, the expanded amount of public assistance hastened the demise of many traditional two-parent families.[37] Women who before the Great Society were dependent on spousal financial support increasingly divorced their husbands – or even more often had children out of wedlock – thinking the government would provide financial assistance. Poverty rates are routinely twice as high or more in households having a single female head. When family life becomes dysfunctional, people fall into poverty.[38]

Looking at the poverty experience, Lowell Gallaway and I, sometimes with Therese Foster, in the 1980s discovered what we called "the poverty-welfare curve."[39] As illustrated in Figure 5.3, data indicate that when public assistance payments are small, modest increases in those payments will likely reduce poverty, because some people are pushed above the poverty line, and the unintended negative consequences from work disincentive effects and damage to traditional family structures are very small. At some point, however, incremental welfare spending becomes counterproductive: the gains from pushing some people above the poverty line are more than offset by the increasingly negative effects of such expenditures on the work effort of welfare recipients, as well as the growth in single-parent (mostly female) households.

In our writings in the mid-1980s, we observed that the data for the postwar period very clearly supported the existence of the poverty–welfare curve. A generation later, after some significant reforms in the welfare system in the 1990s (putting time limits on payments, requiring able-bodied welfare recipients to work), does the poverty–welfare curve still hold? Lowell Gallaway and Daniel Garret replicated the earlier empirical results recently, finding that the curve is still valid.[40]

In the 1990s, there was an increasing bipartisan recognition that the welfare system had failed; candidate Bill Clinton as early as 1991 promised to "end welfare as we have come to know it."[41] The 1996 welfare reform was passed by a Republican Congress with modest Democratic support, but signed by Democrat Clinton. It restricted the ability of persons to indefinitely receive welfare payments, gave states the right to experiment with alternative approaches, and replaced the AFDC program with Temporary Assistance for Needy Families (TANF), with more restrictions and requirements, including work expectations.

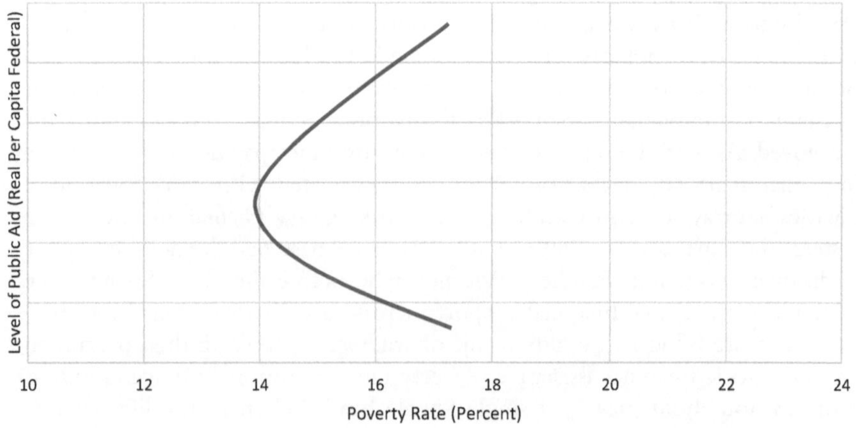

Figure 5.3 Poverty–welfare curve

Leftish politicians and commentators predicted massive hardships. One writer said: "[T]he repeal of the welfare system is merely the latest manifestation of the class warfare the Democrats and Republicans have waged on behalf of their corporate financial backers. . . . [T]he legislation blames poor people for their plight."[42] What did actually happen? The number of people classified poor by the Census Bureau fell by nearly five million from 1996 to 2000; the 2000 poverty rate of 11.3% came close to matching the 1973 all-time low rate.

The welfare reforms of the 1990s did not impact many public assistance programs, which continued to grow. I have argued that the explosion of participation in programs like food stamps (numbers nearly tripling after 2000) and Social Security disability (a tripling in numbers after 1990) led to a sharp decline in the best and most effective cure for poverty: work.[43] Thus, the poverty rate has never returned to the 1973 or even 2000 level.

IV.III. Right-to-work laws

Supreme Court Justice Louis Brandeis famously once said: "a state may, if its citizens choose, serve as a laboratory; and try novel social and economic experiments without risk to the rest of the country."[44] The 1947 Taft–Hartley Act amending the Wagner Act gave states the option of passing legislation that made it illegal to make labor union membership a condition of employment, outlawing union shop labor agreements. Unlike the other policies discussed in this chapter, the RTW alternative permitted states to opt for contractual arrangements closer to those found in classical liberal economic settings, such as the United States before the Great Depression. The fact that states differed in how they reacted to this option provided one of those "economic experiments" comprising American federalism's "laboratories of democracy."

There are currently 28 RTW states. In 2017, for the first time in the 70 years since the passage of Taft–Hartley, a majority (52%) of the American population lived in RTW states, compared to less than 30% in 1970. Some 18 states chose the RTW route by 1960, mostly in the South, West, and Midwest. Then there was a half century drought, when only four more states adopted RTW laws, bringing the total to 22. In the six years from 2011 forward, however, six more states in the Midwest or its periphery became RTW jurisdictions. A political equilibrium had existed for decades, whereby the forces favoring RTW were counteracted roughly equally by those opposing that legislation, so little change occurred. Since 2010, however, the RTW forces have become stronger because labor unions, the prime opponents of RTW, have lost membership and strength. A majority of the 22 non-RTW states are in New England or Mid-Atlantic states or are in the five states bordering the Pacific Ocean. "Flyover" country (noncoastal states) is strongly RTW in its orientation.

Opponents of RTW laws argue they are anti-union, and union protection of workers leads to higher wages and lower poverty. Proponents of the legislation suggest RTW laws provide greater workplace freedom to employees and a better investment climate for business, leading to more employment and probably higher productivity of workers, and with that, in the long run to higher incomes.

There is a good deal of empirical evidence supporting RTW laws. Statistical examination of the relationship between RTW laws and economic growth, controlling for other determinants of growth, shows the laws are growth-enhancing.[45] Incomes rise faster, other things equal, in RTW jurisdictions, even after controlling for population change. Moreover, there is substantial in-migration into RTW states. For example, in the seven years from July 2010 through June 2017, 3,242,683 on net moved into the 22 states that were RTW throughout the period – 52 for every hour of each day! Meanwhile, major non-RTW states like New York and Illinois had sizable out-migration (over one million in the case of New York). When people move into a state, they are presumably expecting to improve the quality of their lives. Moreover, the in-migration of capital resources means not only more jobs but also higher worker productivity.[46]

IV.IV. Unemployment insurance benefits

One of the first manifestations of the welfare state internationally was the creation of unemployment insurance benefits, most famously after 1911 in Great Britain (National Insurance Act) and by the early 1930s elsewhere (e.g., Germany). A state unemployment insurance law was enacted in Wisconsin in 1932, but the modern American system arises from the 1935 Social Security Act.

Advocates of unemployment compensation schemes argue they provide a layer of protection against the risks of income loss in periods of high unemployment. Keynesian economists also argue that unemployment insurance is an "automatic stabilizer," a device that mitigates the volatility of incomes, by taxing employers in prosperous times, allowing insurance funds to rise, while on balance making payments to unemployed workers during downturns.

While the principle of providing an element of income security to workers seems sound and today is relatively noncontroversial, there are some rather serious negative effects of the system. The payment of workers for *not* working is the essence of unemployment insurance, and therefore somewhat of a disincentive to work. There is strong evidence that high British unemployment in the interwar period was largely a consequence of Britain's unemployment insurance provision.[47] In the United States, pioneering empirical studies in the 1970s, first by Gene Chapin and then by the late Martin Feldstein, showed that there were some unemployment-creating effects of unemployment compensation.[48] Subsequent research has shown that extending unemployment benefits over longer time periods has significant unemployment effects.[49] In recognition of that, the American law limited the payment of unemployment benefits to 26 weeks – the idea was that a helping hand would be provided for up to six months, after which the beneficiary would be expected to obtain another job.

I would argue that the Great Recession of 2008 was prolonged considerably by the extraordinary extension of unemployment benefits, in some cases for as long as 99 weeks (nearly two years). This contributed to a very sluggish growth in employment during the recovery. When the U.S. Congress abruptly and somewhat unexpectedly eliminated extended unemployment benefits in 2013, this unleashed a torrent of labor market activity. One study estimated two million jobs were added as a consequence of eliminating extended benefits.[50] In 2012, with prolonged unemployment insurance benefits, the average duration of unemployment was 39.4 weeks (over nine months), and over 41% of the unemployed had been out of work at least 27 weeks; three years later, in 2015, with unemployment insurance benefits existing only for 26 weeks, the average duration of unemployment had fallen over 10 weeks (more than 25%), to 29.2 weeks, and only about 28% were out of work over 27 weeks.[51] Clearly, unemployment insurance prolongs the search for jobs by the unemployed; facing several months of government-provided benefits, unemployed workers have a higher reservation wage (minimally acceptable compensation) than they would otherwise have, prolonging their spells of joblessness.

IV.V. Government health care provision

This *tour de horizon* of government labor policies is not long enough to allow for a detailed exposition of health care legislation. Yet most Americans have employer-provided health care insurance, and health care is thus a major cost item to business. Rather than get into the weeds of Obamacare, Medicaid expansion, and other relevant topics, I simply wish to ask a rather fundamental question: is the health of Americans today significantly better than it would have been if the federal government had not gotten so deeply involved in the provision of health care? Evaluating counterfactual propositions is tricky, but at least some evidence suggests that the lengthening of the quantity of life – probably the most fundamental goal of health care – has not accelerated, and indeed actually has declined, in the era of significant federal health care involvement.

It was the presence of an anti-free market government policy, World War II wage controls, that led to the widespread expansion of employer-provided health insurance in the first place, coupled with favorable tax treatment of that benefit.[52] But really important federal involvement in health care begins with the Great Society Medicare and Medicaid programs of the 1960s. Probably the most obvious "bottom line" of helping the sick and the injured in society is keeping them alive – prolonging their life. What has happened to life expectancy, first during periods of relative *laissez-faire* in health care, say from 1900 to 1965, and then during periods of increasing governmental involvement since?[53]

Figure 5.4 looks at increases in life expectancy in five periods in American history, encompassing the 20th and early 21st centuries. In the first three periods, from 1900 to 1965, on average in every year, life expectancy at birth grew by well over 100 days, going from 47.3 years in 1900 to 70.2 years by 1965. In the last two periods, 1965–2015, life expectancy has risen by sharply diminishing amounts, to less than 50 days added expectancy for each year in the most recent period. During the entire half century, life expectancy rose by 8.6 years, to 78.8 years in 2015.

In the era of governmental health care activism since 1965, life expectancy has risen far less rapidly than in the earlier period of largely free markets with very limited governmental supervision. Two caveats are in order. First, some diminution in the growth of life expectancy might be expected – the low-hanging fruit in terms of extending life, such as the development of antibiotics, came when life expectancy was relatively low. Second, life expectancy is partly determined by factors not directly related to the health care system, such as, to name three, smoking, premature death from drug addiction, and the eating habits of the population.

With these caveats in mind, the data in Figure 5.4 call into doubt the notion that federal health care provision has dramatically *improved* the nation's health. A decent case can be made that it has in some respects *worsened* it: for example, superb potential physicians avoid medicine because of the massive paperwork

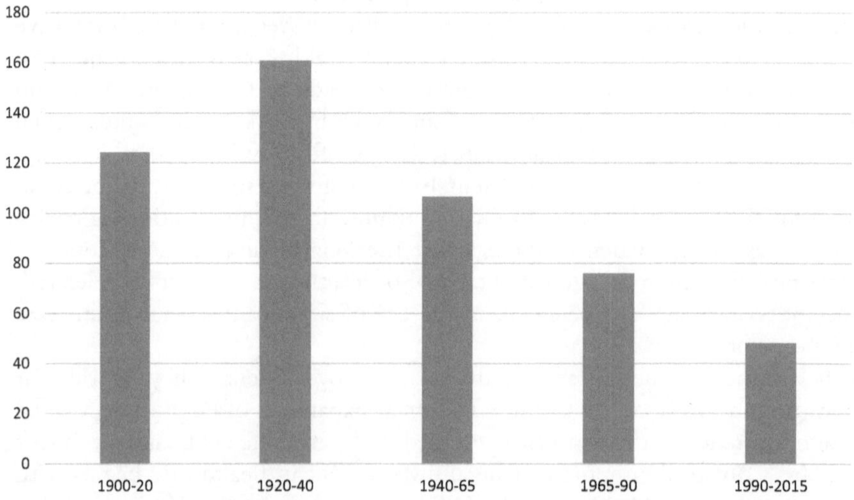

Figure 5.4 Average number of days of expected additional life at birth annually, 1900–2015

Source: U.S. Census Bureau, *Historical Statistics of the United States*, National Center for Health Statistics; author's calculations

from government mandates, high progressive income taxes to finance the welfare state, and the potential legal liabilities from abandoning the traditional doctrine of *caveat emptor* (let the buyer beware); life-saving drugs and therapies are sometimes prohibited by an overly risk-averse Food and Drug Administration; poor people sometimes cannot get medical treatment owing to the fact that many doctors will not accept Medicaid or even Medicare patients because of too much paperwork and too low compensation.

IV.VI. Affirmative action

No one seriously doubts that there was a great amount of racial discrimination in mid-20th-century America, and some gender, ethnic, and sexual preference discrimination also existed. Legitimate concerns led to the Civil Rights Act of 1964 and related legislation. Fast-forward more than one-half century. We have had an African-American serving as president, with several others having served as Secretary of State or Supreme Court justices. A growing number of corporate CEOs are black, and an even greater number are women. Minorities are disproportionately represented in other high-paying jobs, such as professional athletics or as high-profile entertainers. Was this a consequence of legislation and affirmative action, or of labor markets working?

As economists have long recognized, racial (or other) discrimination imposes significant costs on profit-maximizing entrepreneurs.[54] Suppose a firm considering hiring an additional worker has two applicants: a highly productive black person, and a less productive white person. A prejudicial employer selecting the white person will sacrifice output, raising per unit costs, lowering profits, and putting him or her at a competitive disadvantage. Perhaps partly because of that, *blacks were making very significant employment inroads long before civil rights legislation became important.* To cite one factoid: in the six years *before* the passage of the Civil Rights Act of 1964, employment of blacks and other nonwhites in relatively high-paying "professional and technical" jobs rose an extraordinary 90%, while the number working in relatively low-paid jobs as "private household workers" or "farm laborers" fell by 5%.[55] Yet another: from 1947 to 1964, before significant affirmative action legislation, real median family income rose 56% for whites – but a much more robust 71% for blacks and other races.[56]

Moreover, there were some adverse unintended consequences of federal civil rights activism for low-income people. In the *Griggs v. Duke Power* case (1971), the Supreme Court, citing the Civil Rights Act, strongly limited employer testing of prospective employees, leading them to rely more on degree certification, pushing up the demand and price of college degrees, hurting especially poor and minorities – there is a smaller percent of low-income Americans (bottom quartile of the income distribution) among recent college graduates today than before *Griggs*.[57]

Additionally, there is substantial evidence that affirmative action-inspired preferential treatment of minorities often has other adverse unintended consequences. For example, Richard Sander and Stuart Taylor have shown that minority law students at top law schools who received preferential treatment failed the bar exam (or even to graduate) at much higher rates than others but likely would have fared better had they attended less prestigious law schools where they would have been more academically competitive.[58]

IV.VII. Other governmentally imposed labor market distortions

Space does not allow a detailed discussion of other labor market distortions. Classical liberal policies in the 19th century led to the greatest human migration ever experienced to the New World. Restrictions, ironically often promoted by relatively conservative or even libertarian politicians, imposed in the 20th century that persist today have reduced those inflows. Yet even opponents of expansive immigration like Harvard's George Borjas (himself an immigrant) have argued that on balance immigration has positive welfare effects.[59] The late Julian Simon demonstrated the impressive long-term positive effects of immigration.[60] A recent study concluded: "We find that locations with more historical immigration today have higher incomes, less poverty, less unemployment, higher rates of urbanization, and greater educational attainment."[61]

We have neglected detailed analysis of several other labor market interventions, such as the Davis–Bacon Act, or mostly state-based occupational licensing laws, including teacher certification, and partially ignored one huge one, namely, the pension provisions of the Social Security Act of 1935. In virtually every case, there are bad unintended consequences: for example, the Davis–Bacon Act raises construction costs, burdening taxpayers; the Social Security Act no doubt reduced personal saving and a sense of individual responsibility that largely propelled American economic exceptionalism. Occupational licensing has been a barrier to many qualified persons to acquire jobs, and have raised costs to consumers and taxpayers.

V. A final word

Very often, the motive behind federal encroachments into labor market activities are well meaning, designed to ameliorate perceived problems or injustices, such as excessive poverty. Most often, however, the cure is worse than the disease because of the unintended consequences of actions taken. The powerful resource allocation properties of the market are seldom rivaled in their ability to improve the human condition.

Notes

1 The term is used in McCloskey's magisterial three-volume "Bourgeois" trilogy. Deidre N. McCloskey, *The Bourgeois Virtues: Ethics for an Age of Commerce* (Chicago: University of Chicago Press, 2006); Deidre N. McCloskey, *Bourgeois Dignity: Why Economics Can't Explain the Modern World* (Chicago: University of Chicago Press, 2010); Deidre N.

McCloskey, *Bourgeois Equality: How Ideas, Not Capital or Institutions, Enriched the World* (Chicago: University of Chicago Press, 2016).

2 Arnold Toynbee, *Lectures on the Industrial Revolution* (London: Rivington, 1884), p. 85.

3 See Phyllis Deane, *The First Industrial Revolution*, 2nd ed. (Cambridge: Cambridge University Press, 1979), p. 220.

4 Adam Smith, *An Inquiry into the Natures and Causes of the Wealth of Nations* (Oxford: Oxford University Press, 1976), p. 136.

5 A very strong case can be made that the Enlightenment that helped bring about classical liberal ideas also provided both an intellectual and a legal environment encouraging technological change. Joel Mokyr makes that point forcefully, first in his *The Enlightened Economy: An Economic History of Britain 1700–1850* (New Haven: Yale University Press, 2009) and then in his *Culture of Growth: The Origins of the Modern Economy* (Princeton, NJ: Princeton University Press, 2016).

6 See, for example, Joseph Schafer, "Was the West a Safety Valve for Labor?" *Mississippi Valley Historical Review* 24 (December 1937): 299–314.

7 Frederick Jackson Turner, *The Frontier in American History* (New York: Henry Holt and Co., 1920). Many historians ultimately rejected the safety-valve doctrine. See, for example, Fred A. Shannon, "A Post Mortem on the Labor Safety-Valve Theory," *Agricultural History* 19 (January 1945): 31–37.

8 Angus Maddison estimates that the American gross domestic product exceeded that of the United Kingdom for the first time in 1872. See his *The World Economy: Historical Statistics* (Paris: Organization of Economic Cooperation and Development, 2003), p. 48, 84. On a per capita basis, the United States surpassed Britain first in 1901, the year of Queen Victoria's death. See *The World Economy*, pp. 61, 88.

9 198 U.S. 45, 25 S. Ct. 539.

10 The best account of the Pullman Strike is Almont Lindsey, *The Pullman Strike: The Story of a Unique Experiment and of a Great Labor Upheaval*, revised ed. (Chicago: University of Chicago Press, 1964).

11 For a much fuller accounting, see Richard Vedder and Lowell Gallaway, *Cracked Foundation: Repealing the Davis-Bacon Act* (St. Louis: Center for the Study of American Business, Washington University, November 1995).

12 See Richard K. Vedder and Lowell E. Gallaway, *Out of Work: Unemployment and Government in Twentieth-Century America* (New York: New York University Press, 1997) for a detailed discussion of federal labor policies and how they impacted employment and overall output growth.

13 Especially influential were Michael Harrington, *The Other America: Poverty in the United States* (New York: Macmillan, 1962); Harry Caudill, *Night Comes to the Cumberlands: A Biography of a Depressed Area* (Boston, MA: Little, Brown, 1963).

14 Data on personal income and its disposition are available via www.bea.gov.

15 See U.S. Bureau of the Census, *Income and Poverty in the United States: 2017*. Available at www.census.gov/library/publications/2016/demo/p60-256.html.

16 Although there is a voluminous literature relating to this point, the classic paper is by Paul A. Samuelson. See his "International Trade and the Equalisation of Factor Prices," *Economic Journal* 58 (June 1948): 163–184.

17 For state per capita income data from 1929 to the present, go to the Bureau of Economic Analysis web site available at www.bea.gov.

18 The most authoritative data on consumption is provided by the Consumer Expenditure Survey of the U.S. Bureau of Labor Statistics.

19 Charles Murray, *Coming Apart: The State of White America, 1960–2010* (New York: Crown Forum, 2012).

20 The literature on intergenerational income mobility is immense. Two representative but quite different well-cited papers include Gary S. Becker and Nigel Tomes, "An Equilibrium Theory of the Distribution of Income and Intergenerational Mobility," *Journal of Political Economy* 87 (December 1979): 1153–1189; and Miles Corak, "Income

Inequality, Equality of Opportunity, and Intergenerational Mobility," *Journal of Economic Perspectives* 27 (July 2013): 79–102.

21 Progressive economists, however, cite evidences (see Corak above) that show a positive relationship between income equality and income mobility – rich people use some of their income to enhance the success of their children, reducing intergenerational income mobility.

22 See, of course, Alexis de Tocqueville, *Democracy in America* (New York: George Dearborn, 1838); the enormous popular Horatio Alger (1832–1899) novels showed how poor boys could achieve success through hard work, honesty, discipline, determination, etc.

23 For a chart providing the history of changes in the minimum wage, go to the World Wide Web. Available at https://dol.gov/whd/minwage/chart.htm.

24 An excellent summary of the bill is John S. Forsythe, "Legislative History of the Fair Labor Standards Act," a Duke University study obtainable by Googling "legislative history of the Fair Standards Act."

25 Monthly unemployment rates were not yet estimated by the Bureau of Labor Statistics. These were estimates I previously did with Lowell Gallaway, *See Out of Work: Unemployment and Government in Twentieth-Century America* (New York: New York University Press, 1997), p. 77.

26 George Stigler, "The Economics of Minimum Wage Legislation," *American Economic Review* 36 (June 1946): 358–365.

27 Joseph Stiglitz, *Economics* (New York: Norton, 1993), p. 133.

28 See David Neumark and William Wascher, "Minimum Wages and Employment: A Review of Evidence on Minimum Wage Research," National Bureau of Economic Research Working Paper 12663, issued in November 2006, or their more comprehensive *Minimum Wages* (Cambridge, MA: MIT Press, 2008). The claims that minimum wages do not have negative employment effects arose from the work of David Card and Alan Krueger, based on a study of differential state minimum wage laws and its impact on restaurant employment. See their *Myth and Measurement: The New Economics of the Minimum Wage* (Princeton, NJ: Princeton University Press, 1997). Their methodology has been widely criticized and has found few adherents among researchers on minimum wages.

29 This is based on May 2017 data, as published by the Bureau of Labor Statistics. See their monthly unemployment release at www.bls.gov.

30 Using the 1930 Census data, Lowell Gallaway and I estimated the unemployment rate of African-Americans as of April 1930 to be 6.07%, actually lower than the 6.59% rate for whites. In the postwar era (with the federal and some state minimum wage laws well established), the black unemployment rate has been consistently close to twice the rates for whites. See our "Racial Differences in Unemployment in the United States, 1890–1990," *Journal of Economic History* 52 (September 1992): 696–702.

31 Milton Friedman, "Minimum Wage Rates," *Newsweek*, September 26, 1966.

32 I am indebted to Justin Strehle for his superb assistance here.

33 Ekaterina Jardim, Marck C. Long, Robert Plotnick, Emma van Inwegen, Jacob Vigdor, and Hilary Wething, *Minimum Wage Increases, Wages and Low-Wage Employment, Evidence for Seattle*. National Bureau of Economic Research Working Paper 23532 (Cambridge, MA: NBER, June 2017).

34 This is not the first time I observed that the minimum wage was an ineffective poverty reduction device. See Richard Vedder and Lowell Gallaway, *Does the Minimum Wage Reduce Poverty?* (Washington, DC: Employment Policies Institute, June 2001).

35 As quoted by Friedman's *Newsweek* article cited above.

36 Three examples: Carl T. Brehm and Thomas R. Saving, "The Demand for General Assistance Payments," *American Economic Review* 54 (December 1964): 1002–1018: Lowell E. Gallaway, "Negative Income Taxes and the Elimination of Poverty," *National Tax*

Journal 19 (September 1966): 298–307; Hirschel Kasper, "Welfare Payments and Work Incentive: Some Determinants of the Rate of General Assistance Payments," *Journal of Human Resources* 3 (Winter 1968): 86–110.

37 Charles Murray, *Losing Ground: American Social Policy* (New York: Basic Books, 1984).

38 A contemporary book that illustrates this vividly is J. D. Vance, *Hillbilly Elegy* (New York: Harper, 2016).

39 The shortest version, and most read, is Lowell Gallaway and Richard Vedder, "AFDC and the Laffer Principle," *Wall Street Journal*, March 26, 1986. The most comprehensive treatment is found is our monograph *Poverty, Income Distribution, The Family and Public Policy*. Joint Economic Committee of the U.S. Congress (Washington, DC: Government Printing Office, December 19, 1986).

40 Lowell E. Gallaway and Daniel G. Garrett, "The Unintended Consequences of the War on Poverty," *Cato Journal* 36 (Winter 2016): 33–45. There has been surprisingly little criticism of the poverty–welfare curve findings. One example, however, is Sanford F. Schram and Paul H. Wilken, "It's No 'Laffer Matter': Claim That Increasing Welfare Aid Breeds Poverty and Dependence Fails Statistical Test," *American Journal of Economics and Sociology* 48 (April 1989): 203–217.

41 Bill Clinton, "The New Covenant: Responsibility and Rebuilding the American Community," remarks to students at Georgetown University, October 23, 1991.

42 Mark Dunlea, "'Welfare Reform': Clinton Kills the Safety Net," *Synthesis/Regeneration* 12 (Winter 1997).

43 Richard Vedder, *Wall Street Journal*, January 16, 2013.

44 *New State Ice Co. v. Liebmann*, 285 U.S. 262, 1932.

45 Working with coauthors, I have produced at least five such studies. Perhaps the most accessible is Richard Vedder, "Right-to-Work Laws: Liberty, Prosperity, and the Quality of Life," *Cato Journal* 30 (Winter 2010): 171–180. For a shorter account, see my "Income Rises When Right-to-Work Laws Are Passed," *New York Times*, March 14, 2015.

46 The productivity and population-enhancing dimensions of RTW laws are empirically verified by Michael J. Hicks, Michael LaFaive, and Srikant Devaraj, "New Evidence on the Effect of Right-to-Work Laws and Productivity and Economic Growth," *Cato Journal* 36 (Winter 2016): 101–120.

47 Daniel Benjamin and Levis Kochin, "Searching for an Explanation of Unemployment in Interwar Britain," *Journal of Political Economy* 87 (June 1979): 441–478.

48 Gene Chapin, "Unemployment Insurance, Job Search, and the Demand for Leisure," *Economic Inquiry* (March 1971): 102–107; Martin Feldstein, "Unemployment Compensation: Adverse Incentives and Distributional Anomalies," *National Tax Journal* 27 (June 1974): 231–244, and his "The Effect of Unemployment Insurance on Temporary Layoff Unemployment," *American Economic Review* 68 (December 1978): 834–846.

49 Two examples selected almost at random from the literature: Jean B. Grossman, "The Work Disincentive Effect of Extended Unemployment Compensation: Recent Evidence," *Review of Economics and Statistics* 71 (February 1989): 159–164; Knut Roed and Tao Zhang, "Does Unemployment Compensation Affect Unemployment Duration?" *Economic Journal* 113 (January 2003): 190–206.

50 Marcus Hagedorn, Iourii Manovskii, and Kurt Mitman, *The Impact of Unemployment Benefit Extensions on Employment: The 2014 Employment Miracle*. Working Paper No. 20884 (Cambridge, MA: National Bureau of Economic Research, January 2015).

51 Data are from the U.S. Department of Labor, Bureau of Labor Statistics.

52 While strict limits were put on wage increases, the wage control authorities created a loophole, allowing larger increases in fringe benefits (until then, a minor item).

53 The comprehensive analysis of current life expectancy, with some historical data, is from the National Center for Health Statistics, *Health, United States, 2016: With Chartbook on Long-Term Trends* (Washington, DC: U.S. Government Printing Office, 2017).

54 The standard account is Gary S. Becker, *The Economics of Discrimination*, revised ed. (Chicago: University of Chicago Press, 1957 [1971]). A similar perspective placed in a historical context is provided by Robert Higgs, *Competition and Coercion: Blacks in the American Economy, 1865–1914* (Chicago: University of Chicago Press, 1980).

55 U.S. Department of Labor, *Manpower Report of the President* (Washington, DC: Government Printing Office, 1970), p. 227.

56 U.S. Bureau of the Census, *Money Income of Households, Families and Persons in the United States: 1984* (New York: U.S. Bureau of the Census, 1984), pp. 29–30, and author's calculations.

57 See Bryan O'Keefe and Richard Vedder, *'Griggs v. Duke Power': Implications for College Credentialing* (Washington, DC: John William Pope Center for Higher Education Policy (NJ1), 2008).

58 Richard Sander and Stuart Taylor, *Mismatch: How Affirmative Action Hurts Students It's Intended to Help, and Why Universities Won't Admit It* (New York: Basic Books, 2012). For a more comprehensive treatment of the problems of affirmative action, see Stephen Thernstrom and Abigail Thernstrom, *America in Black and White: One Nation, Indivisible* (New York: Simon and Schuster, 1997).

59 George J. Borjas, *Heaven's Door: Immigration Policy and the American Economy* (Princeton, NJ: Princeton University Press, 1999).

60 Julian L. Simon, *The Economic Consequences of Immigration* (Ann Arbor: University of Michigan Press, 1999).

61 Sandra Sequeira, Nathan Nunn, and Nancy Qian, *Migrants and the Making of America: The Short- and Long-Run Effects of Immigration During the Age of Mass Migration*. Working Paper 23289 (Cambridge, MA: National Bureau of Economic Research, March 2017).

References

Becker, G. S. 1957 [1971]. *The Economics of Discrimination*. Chicago: University of Chicago Press.

Becker, G. S., and N. Tomes. 1979. "An Equilibrium Theory of the Distribution of Income and Intergenerational Mobility." *Journal of Political Economy* 87 (6): 1153–1189.

Benjamin, D. K., and L. A. Kochin. 1979. "Searching for an Explanation of Unemployment in Interwar Britain." *Journal of Political Economy* 87 (3): 441–478.

Borjas, G. J. 2011. *Heaven's Door: Immigration Policy and the American Economy*. Princeton, NJ: Princeton University Press.

Brehm, C. T., and T. R. Saving. 1964. "The Demand for General Assistance Payments." *The American Economic Review* 54 (6): 1002–1018.

Card, D., and A. B. Krueger. 1995. *Myth and Measurement*. Princeton, NJ: Princeton University Press.

Chapin, G. 1971. "Unemployment Insurance, Job Search, and the Demand for Leisure." *Economic Inquiry* 9 (1): 102–107.

Claudill, H. M. 2015. *Night Comes to the Cumberlands: A Biography of a Depressed Area*. New York: Pickle Partners Publishing.

Clinton, B. 1991. *The New Covenant: Responsibility and Rebuilding the American Community*. Remarks to students at Georgetown University. Speech. Washington, DC: Georgetown University, October 23.

Corak, M. 2013. "Income Inequality, Equality of Opportunity, and Intergenerational Mobility." *Journal of Economic Perspectives* 27 (3): 79–102.

De Tocqueville, A. 1838. *Democracy in America*, Henry Reeve, trans., vol. 1. New York: George Dearborn and Co.

Dunlea, M. 1997. "Welfare Reform: Clinton Kills Safety Net." *Synthesis/Regeneration*, 12, Winter. Available at www.greens.org/s-r/12/12-15.html.

Feldstein, M. 1974. "Unemployment Compensation: Adverse Incentives and Distributional Anomalies." *National Tax Journal*: 231–244.

Feldstein, M. 1978. "The Effect of Unemployment Insurance on Temporary Layoff Unemployment." *The American Economic Review* 68 (5): 834–846.

Forsythe, J. S. 1939. "Legislative History of the Fair Labor Standards Act." *Law and Contemporary Problems* 6: 464.

Friedman, M. 1966. "Minimum Wage Rates." *Newsweek*, September 26.

Gallaway, L. E. 1966. "Negative Income Tax Rates and the Elimination of Poverty." *National Tax Journal* 19 (3): 298–307.

Gallaway, L. E., and D. G. Garrett. 2016. "The Unintended Consequences of the War on Poverty." *Cato Journal* 36: 33.

Gallaway, L. E., and R. Vedder. 1986. "Poverty, Income Distribution, the Family, and Public Policy." In *Study, Joint Economic Committee of Congress*. Washington, DC: Government Printing Office, December.

Griggs v Duke Power Co. 401 U.S. 424 (1971).

Grossman, J. B. 1989. "The Work Disincentive Effect of Extended Unemployment Compensation: Recent Evidence." *The Review of Economics and Statistics* 159–164.

Hagedorn, M., Manovskii, I., and K. Mitman. 2015. *The Impact of Unemployment Benefit Extensions on Employment: The 2014 Employment Miracle?* No. w20884. Washington, DC: National Bureau of Economic Research.

Harrington, M. 1962. *The Other America: Poverty in the United States*. New York: Macmillan.

Hicks, M. J., LaFaive, M., and S. Devaraj. 2016. "New Evidence on the Effect of Right-to-Work Laws on Productivity and Population Growth." *Cato Journal* 36: 101.

Higgs, R. 1980. *Competition and Coercion: Blacks in the American Economy 1865–1914*. Chicago: University of Chicago Press.

Jardim, E., Long, M. C., Plotnick, R., Van Inwegen, E., Vigdor, J., and H. Wething. 2017. *Minimum Wage Increases, Wages, and Low-Wage Employment: Evidence from Seattle*. No. w23532. Washington, DC: National Bureau of Economic Research.

Kasper, H. 1968. "Welfare Payments and Work Incentive: Some Determinants of the Rates of General Assistance Payments." *Journal of Human Resources* 86–110.

King v Burwell. 576 U.S. 988 (2015).

Lindsey, A. 1943 [1964]. *The Pullman Strike: The Story of a Unique Experiment and of a Great Labor Upheaval*. Chicago: University of Chicago Press.

Lochner v. New York, 198 U.S. 45, 1905.

Maddison, A. 2003. *Development Centre Studies the World Economy: Historical Statistics*. Paris: OECD Publishing.

Maddison, A. 2007. *The World Economy Volume 1: A Millennial Perspective Volume 2: Historical Statistics*. London: Academic Foundation, pp. 61, 88.

McCloskey, D. N. 2006. *The Bourgeois Virtues: Ethics for an Age of Commerce*. Chicago: University of Chicago Press.

McCloskey, D. N. 2010. *Bourgeois Dignity: Why Economics Can't Explain the Modern World*. Chicago: University of Chicago Press.

McCloskey, D. N. 2016. *Bourgeois Equality: How Ideas, Not Capital or Institutions, Enriched the World*. Chicago: University of Chicago Press.

Mokyr, J. 2009. *The Enlightened Economy: An economic history of Britain 1700–1850*. New Haven, CT: Yale University Press.

Mokyr, J. 2016. *Culture and Growth: The Origins of the Modern Economy*. Princeton, NJ: Princeton University Press.

Murray, C. 2008. *Losing Ground: American Social Policy, 1950–1980*. New York: Basic Books.

Murray, C. 2013. *Coming Apart: The State of White America, 1960–2010*. New York: Three Rivers Press.

National Center for Health Statistics (US). 2016. *Health, United States, 2016: With Chartbook on Long-Term Trends in Health*. Hyattsville, MD: National Center for Health Statistics.

Neumark, D., and W. L. Wascher. 2007. "Minimum Wages and Employment: Foundations and Trends®." *Microeconomics* 3 (1–2): 1–182.

Neumark, D., and W. L. Wascher. 2008. *Minimum Wages*. Cambridge, MA: MIT Press.

New State Ice Co. v. Liebmann, 285 U.S. 262, 1932.

O'keefe, B., and R. Vedder. 2008. *'Griggs v. Duke Power': Implications for College Credentialing*. Washington, DC: John William Pope Center for Higher Education Policy (NJ1).

Proctor, B. D., Semega, J. L., and M. A. Kollar. 2016. *Income and Poverty in the United States: 2015*, September 13. Available at www.census.gov/library/publications/2016/demo/p60-256.html.

Røed, K., and T. Zhang. 2003. "Does Unemployment Compensation Affect Unemployment Duration?" *The Economic Journal* 113 (484): 190–206.

Samuelson, P. A. 1948. "International Trade and the Equalisation of Factor Prices." *The Economic Journal* 58 (230): 163–184.

Sander, R., and S. Taylor. 2012. *Mismatch: How Affirmative Action Hurts Students Its Intended to Help, and Why Universities Won't Admit It*. New York: Basic Books.

Schafer, J. 1937. "Was the West a Safety Valve for Labor?" *The Mississippi Valley Historical Review* 24 (3): 299–314.

Schram, S. F., and P. H. Wilken. 1989. "It's No Laffer' Matter: Claim That Increasing Welfare Aid Breeds Poverty and Dependence Fails Statistical Test." *American Journal of Economics and Sociology* 48 (2): 203–217.

Sequeira, S., Nunn, N., and N. Qian. 2017. *Migrants and the Making of America: The Short- and Long-Run Effects of Immigration During the Age of Mass Migration*. No. w23289. Washington, DC: National Bureau of Economic Research.

Shannon, F. A. 1945. "A Post Mortem on the Labor-Safety-Valve Theory." *Agricultural History* 19 (1): 31–37.

Simon, J. L., and S. Moore. 1999. *The Economic Consequences of Immigration*. Ann Arbor, MI: University of Michigan Press.

Smith, A. 1976. *An Inquiry into the Natures and Causes of the Wealth of Nations*. Oxford: Oxford University Press, p. 136.

Stigler, G. J. 1946. "The Economics of Minimum Wage Legislation." *The American Economic Review* 36 (3): 358–365.

Stiglitz, J. E. 1993. *Economics*. New York: Norton, p. 133.

Toynbee, A. 1884. *Lectures on the Industrial Revolution*. London: Dodo Press, p. 85.

Turner, F. J., and A. G. Bogue. 2010. *The frontier in American history*. Chelmsford: Courier Corporation.

U.S. Bureau of the Census. 1984. *Money Income of Households, Families and Persons in the United States: 1984*. New York: U.S. Bureau of the Census, pp. 29–30.

U.S. Department of Labor. 1970. *Manpower Report of the President*. Washington, DC: Government Printing Office, p. 227.

Vance, J. D., and J. D. Vance. 2016. *Hillbilly Elegy*. New York: HarperCollins.

Vedder, R. K., and L. Gallaway. 1986. "AFDC and the Laffer Principle." *Wall Street Journal*.

Vedder, R. K., and L. Gallaway. 1992. "Racial Differences in Unemployment in the United States, 1890–1990." *The Journal of Economic History* 52 (3): 696–702.

Vedder, R. K., and L. E. Gallaway. 1995. *Cracked Foundation: Repealing the Davis-Bacon Act.* No. 127. Washington, DC: Center for the Study of American Business, Washington University.

Vedder, R. K., and L. E. Gallaway. 1997. *Out of Work: Unemployment and Government in Twentieth-Century America.* New York: New York University Press.

6 Government and the economic history of American income inequality

Vincent Geloso

I. Introduction

At the end of the 1990s, the subject of inequality was more or less a marginal subfield within the discipline of economics. Since then, thanks largely to the quantitative efforts of Thomas Piketty, Tony Atkinson, Emmanuel Saez, and Edward Wolff, the topic has risen to prominence and now occupies center stage within the discipline. This greater prominence should not be bemoaned but welcomed; though not, as I will argue in this chapter, for the reasons often put forward.

In addition to the efforts of the scholars mentioned above, the crisis of 2008 and the ensuing Great Recession also contributed significantly to inequality's rise to prominence. The oft-discussed growth slowdown that accompanied the recession served to focus the attention of the profession on the gap between the rich and the poor and has given rise to a sizeable literature with differing views on the subject. Some scholars, for instance, argue that the years since the crisis have seen the rich get richer, with the poor lagging behind (Piketty and Saez 2003, 2007, 2014; Kopczuk et al. 2010; Atkinson 2015; Kopczuk 2015; Piketty et al. 2016; Saez and Zucman 2016). Others, meanwhile, have emphasized that the rise of inequality caused the growth slowdown (Bowles 2012; Ostry et al. 2014), while some have taken the bolder step of linking inequality to a wider array of social problems (Wilkinson and Pickett 2010).[1]

Some scholars argue that the rise in inequality since the crisis is part of a broader historical pattern. To do so, they point to a U-curve of inequality where inequality was high in the 19th and early 20th centuries, fell progressively until the 1970s, and then started increasing back to the earlier levels (Lindert and Williamson 2016a, 2016b). Attached to this narrative is the idea that the tails of the U-curve are eras of small government when taxes were low and there was little redistribution toward the poor. The middle of the U-curve on the other hand was a period of high taxes that served to redistribute incomes and fund programs that were meant to increase upward mobility (Lindert 2004). In essence, the U-curve narrative embeds a narrative regarding public policy where more (less) government intervention reduces (increases) inequality.

In this chapter, I intend to question this broad narrative in three different ways. First, I analyze the empirical foundations of the U-curve narrative more closely. Based on this investigation, I argue that some of the rise of inequality in recent decades is overestimated. Second, I take a closer look at some of the underlying causes that explain the U-curve. As mentioned earlier, according to the most popular explanations, falling inequality is said to be the result of rising government intervention and regulation, and vice versa. I challenge this view in two ways. First, I argue that the relationship between government intervention and the level of inequality has, in fact, often been exactly the reverse: numerous regulations and interventions have led to rising and not falling inequality. And second, reductions in inequality have often been the result of the operation of market forces. Finally, I argue that some of the recent increases in inequality have been the result of factors that are welfare and/or growth enhancing. Such "good" inequality, I argue, is not problematic and need not be addressed through policy measures.

II. A question of degree: the fall and rise of inequality

II.I. Prices

Indicators of inequality consistently show an increase in market income inequality since the 1970s.[3] The same is true of the inequality of incomes after taxes and transfers; it has been increasing in most Western countries. The upward direction of inequality is *not* in dispute. What is in dispute is the magnitude of the increase. The assessment of the evolution of inequality is plagued with measurement problems with regards to (a) the price indices used to deflate real incomes and (b) the measurement of income.

Despite the fact that the problem of price indices is the less discussed of the two, it could be argued that, on certain margins, it is the more important problem confronting the measurement of inequality. First of all, there is a well-known bias in price indices that tends to overstate the level of inflation. Since the 1990s, thanks to the work of the Boskin Commission, we are aware that the CPI overstates inflation by roughly 1.1 percentage points; a figure that Boskin later updated to 0.8 percentage points (Boskin 2005). One part of this bias is a substitution bias: the CPI does not adequately capture changes in relative prices that induce consumers to substitute goods that are relatively cheaper for those that are more expensive. The other part arises from problems thrown up by changes in the quality of goods, the idea being that increases in prices linked with increases in quality should not be considered an increase in the cost of living.

The most significant effort to estimate these biases that stem from quality and substitution and their impact on measures of inequality has been put forward by Broda et al. (2009) and Broda and Weinstein (2008). They point out that price measurement errors are larger at the bottom of the income ladder. Upon substituting the conventional urban CPI, which indicates no growth in real wages at the 10th percentile between 1979 and 2005, for their index that corrects for the substitution bias, they find an increase of 13% in real wages at the 10th percentile. When they factor in quality improvements, these real gains rise to 30% (Broda and Weinstein 2008: 24–25). Moreover, they also find that their corrections reduce the level of inequality between the 10th and 90th percentile by 5%.

Importantly, the choice of the price index used to deflate nominal income measures seems to have a significant impact on the time trend of inequality estimates. That this crucially affects our perception of the history of inequality is shown by Costa (2001), who finds that between 1888 and 1919 the price index *underestimates* inflation by 0.1 percentage point and that the peak of this mismeasurement is between 1972 and 1982, when it overestimates price changes by 2.7 percentage points. Thus, if the point made by Broda and Weinstein could be extended backward, then the evolution of inequality would probably appear less dramatic.

Adjusting for these biases in the measurement of inflation also affects estimates of income mobility. In their work on the absolute income mobility of Americans, Chetty et al. (2017) initially show that roughly 90% of the children born in 1940 earned more than their parents, as opposed to close to 50% for those born after 1980. However, they then also show that shifting to the GDP deflator attenuates the fall in mobility by a few percentage points and that shifting to the CPI minus 2% (a high-bound estimate of the measurement bias) attenuates the fall by close to 20%.

A second problem related to prices is that they are not equal between the different regions of a country. While it is true that prices for tradable homogeneous goods tend to equalize, prices for housing and services tend to diverge across regions, resulting in differences in the price levels that prevail in different regions. An income of $10,000 in Bozeman, Montana, for instance, commands a greater purchasing power than the same amount in New York City. Thus, to truly compare the inequality between the residents of Bozeman and New York City, one needs to make some corrections.

Adjusting for state-level price differences reduces the level of income inequality in the United States by 0.5% while also dramatically changing the spatial distribution of those in the bottom 10% of the income distribution (Geloso and Msaid 2017). Similar results were found at a more granular level of regional price adjustments: when adjusting for prices at the metropolitan level, returns from going to college (a key ingredient in growing wage inequality) are reduced by somewhere between a third and a half (Moretti 2013).

In addition, these differences will also affect trends over time. Since the 1970s, differences in price levels within the United States have increased. This creates a statistical bias that overestimates the increase in inequality over time.[2] In fact, we are not only overestimating the increase in inequality since the 1970s, we are also overestimating the fall in inequality prior to that point. Indeed, from the late 19th century to the mid-20th century, price differences between regions fell (Mitchener and McLean 1999), and a failure to correct for this leads to an overestimation of the fall of inequality prior to that point. As such, trends in regional price differences also tend to follow a U-shape curve over time, which, if ignored, leads to an overly pronounced U-curve of income inequality in the United States over the 20th century.

II.II. Incomes

A large share of the inequality literature has relied on the use of tax records to measure top incomes. This method definitely has some advantages. Most importantly, its focus on the top layers of the income distribution means that one can arrive at a measure of inequality without having to measure the entire income distribution. However, the use of tax data to arrive at inequality estimates is also fraught with numerous complications.

Tax codes offer many ways to move income and reduce tax burdens. Consider, for example, a tax code where there is a significant difference between the corporate and personal income tax rates. In such a scenario, individuals have an incentive to change or shift the way they report incomes in order to pay fewer taxes.

Prior to 1986, the difference between the corporate and personal income tax rates meant that individuals had the incentive to report personal income as corporate income. After the tax reforms of 1986 in the United States, which reversed this situation, individuals shifted incomes between the corporate and personal accounts in the opposite direction.[3] After accounting for these changes in the relative heights of the corporate and personal income tax rates, Mechling et al. (2017) found that the trends of inequality as presented in the works of Piketty and Saez (2003) are flawed. Their adjustments, which adjust the pretax reform measurements so that they properly reflect true (personal) incomes, raised the income shares of the top 1% by as much as 4 percentage points. This means that not only is the U-curve less pronounced (as its bottom point is higher than depicted) but that the increase since the 1970s is smaller than often portrayed. Similar results have been found by Auten et al. (2016) and Auten and Splinter (2017).

Similar issues exist for the 1920s, where there were many more channels for tax avoidance. For example, the interest on numerous types of securities (like municipal bonds) was exempt from the personal income tax (Smiley and Keehn 1995: 289). This offered an easy channel for evading the high tax rates that prevailed between 1917 and 1923 and between 1932 and 1941. Thus, the large tax changes of the 1920s and 1940s[4] led to large changes in tax avoidance, which in turn affected the quality of the data on inequality reported from tax returns. Adjustments for tax avoidance during the era show that inequality trends for that period were modestly overestimated (Smiley 1983, 1998, 2000). Recent adjustments and expansions to the Smiley method that were meant to make it comparable in methodology to the method used by Piketty and Saez (2003) show that the level of inequality is also overestimated, an effect that is compounded by a series of corrections to the assumption used to make incomes uniform across the pre-1943 era (Geloso et al. 2017).[5]

Measurements of incomes are further complicated by the issue of household size. If a household grows from one to three members, this tripling of size does not result in a tripling of expenditures due to the presence of economies of scale. It follows that one must adjust for these economies of scale to get to the right level of income per "adult equivalent." Now, if the structure of households does not change over time, then this issue poses no problem to estimates of the trend of income and income inequality. However, household sizes have grown increasingly heterogeneous (across the OECD), with richer households getting larger over time. As a result, estimates of the trend of income are also affected.

Adjustments to household size to reflect these economies of scale heavily attenuate the levels and trends of inequality. For example, in their work on absolute income mobility Chetty et al. (2017) found that instead of 50% of children born in 1980 earning more than their parents, 60% of them do so once adjustments to household size are made. Another paper found that after adjusting for household size, the increase in the inequality of disposable income between 1979 and 2007 is heavily reduced (Armour et al. 2014). In fact, that same study found that when these adjustments are compounded to other sources of measurement errors, inequality *fell* between 1989 and 2007 (but not enough to offset the increase between 1979 and 1989).

Moreover, monetary income is not a perfect measure of inequality. In the United States, for example, a rising share of total compensation has taken the form of nonmonetary benefits like nontaxable employer-provided health insurance (Feldstein 2008). As health insurance provided by employers costs the same regardless of income, rising health insurance premiums mean that this portion of compensation is rising more rapidly than monetary earnings. However, since this equal per worker cost tends to represent a larger share of total compensation for low-paid workers than high-paid workers, earnings inequality will increase faster than total compensation inequality.[6]

Thus, whereas the growth of earnings at the 99th percentile was equal to 1.29 times that of the 30th percentile between 1992 and 2010, the corresponding figure for total compensation stood at 1.18 (Warshawsky 2017). A wide array of studies have confirmed this core result that we are unevenly underestimating all incomes (Burtless and Svaton 2010; Burkhauser and Simon 2010; Kaestner and Lubotsky 2016; Meyer and Sullivan 2013, 2017).

There are also issues with using cross-sectional snapshots of incomes to measure actual inequality. Some individuals, for instance, may have very high incomes at certain points in their lives and then see their incomes fall for a short period as they transition to a different career path. Changes in demographic composition can also be problematic. For example, an aging population means an increase in the share of older individuals who are near the top of their earnings paths, which, by definition, will create a measurement bias that leads us to see more inequality. Moreover, there is also the fact that government welfare payments flow disproportionately to the relatively older segments of the population.

All these factors suggest that the focus of inequality measurements should revolve around lifetime income inequality (Friesen and Miller 1983). The existing measures of lifetime earnings inequality suggest that for the United States (using the standard deviation of the log of earnings), there has been only a modest increase in inequality (Guvenen et al. 2017).[7] A similar result has been found in the case of Britain (Levell et al. 2015), while results for Germany suggest that lifetime inequality is increasing at the same pace as cross-sectional measures of inequality but that the former is at a substantially lower level (Bönke et al. 2014). For Canada, such a measure does not exist, but Grubel (2016) used a measure of longitudinal inequality (following the same group of people over time) and found that there was actually a reduction in inequality.[8]

While measurements of lifetime income inequality represent a close-to-ideal measurement, such data are not always available, which means we have to fall back on a substitute. In this case, consumption offers a stable measure of well-being, and hence a better measure of inequality as individuals tend to smooth their consumption, something that government transfers contribute to. While Meyer and Sullivan (2017) find that consumption inequalities since the 1960s have either flat-lined, modestly decreased, or modestly increased, their range of trends in inequality are well below those of income inequality. Similar results have been found for Canada (Pendakur 1998; Sarlo 2009; Brzozowski et al. 2010), Britain (Blundell and Etheridge 2010), Germany (Fuchs-Schündeln et al. 2010), and Italy (Jappelli and Pistaferri 2010).[9]

Some of the elements presented are debated (notably on consumption inequality) and much more research is needed to arrive at more accurate depictions of the situation.[10] Nonetheless, taken together, these elements of the literature moderate the increase in inequality. They do not deny the existence of a recent increase, nor do they repudiate the idea of a decline prior to the 1970s. Indeed, the wealth of evidence that exists indicates that, as a stylized fact, there was a U-curve of inequality in the United States between the late 19th century and today. The only debate is how pronounced its shape truly is.

III. Interpreting the fall of inequality from the late 19th century to the mid-1970s

While the evidence does suggest the existence of U-curve, albeit a modest one, there is room for a different interpretation of the usual causes attributed to it. Consider the first part of the U-curve of inequality – the one from the high ceiling of the late 1800s to the low point of the 1970s.

First, we should be careful not to interpret the high levels of inequality of the late 19th and early 20th centuries as necessarily welfare-reducing. As Galor and Moav (2004) point out, inequality in a world dominated by physical capital means that resources tend to be channeled toward those with great propensity to save and invest. As such, inequality in such a world stimulates development. This is what the late 19th and early 20th centuries looked like. Inequality may have been high, but there were important investments and technological innovations that were made, which led to rapid increases in living standards at the bottom of the income ladder (Smil 2005). This can be seen, in part, by the fact there are some signs (which are not conclusive) that inequalities in life expectancy and mortality fell during the period (Ho et al. 2012; Molitoris and Dribe 2016).

Second, one should be careful before adopting the conventional narrative regarding the leveling of inequality. According to this narrative, the Progressive and New Deal eras led to the creation of numerous government schemes to redistribute income, which did reduce inequality. The substantial increase in tax rates (from a top marginal rate of 24% in 1929 to a top marginal rate of 94% in 1944) served to finance these programs. However, the increase in revenues also came at the expense of lower-income households. While tax rates on the rich increased, the tax system of the United States was expanded to include a growing number of lower-income households. The top tax rate in 1929 was 64 times the bottom tax rate. By 1944, that ratio had fallen to 4.1. It is important to note that the personal exemption threshold was constantly lower *de jure* and *de facto* through inflation, which allowed more and lower-income households to enter a tax system that in 1913 collected revenues from only 2% of Americans (Smiley and Keehn 1995: 285). Basically, lower income brackets were dragged into the tax system (especially after the implementation of withholding). Furthermore, many of the programs of the New Deal era were funded through excise taxes on common staple goods, which is a form of regressive taxation (Schmitz and Fishback 1983).

Additionally, the programs that the government funded were sometimes explicitly regressive. For example, Katznelson (2005) and Rothstein (2017) point out that many public welfare and housing and employment programs explicitly discriminated against blacks. Rothstein in particular points out that public housing programs actively promoted segregation. The Federal Housing Administration, founded in 1934, refused to insure mortgages in and near African-American neighborhoods, which furthered segregationist ends. The Public Housing Act of 1949 was also adopted with explicit segregationist rules.[11]

Third, many sources of the decline in inequality were from "mundane," market-driven sources. For example, in spite of the Jim Crow laws, Black Americans did catch up with White Americans. The per capita income of blacks as a percentage of the same for White Americans increased from between 25% and 30% in 1870 to between 34% in 38% in 1940 (Higgs 1977; Margo 2016). This was in large part because Black Americans migrated from the low-wage south to the high-wage North. When this migration became a deluge after 1940, the convergence of Black Americans accelerated (Boustan 2016). Simultaneously, there was an important reduction in the differences in income between the different regions of the United States.

As Lindert and Williamson (2016a) pointed out, a nonnegligible share of income inequality in the United States before 1970 emanated from differences between regions rather than differences within regions. However, these differences were reduced between the late 19th and mid-20th centuries (Mitchener and McLean 1999; Klein 2013). One of the main reasons for this convergence between states was largely because capital moved to where the returns were greater, as standard growth theory suggests (Turner et al. 2013).

Another source of inequality reduction was the convergence of the living standards of women relative to men (Goldin 1990). Several factors behind this relative improvement of the well-being of women were mundane: the contraceptive pill (Bailey 2006), running water (Cardia et al. 2008), household appliances (Coen-Pirani et al. 2010), and technological changes affecting the workplace (Philips 1982). These factors incited the transition from the family economy to the market economy (Rotella 1980) which, inadvertently, reduced inequality.

Finally, it is also necessary to highlight the role of government restrictions on immigration. Severe curtailments of migration after the 1910s led to a considerable fall in the immigrant share of the U.S. population (from 13.2% in 1920 to 4.7% in 1970). Immigration tends to increase inequality for purely mathematical reasons. As long as the distribution of immigrants is different from the local host population, they will shift the distribution in ways that unavoidably increase inequality. If the immigrants are unskilled, they swell inequality by entering at the bottom. If the immigrants are skilled, they swell inequality by entering at the top. Only the immigrant equal to the median or the average has virtually no effect on measured inequality (see more in Section V). Reducing immigration will, by definition, reduce inequality. The restrictions that began in the 1910s and 1920s had this effect, and this is commonly acknowledged in the mainstream (see notably Lindert and Williamson 2016b: 230, 245).

While governments probably did contribute, by taxing and redistributing, to a fall in inequality (Lindert 2004; Piketty and Saez 2003), it seems that this contribution was modest. Many mundane factors, unrelated to government policies, played more prominent roles. Internal migration of capital and labor is indeed a mundane, market-driven force, but most economists would agree that the ability to exit bad environments is one of the most powerful forces for equalizing incomes. The emancipation of women and blacks, while seemingly less mundane in popular imaginations, actually occurred *in spite* of government restrictions on their rights (especially in the case of Black Americans). In fact, the only way to increase the share of the fall attributable to government is to assume that the immigration restrictions were beneficial. However, it is doubtful that this was beneficial and the effect of immigration restrictions is the result of a purely mathematical reality that reduces economic welfare (see more in Section V).

IV. Interpreting the increase in inequality after the mid-1970s

What about the increase of inequality since the 1970s? As much as falling immigration levels before then may contribute to reducing measures of inequality, rising immigration must increase them. The loosening of immigration restrictions that started in the United States and other Western countries around the 1960s and 1970s acted in ways to increase inequality (again, from a purely mathematical reality – see Section V). For the United States, the rise of immigration levels explains 5% of the increase in income inequality (Card 2009). For Canada, which has had a much more pronounced increase in immigration levels than the United States, the exclusion of immigrants from the census population used to calculate inequality dramatically reduces the pace of inequality increase (Moore and Pacey 2003). Given that immigration levels were much higher in the past relative to local populations (especially in the case of the United States, Australia, New Zealand, and Canada), these would have also contributed to higher levels of inequality in the past.

However, in many ways, government policies probably *contributed* to the increase. Restrictions on land-use represent a good illustration. By making the supply of housing more inelastic, these restrictions tend to push prices up. Given that money spent on acquiring shelter represents a larger share of the expenditures of poor households, the increase in housing prices does not affect households across the income distribution equally. It affects poorer households much more than it does the richer households. Probably the most competent study of the effects of these restrictions is Hilber and Vermeulen (2016), which analyzes the housing market of the United Kingdom during the period between 1974 and 2008. These authors found that, absent the regulatory restrictions on new constructions, the level of housing prices would be 35% lower (in real terms) than that observed in 2008. Similar results are echoed in the literature regarding the United States (see notably Glaeser et al. 2005, 2008).

High housing costs also create a mobility barrier that stops poor people from moving into areas with higher housing prices. Because such areas also tend to be characterized by higher levels of productivity, poorer workers are thus denied the opportunity of achieving higher wages by moving there. Moreover, the high prices also succeed in pushing out incumbent poor workers from these areas. As noted by Ganong and Shoag (2017), the limited mobility of poor workers caused by increased housing prices alone explains 10% of the increase in inequality in the United States since 1980. These barriers to mobility have also contributed to a modest reversal in regional integration across U.S. states. In fact, according to Young et al. (2008), policies preventing mobility have actually led to an increase in the inequality *between* states from 1970 to 2008.

Occupational licensing is another government policy that has been a significant source of increasing inequality. Licensing regulations, usually enacted at the behest of incumbent producers to limit competition from potential market entrants, are most prevalent in relatively unskilled professions such as hairdressing, landscaping, and construction work that are easily accessible to low-income individuals. As such, these regulations conspire to heavily curtail upward mobility for low-income workers (Carpenter et al. 2015; Hall and Pokharel 2016; Lloyd and Payne 2017; Kleiner and Vorotnikov 2017). In addition to these licensing regulations, numerous regulations on products have also tended to be relatively regressive, exacerbating income inequality. Product regulations, which have also been increasing, tend to affect goods that are more heavily represented in the budgets of poor individuals, thereby increasing the cost of living disproportionately for the poor (Chambers and Collins 2016).

Finally, there is the war on drugs, which has led to a significant increase in incarceration rates, and has thereby led to an increase in inequality. At first sight, it should be obvious why a rising share of the population in jail at any given time should lead to increased inequality. Former convicts tend to be penalized in the form of lower wages and slower wage growth: a first conviction reduces the probability of being employed by 5% and reduces income by as much as 30% (Waldfogel 1994). These effects are especially large for those who enter prison when they are prime-age workers (Nagin and Waldfogel 1998) as prison cuts their careers in half and deprives them of the chance to work when their incomes should be at their peak.

The regressive nature of the war on drugs is exacerbated by the fact that Black Americans, who are socioeconomically disadvantaged, are disproportionately represented within the inmate population. Nevertheless, earnings convergence between Blacks and Whites appears to have continued (Margo 2016) despite the drug war's effect on incarceration. The official statistics of earnings, however, are misleading largely because of selection problems regarding the black population surveyed. Indeed, the rising rate of incarceration, which affects Blacks in larger proportions than their overall demographic weight, implies that Blacks who have lower than average incomes tend to be left out of the survey population. When corrections are made to the official statistics, there are actually signs of a *reversal* in the relative living standards of Black Americans since the 1960s (Pettit and Western 2004; Western and Pettit 2005; Western 2007), giving us a glimpse into how government policies are contributing to the increase in inequality.

V. Good and bad inequality

What movements in inequality should we shrug off as nonproblematic? Some readers might be offended by the proposition that some inequalities are not problematic. However, who would argue that the inequality of income between a Benedictine monk who has made vows of poverty and a hedge fund banker is problematic? After all, both individuals are maximizing well-being on different planes of existence. From the perspective of an economist, if the monk refuses to change positions with the banker despite the substantial increase in earnings involved, he has signaled that the opportunity cost of these greater earnings is too high for him. As such, income inequality tells us very little in this case about the well-being of these two individuals (Buchanan 1979). In fact, if the banker were to discover that he prefers to leave the bank and become a monk himself, he would increase inequality, but he would have expressed that he prefers this alternative. Thus, inequalities in income stemming from such sources are welfare enhancing and can be classified as "good" inequalities (Geloso and Horwitz 2017).

To see another instance of "good" inequality, consider the effects of immigration. If the average Haitian, whose income is roughly the equivalent of

$1,600, comes to the United States, his income will increase dramatically even if he earns just $12,457, which is the average income of those in the bottom quintile in America.[12] Few people would frown upon such an improvement in the average Haitian's living standards, although it would increase income inequality in the United States.

Unless entrants into a country have an income distribution identical to that of the overall population, inequality will increase for purely mathematical reasons. If the entrants earn incomes equal to those at the bottom of the income ladder in the host country, they will increase the inequality at the bottom of the distribution. If, on the other hand, they were to enter at the top of the income ladder, inequality in the higher reaches of the income distribution will increase. Yet, who would be reluctant to consider such increases in inequality as welfare-enhancing and nonproblematic?[13] The immigrant gains massively and there is limited evidence that it harms the host population, with the bulk of the evidence pointing to a gain for them. In fact, from a *global, worldwide* perspective, migration *reduces* inequality (Sala-i-Martin 2006).

Inequality that stems from an aging population is another example of "good" inequality. When the population of a country ages, older individuals, who tend to have greater earnings and wealth, represent a growing share of the population. As a result, inequality tends to increase. The case for adjusting for the age structure of the population has been made for decades (Paglin 1975; Friesen and Miller 1983), and it is always worthwhile to make it again. Indeed, adjusting for changes in the age structure accentuates the decrease in inequality between 1947 and 1971 (Paglin 1975) and reduces the increase thereafter (Schirle et al. 2012), to the extent that there is very little actual increase in inequality in the period after 1971 (Almås et al. 2011; Almås and Mogstad 2012, 2015).

A rapidly innovating economy would also tend to show high levels of "good" inequality (Watson 2015). When a firm innovates, it aims to conquer wide market shares in order to generate large fortunes (McKenzie and Lee 2008). These large fortunes emanate from the ability to convince large masses of consumers to adopt a given product. Ask anyone how much you would have to pay them to get rid of their smartphones for a year and the price asked will likely be much greater than the price they actually pay for the phone, thus implying that the price paid understates the value created to consumers. This is reflective of the point made by William Nordhaus (2004) that only 2.2% of the benefits from innovation accrue to the innovators, with the rest being shared among the greater public. However, the monetary profits made by inventors are likely to be substantial, which will increase inequality. In this situation of rapid innovation that increases utility in many ways, there can be a disconnect between dollar-based measures of inequality and actual inequalities in comfort and well-being.

The point here is that inequality resulting from individuals who are able to select how to maximize their well-being is a good form of income inequality. A strong indication that these inequalities might be "good" (or at the very least not problematic) is the fact that while income (and wealth) inequality has increased in recent decades, inequality of reported life satisfaction and happiness has declined (Stevenson and Wolfers 2008, 2012). This is complemented by the fact that there is evidence that individuals are not too bothered by "unequal" distributions as they seem to prefer what they deem as "fair" distributions (Starmans et al. 2017). A "fair" distribution can be said to encompass this greater definition of human well-being where income is not equated as one would expect from the opening example of the monk and the banker. In short, our normative assessment of inequality should be constrained by the nature of the choices made by individuals: if individuals make free choices that reduce income inequality, then so much the better. If individuals make choices that reflect their well-being (like in the case of the monk and the banker) in ways that increase income inequality, no one should care.

However, there are also "bad," welfare-reducing forms of inequality. Examples of this include the inequality that is inherited at birth and that which results from government policies. Consider the former category first. Most individuals will admit to being offended by the idea that, at birth and prior to undertaking any action, some individuals have a predetermined and limited set of options, choices, and possibilities that are open them. According to Corak (2013), these disparities constitute a form of "sticky inequality." However, the reality is that while there are still "bad" inequalities that result from birth and they are very high (Lefranc et al. 2008), they have not increased since the 1970s. Indeed, inequality of opportunity explains virtually none of the increase in inequality in the United States between 1968 and 2001 (Pistolesi 2009). This leaves us with the second kind of inequality, which has been discussed in Sections III and IV.

One must ask what government policies exist that are redistributing incomes forcefully from the poor to the rich or that are restricting the ability of the poor to seize opportunities that would make them better off. Most economists (and social scientists, for that matter) care *deeply* about institutions, because they represent the "rules of the game" under which we operate. All our exchanges occur within the boundaries they impose, and our transgressions of these norms and rules result from the incentives that are associated with them. However, all rules can be designed to benefit a group or person (e.g., creating entry barriers to competitors or acquiring subsidies). Institutions that are designed through politics can be co-opted by interest groups that set the rules in their favor.

In Section III, I highlighted how government policies adopted in the middle of the U-curve had contradictory effects. Some were meant to redistribute more resources to the poor. However, the poor were taxed more heavily and many of the programs were designed to *exclude* certain poor groups (notably Black Americans). Moreover, some reduction in inequality took place *in spite* of government actions (i.e., the economic convergence of Black Americans occurred in spite of Jim Crow laws). In Section IV, I highlighted how many government policies after 1970 would have put upward pressures on inequality by hurting the opportunities of the poor more so than those of the rich. These are all examples of "bad" inequality and they are all the result of varying *institutions*. The fact that there are ambiguous effects about the "golden age" where "mundane" (i.e., good sources of changes in inequality like internal migration, the emancipation of women, and black economic convergence) factors play a significant role in reducing inequality should give anyone a fair warning about the role of governments in fighting inequality as it is unclear how much "bad" inequalities they end up creating.

As soon as one accepts the idea that there are different types of inequality, one is forced to accept the idea that the best course of action in terms of public policy is that one should first do no harm.

VI. Conclusion

The fall and rise of income inequality in the United States over the course of the late 19th and 20th centuries should be decomposed according to the sources. Some are mundane and should even be considered good. Others should be considered as more problematic as they either result from birth or from government policies. Viewed through these lenses, it is easier to sort the wheat from the chaff in the evolution of income inequality and tackle only what is truly problematic. The corollary of this view is that it appears like governments played much smaller roles than believed in reducing inequality until 1970 and played a strong role in increasing them after that point.

A policy corollary of such an interpretation is that a policy of "first, do no harm" is warranted. As such, maybe it is time to consider that peeling back government policies would be an improvement.

Notes

1 Readers skeptical of such connections between inequality and a wide array of social problems are invited to read the work of Snowdon (2010), which raises room for important doubt.
2 For Canada (Pendakur 2002) and China (Démurger et al. 2006), adjustments for the evolution of regional price differences have also been shown to reduce the magnitude of the increase in inequality.
3 After World War II, the top marginal rate for personal income pre-1986 was between 50% and 90% compared to between 45% and 55% for corporate income. Since 1986, the statutory rate for corporate income is above most marginal tax rates on personal income.
4 Top marginal rates on personal income between 1917 and 1945 went from a high of 77% in 1918 to a low of 24% in 1929 and back up to 94% in 1944.
5 Another problem is that the top income approach relies on tax units that do not fully overlap with households (there are more tax units than households) and leads to mismeasurement of incomes (Burkhauser et al. 2012).
6 Health insurance represented 7.59% of total compensation at the 30th percentile as opposed to 4.46% in 1992. In 2010, these proportions had risen to 11.62% and 5.73% (Warshawsky 2017).
7 However, the study cited here shows widening inequality on the gender-basis and flatlining annual earnings for men, which means that the moderation of the inequality trend is largely driven by the increase in women's earnings.

8 There are limitations to this analysis of Grubel, but it is valuable in the sense that it shows the extent of the measurement problems caused by lifetime variations.
9 However, it seems that in Spain the reverse is true: income inequality fell and much more so than consumption inequality (Pijoan-Mas and Sánchez-Marcos 2010).
10 One should consult Aguiar and Bils (2015) for a critical overview.
11 In fact, Senator Robert A. Taft attempted to drive a wedge in the act by introducing an amendment that prohibited segregation in public housing. The amendment was refused and the Act passed.
12 Available at www.taxpolicycenter.org/statistics/household-income-quintiles.
13 Some could be tempted to argue that there are small temporary negative effects on the small subset of the population that is most unskilled as a result of the increase in labor supply. However, the effects are *temporary* (i.e. they fade away over time) and they can be minimized through cheaper means-targeted policy (as opposed to minimizing them by restricting immigration). Moreover, this argument is hotly debated because the increase in supply is mitigated by an increase in demand (Longhi et al. 2005; Ottaviano and Peri 2012; Clemens and Hunt 2017).

References

Aaberge, R., and M. Mogstad. 2015. "Inequality in Current and Lifetime Income." *Social Choice and Welfare* 44 (2): 217–230.

Aguiar, M., and M. Bils. 2015. "Has Consumption Inequality Mirrored Income Inequality?" *American Economic Review* 105 (9): 2725–2756.

Almås, I., Havnes, T., and M. Mogstad. 2011. "Baby Booming Inequality? Demographic Change and Earnings Inequality in Norway, 1967–2000." *Journal of Economic Inequality* 9 (4): 629–650.

Almås, I., and Mogstad, M. 2012. "Older or Wealthier? The Impact of Age Adjustment on Wealth Inequality." *The Scandinavian Journal of Economics* 114 (1): 24–54.

Armour, P., Burkhauser, R. V., and J. Larrimore. 2014. "Levels and Trends in US Income and Its Distribution: A Crosswalk from Market Income Towards a Comprehensive Haig-Simons Income Approach." *Southern Economic Journal* 81 (2): 271–293.

Atkinson, A. 2015. *Inequality*. Cambridge, MA: Harvard University Press.

Auten, G., and D. Splinter. 2017. *Income Inequality in the United States: Using Tax Data to Measure Long-Term Trends*. Technical Report. Washington, DC: U.S. Department of Treasury.

Auten, G., Splinter, D., and S. Nelson. 2016. "Reaction of High-Income Taxpayers to Major Tax Legislation." *National Tax Journal* 69 (4): 935–964.

Bailey, M. J. 2006. "More Power to the Pill: The Impact of Contraceptive Freedom on Women's Life Cycle Labor Supply." *The Quarterly Journal of Economics* 121 (1): 289–320.

Blundell, R., and B. Etheridge. 2010. "Consumption, Income and Earnings Inequality in Britain." *Review of Economic Dynamics* 13 (1): 76–102.

Bönke, T., Corneo, G., and H. Lüthen. 2014. "Lifetime Earnings Inequality in Germany." *Journal of Labor Economics* 33 (1): 171–208.

Boskin, M. J. 2005. "Causes and Consequences of Bias in the Consumer Price Index as a Measure of the Cost of Living." *Atlantic Economic Journal* 33 (1): 1–13.

Boustan, L. P. 2016. *Competition in the Promised Land: Black Migrants in Northern Cities and Labor Markets*. Princeton, NJ: Princeton University Press.

Bowles, S. 2012. *The New Economics of Inequality and Redistribution*. Cambridge: Cambridge University Press.

Broda, C., Leibtag, E., and D. E. Weinstein. 2009. "The Role of Prices in Measuring the Poor's Living Standards." *Journal of Economic Perspectives* 23 (2): 77–97.

Broda, C., and D. E. Weinstein. 2008. *Prices, Poverty, and Inequality: Why Americans Are Better Off Than You Think.* Washington, DC: AEI Press.

Brzozowski, M., Gervais, M., Klein, P., and M. Suzuki. 2010. "Consumption, Income, and Wealth Inequality in Canada." *Review of Economic Dynamics* 13 (1): 52–75.

Buchanan, J. M. 1979. *Cost and Choice: An Inquiry in Economic Theory*. Chicago: University of Chicago Press.

Burkhauser, R. V., Larrimore, J., and K. I. Simon. 2012." A 'Second Opinion' on the Economic Health of the American Middle Class." *National Tax Journal* 65 (1): 7–35.

Burkhauser, R. V., and K. I. Simon. 2010. *Measuring the Impact of Health Insurance on Levels and Trends in Inequality*. Technical Report. Washington, DC: National Bureau of Economic Research.

Burtless, G., and P. Svaton. 2010. "Health Care, Health Insurance, and the Distribution of American Incomes." *Forum for Health Economics & Policy* 13: 1.

Card, D. 2009. "Immigration and Inequality." *American Economic Review* 99 (2): 1–21.

Cardia, E., et al. 2008. "Household Technology: Was It the Engine of Liberation?" In *2008 Meeting Papers*. No. 826. New York: Society for Economic Dynamics.

Carpenter, D. M., Knepper, L., Erickson, A. C., and J. K. Ross. 2015. "Regulating Work: Measuring the Scope and Burden of Occupational Licensure Among Low-and Moderate-Income Occupations in the United States." *Economic Affairs* 35 (1): 3–20.

Chambers, D., and C. A. Collins. 2016. *How Do Federal Regulations Affect Consumer Prices? An Analysis of the Regressive Effects of Regulation.* Technical Report. Mercatus Working Paper. Arlington, VA: Mercatus Center at George Mason University.

Chetty, R., Grusky, D., Hell, M., Hendren, N., Manduca, R., and J. Narang. 2017. "The Fading American Dream: Trends in Absolute Income Mobility Since 1940." *Science* 356 (6336): 398–406.

Clemens, M. A., and J. Hunt. 2017. *The Labor Market Effects of Refugee Waves: Reconciling Conflicting Results.* Technical Report. Washington, DC: National Bureau of Economic Research.

Coen-Pirani, D., León, A., and S. Lugauer. 2010. "The Effect of Household Appliances on Female Labor Force Participation: Evidence from Microdata." *Labour Economics* 17 (3): 503–513.

Corak, M. 2013. "Income Inequality, Equality of Opportunity, and Intergenerational Mobility." *The Journal of Economic Perspectives* 27 (3): 79–102.

Costa, D. L. 2001. "Estimating Real Income in the United States from 1888 to 1994: Correcting CPI Bias Using Engel Curves." *Journal of Political Economy* 109 (6): 1288–1310.

Démurger, S., Fournier, M., and S. Li. 2006. "Urban Income Inequality in China Revisited (1988–2002)." *Economics Letters* 93 (3): 354–359.

Feldstein, M. 2008. "Did Wages Reflect Growth in Productivity?" *Journal of Policy Modeling* 30 (4): 591–594.

Friesen, P. H., and D. Miller. 1983. "Annual Inequality and Lifetime Inequality." *Quarterly Journal of Economics* 98 (1): 139–155.

Fuchs-Schündeln, N., Krueger, D., and M. Sommer. 2010. "Inequality Trends for Germany in the Last Two Decades: A Tale of Two Countries." *Review of Economic Dynamics* 13 (1): 103–132.

Galor, O., and O. Moav. 2004. "From Physical to Human Capital Accumulation: Inequality and the Process of Development." *The Review of Economic Studies* 71 (4): 1001–1026.

Ganong, P., and D. W. Shoag. 2017. *Why Has Regional Income Convergence in the US Declined?* Technical Report. Washington, DC: National Bureau of Economic Research.

Geloso, V., and S. Horwitz. 2017. "Inequality: First, Do No Harm." *Independent Review* 22 (1): 121–134.

Geloso, V., Magness, P. W., Moore, J. A., and P. D. Schlosser. 2017. "Is the U-Curve That Pronounced? Revisiting Income Inequality in the United States, 1917–1945." *SSRN Electronic Journal*. Doi:10.2139/ssrn.2985234.

Geloso, V., and Y. Msaid. 2017. "Adjusting Inequalities for Regional Price Parities: Importance and Implications." *Journal of Regional Analysis and Policy* 4.

Glaeser, E. L., Gyourko, J., and A. Saiz. 2008. "Housing Supply and Housing Bubbles." *Journal of Urban Economics* 64 (2): 198–217.

Glaeser, E. L., Gyourko, J., and R. E. Saks. 2005. "Urban Growth and Housing Supply." *Journal of Economic Geography* 6 (1): 71–89.

Goldin, C. 1990. *The Gender Gap: An Economic History of American Women*. New York: Cambridge University Press.

Grubel, H. 2016. *Income Mobility: The Rich and Poor in Canada*. Technical Report. Vancouver: Fraser Institute.

Guvenen, F., Kaplan, G., Song, J., and J. Weidner. 2017. *Lifetime Incomes in the United States over Six Decades*. Technical Report. Washington, DC: National Bureau of Economic Research.

Hall, J. C., and S. B. Pokharel. 2016. "Barber Licensure and the Supply of Barber Shops: Evidence from US States. *Cato Journal* 36: 647.

Higgs, R. 1977. *Competition and Coercion: Blacks in the American Economy 1865–1914*. Cambridge: Cambridge University Press.

Hilber, C. A., and W. Vermeulen. 2016. "The Impact of Supply Constraints on House Prices in England." *The Economic Journal* 126 (591): 358–405.

Ho, B., et al. 2012. "An Alternative Perspective on Health Inequality." *Economics Bulletin* 32 (4): 3182–3196.

Jappelli, T., and L. Pistaferri. 2010. "Does Consumption Inequality Track Income Inequality in Italy?" *Review of Economic Dynamics* 13 (1): 133–153.

Kaestner, R., and D. Lubotsky. 2016. "Health Insurance and Income Inequality." *The Journal of Economic Perspectives* 30 (2): 53–77.

Katznelson, I. 2005. *When Affirmative Action Was White: An Untold History of Racial Inequality in Twentieth-Century America*. New York: Norton.

Klein, A. 2013. "New State-Level Estimates of Personal Income in the United States, 1880–1910." *Research in Economic History* 29: 191–255.

Kleiner, M. M., and E. Vorotnikov. 2017. "Analyzing Occupational Licensing Among the States." *Journal of Regulatory Economics*: 1–27.

Kopczuk, W. 2015. "What Do We Know About the Evolution of Top Wealth Shares in the United States?" *Journal of Economic Perspectives* 29 (1): 47–66.

Kopczuk, W., Saez, E., and J. Song. 2010. "Earnings Inequality and Mobility in the United States: Evidence from Social Security Data Since 1937." *Quarterly Journal of Economics* 125 (1): 91–128.

Lefranc, A., Pistolesi, N., and A. Trannoy. 2008. "Inequality of Opportunities vs. Inequality of Outcomes: Are Western Societies All Alike?" *Review of Income and Wealth* 54 (4): 513–546.

Levell, P., Roantree, B., and Shaw, J. 2015. *Redistribution from a Lifetime Perspective*. Technical Report. IFS Working Papers. London: IFS.

Lindert, P. H. 2004. *Growing Public: Volume 1, the Story: Social Spending and Economic Growth Since the Eighteenth Century*, vol. 1. Cambridge: Cambridge University Press.

Lindert, P. H., and J. G. Williamson. 2016a. "Inequality in the Very Long Run: Malthus, Kuznets, and Ohlin." *Cliometrica* 1–7.

Lindert, P. H., and J. G. Williamson. 2016b. *Unequal Gains: American Growth and Inequality Since 1700*. Princeton, NJ: Princeton University Press.

Lloyd, C., and J. Payne. 2017. "Licensed to Skill? The Impact of Occupational Regulation on Fitness Instructors." *European Journal of Industrial Relations*. DOI:10.1177/0959680117701016.

Longhi, S., Nijkamp, P., and J. Poot. 2005. "A Meta-Analytic Assessment of the Effect of Immigration on Wages." *Journal of Economic Surveys* 19 (3): 451–477.

Margo, R. A. 2016. "Obama, Katrina, and the Persistence of Racial Inequality." *The Journal of Economic History* 76 (2): 301–341.

McKenzie, R. B., and D. R. Lee. 2008. *In Defense of Monopoly: How Market Power Fosters Creative Production*. Ann Arbor: University of Michigan Press.

Mechling, G., Miller, S., and R. Konecny. 2017. "Do Piketty and Saez Misstate Income Inequality? Critiquing the Critiques." *Review of Political Economy* 29 (1): 30–46.

Meyer, B. D., and J. X. Sullivan. 2013. *Winning the War: Poverty from the Great Society to the Great Recession*. Technical Report. Washington, DC: National Bureau of Economic Research.

Meyer, B. D., and J. X. Sullivan. 2017. *Consumption and Income Inequality in the US Since the 1960s*. Technical Report. Washington, DC: National Bureau of Economic Research.

Mitchener, K. J., and I. W. McLean. 1999. "US Regional Growth and Convergence, 1880–1980." *Journal of Economic History* 59 (4): 1016–1042.

Molitoris, J., and M. Dribe. 2016. "Industrialization and Inequality Revisited: Mortality Differentials and Vulnerability to Economic Stress in Stockholm, 1878–1926." *European Review of Economic History* 20 (2): 176–197.

Moore, E. G., and M. A. Pacey. 2003. "Changing Income Inequality and Immigration in Canada, 1980–1995." *Canadian Public Policy/Analyse de Politiques*: 33–52.

Moretti, E. 2013. "Real Wage Inequality." *American Economic Journal: Applied Economics* 5 (1): 65–103.

Nagin, D., and J. Waldfogel. 1998. "The Effect of Conviction on Income Through the Life Cycle." *International Review of Law and Economics* 18 (1): 25–40.

Nordhaus, W. D. 2004. *Schumpeterian Profits in the American Economy: Theory and Measurement*. Technical Report. Washington, DC: National Bureau of Economic Research.

Ostry, M. J. D., Berg, M. A., and M. C. G. Tsangarides. 2014. *Redistribution, Inequality, and Growth*. Washington, DC: International Monetary Fund.

Ottaviano, G. I., and G. Peri. 2012. "Rethinking the Effect of Immigration on Wages." *Journal of the European Economic Association* 10 (1): 152–197.

Paglin, M. 1975. "The Measurement and Trend of Inequality: A Basic Revision." *The American Economic Review* 65 (4): 598–609.

Pendakur, K. 1998. "Changes in Canadian Family Income and Family Consumption Inequality Between 1978 and 1992." *Review of Income and Wealth* 44 (2): 259–282.

Pendakur, K. 2002. "Taking Prices Seriously in the Measurement of Inequality." *Journal of Public Economics* 86 (1): 47–69.

Pettit, B., and B. Western. 2004. "Mass Imprisonment and the Life Course: Race and Class Inequality in Us Incarceration." *American Sociological Review* 69 (2): 151–169.

Philips, P. 1982. "Gender-Based Wage Differentials in Pennsylvania and New Jersey Manufacturing, 1900–1950." *The Journal of Economic History* 42 (1): 181–186.

Pijoan-Mas, J., and V. Sánchez-Marcos. 2010. "Spain Is Different: Falling Trends of Inequality." *Review of Economic Dynamics* 13 (1): 154–178.

Piketty, T., and E. Saez. 2003. "Income Inequality in the United States, 1913–1998." *Quarterly Journal of Economics* 118 (1): 1–39.

Piketty, T., and E. Saez. 2007. "Income and Wage Inequality in the United States, 1913–2002." In *Top Incomes Over the Twentieth Century*. Oxford: Oxford University Press, pp. 141–226.

Piketty, T., and E. Saez. 2014. "Inequality in the Long-Run." *Science* 344 (6186): 838–843.

Piketty, T., Saez, E., and G. Zucman. 2016. *Distributional National Accounts: Methods and Estimates for the United States*. Technical Report. Washington, DC: National Bureau of Economic Research.

Pistolesi, N. 2009. "Inequality of Opportunity in the Land of Opportunities, 1968–2001." *Journal of Economic Inequality* 7 (4): 411–433.

Rotella, E. J. 1980. "Women's Labor Force Participation and the Decline of the Family Economy in the United States." *Explorations in Economic History* 17 (2): 95–117.

Rothstein, R. 2017. *The Color of Law: The Forgotten History of How Our Government Segregated America*. New York: Norton.

Saez, E., and G. Zucman. 2016. "Wealth Inequality in the United States Since 1913: Evidence from Capitalized Income Tax Data." *Quarterly Journal of Economics* 131 (2): 519–578.

Sala-i-Martin, X. 2006. "The World Distribution of Income: Falling Poverty and . . . Convergence, Period." *The Quarterly Journal of Economics* 121 (2): 351–397.

Sarlo, C. A. 2009. *The Economic Well-Being of Canadians: Is there a Growing Gap?* Vancouver: The Fraser Institute.

Schirle, T. et al. 2012. "Age-Adjusted Measures of Earnings Inequality in the United States, 1980–2010." *Economics Bulletin* 32 (3): 2662–2669.

Schmitz, M., and P. V. Fishback. 1983. "The Distribution of the Income in the Great Depression: Preliminary State Estimates." *The Journal of Economic History* 43 (1): 217–230.

Smil, V. 2005. *Creating the Twentieth Century: Technical Innovations of 1867–1914 and Their Lasting Impact*. Oxford: Oxford University Press.

Smiley, G. 1983. "Did Incomes for Most of the Population Fall from 1923 Through 1929?" *Journal of Economic History* 43 (1): 209–216.

Smiley, G. 1998. "New Estimates of Income Shares During the 1920s." In J. E. Haynes, ed., *Calvin Coolidge and the Coolidge Era: Essays on the History of the 1920s*. Washington, DC: Library of Congress, pp. 215–232.

Smiley, G. 2000. "A Note on New Estimates of the Distribution of Income in the 1920s." *Journal of Economic History* 60 (4): 1120–1128.

Smiley, G., and R. H. Keehn. 1995. "Federal Personal Income Tax Policy in the 1920s." *Journal of Economic History* 55 (2): 285–303.

Snowdon, C. 2010. *The Spirit Level Delusion: Fact-Checking the Left's New Theory of Everything*. London: Democracy Institute.

Starmans, C., Sheskin, M., and P. Bloom. 2017. "Why People Prefer Unequal Societies." *Nature Human Behaviour* 1: 0082.

Stevenson, B., and J. Wolfers. 2008. "Happiness Inequality in the United States." *Journal of Legal Studies* 37 (S2): S33–S79.

Stevenson, B., and J. Wolfers. 2012. "Subjective and Objective Indicators of Racial Progress." *Journal of Legal Studies* 41 (2): 459–493.

Turner, C., Tamura, R., and S. E. Mulholland. 2013. "How Important Are Human Capital, Physical Capital and Total Factor Productivity for Determining State Economic Growth in the United States, 1840–2000?" *Journal of Economic Growth* 18 (4): 319–371.

Waldfogel, J. 1994. " 'Effect of Criminal Conviction on Income and the Trust' Reposed in the Workmen." *Journal of Human Resources* 29 (1): 62–81.

Warshawsky, M. J. 2017. "The Implications of the Rapidly Rising Cost of Employer-Provided Health Insurance for Earnings Inequality." *Benefits Quarterly* 33 (3).

Watson, W. 2015. *The Inequality Trap: Fighting Capitalism Instead of Poverty*. Toronto: University of Toronto Press.

Western, B. 2007. "Mass Imprisonment and Economic Inequality." *Social Research: An International Quarterly* 74 (2): 509–532.

Western, B., and B. Pettit. 2005. "Black-White Wage Inequality, Employment Rates, and Incarceration." *American Journal of Sociology* 111 (2): 553–578.

Wilkinson, R., and K. Pickett. 2010. *The Spirit Level: Why Equality Is Better for Everyone*. London: Penguin.

Young, A. T., Higgins, M. J., and D. Levy. 2008. "Sigma Convergence Versus Beta Convergence: Evidence from us County-Level Data." *Journal of Money, Credit and Banking* 40 (5): 1083–1093.

7 Inequality, monetary policy, and the gold standard

Robert P. Murphy

I. Introduction

The economists who endorse the normative policy prescription to redistribute income *also* typically subscribe to the positive empirical claim that the distribution of income in the United States became much more unequal in the 1980s. Symmetrically, there is a strong correlation between economists who reject "egalitarian" tax and welfare policies and those who argue that many standard measures overstate the concentration of income and wealth among the richest Americans. As a result, the typical arguments about income inequality – at least in the context of the United States – tend to focus on the 1980s, and the normative/positive claims tend to go together as a package deal.

In this chapter, I depart from this traditional arrangement of the camps in the dispute. I stipulate (if only for the sake of argument) some of the key evidence that ostensibly demonstrates the "pro-rich" tilt in U.S. policy that halted the postwar progress of the poor and middle class. However, rather than attribute the abrupt change to the supply-side tax rate reductions (and other "neo-liberal" reforms) of the Reagan era, I focus on the enormous change in *monetary* policy that occurred in 1971.

My alternative hypothesis fits the income data much better than the typical claim that it was the Reagan-era policies that caused the change in workers' fortunes. I show that the alleged divergence between net productivity and average worker pay begins in the early 1970s, which is also when Richard Nixon closed the gold window. (Specifically, he officially ended the U.S. dollar's redeemability in gold on August 15, 1971.) This drastic change in U.S. monetary policy is a far more plausible explanation for the sudden change in the distribution of economic gains rather than the successive reductions of the top marginal income tax rate that would not occur until the early and mid-1980s.

Having noted the remarkable proximity of Nixon's decision and the change in income patterns, in the remainder of the chapter I offer some possible theoretical mechanisms that could explain how the switch to fiat money might have adversely affected the poor and middle class relative to Americans in the top of the income distribution.

The overall purpose of this chapter is *not* to give blanket approval to the typical statistics by which some economists seek to demonstrate that the average worker has been "left behind" as the economy has grown over the last several decades. (Indeed, I agree with many of the critiques that the other contributors to this book have offered in their respective chapters.) Rather, my purpose is to disentangle the normative and positive claims from their typical "package deal" and ask economists to consider each on its own terms. In particular, economists who believe that workers have been left behind cannot automatically blame "neo-liberal" policies, because it may very well have been the increased *monetary* activism unleashed in the 1970s that is the cause. On the other hand, pro-market economists who oppose redistributive policies have nothing to fear from income data that show apparently "unfair" gains accruing at the top, because they could use such evidence to bolster their support for "sound money."

II. Did "The Problem" start in the 1980s – or the 1970s?

It is standard in debates concerning U.S. income inequality to focus attention on the 1980s, specifically the policies of the Reagan Administration. The top marginal income tax rate began at 70% in 1980 and was reduced to 69.13% in 1981, and then 50% in 1982. After the 1986 Tax Reform Act, the top rate was further reduced to 38.5% in 1987, and finally 28% in 1988.[1]

In addition to the bold reductions in tax rates, the Reagan era also heralded a transformation in rhetoric and governing philosophy, with an emphasis on "supply-side" (rather than Keynesian "demand-side") economics. It is thus completely understandable why friends and foes alike of these significant changes would focus their attention on the 1980s in arguments over U.S. income inequality.

Although there are countless examples of this emphasis on the 1980s, we will provide five. First is Thomas Piketty's (2014) discussion in his runaway bestseller, *Capital in the Twenty-First Century*:

> *After experiencing a great passion for equality from the 1930s through the 1970s, the United States and Britain veered off with equal enthusiasm in the opposite direction. Over the past three decades [i.e. 1980s, 1990s, and 2000s – RPM], their top marginal income tax rates, which had been significantly higher than the top rates in France and Germany, fell well below French and German levels . . . .* The Anglo-Saxon countries have played yo-yo with the wealthy since the 1930s. By contrast, attitudes toward top incomes in both continental Europe . . . and Japan have held steady. . . . [P]art of the explanation for this difference might be that the United States and Britain came to feel that they were being overtaken by other countries in the 1970s. *This sense that other countries were catching up contributed to the rise of Thatcherism and Reaganism.* To be sure, the catch-up that occurred between 1950 and 1980 was largely a mechanical consequence of the shocks endured by continental Europe and Japan between 1914 and 1945. The people of Britain and the

> United States nevertheless found it hard to accept: for countries as well as individuals, the wealth hierarchy is not just about money; it is also a matter of honor and moral values. *What were the consequences of this great shift in attitudes in the United States and Britain?*
>
> (Piketty 2014: 508–509, emphasis added)

Next, we quote from a 2013 article co-authored by many of the leading lights in the inequality literature, namely Facundo Alvaredo, Anthony Atkinson, Thomas Piketty, and Emmanuel Saez. After providing a scatterplot covering 18 countries, putting increases since 1960 in the share of income accruing to the top 1% on one axis and reductions in top marginal income tax rates on the other axis, the authors concede:

> The correlation shown in [the figure] between top marginal tax rates and changes in top income shares may of course reflect in part coincidence rather than causality. *The political factors that led to top tax rate cuts – such as those by Reagan and Thatcher in the 1980s in the United States and the United Kingdom* – were accompanied by other legislative changes, such as deregulation, which may have caused top incomes to rise.
>
> (Alvaredo et al. 2013: 10–11, emphasis added)

Once again, the documentation of rising income inequality (since the 1960s) was attributed to tax policy, with an emphasis on the Reagan and Thatcher episodes.

Similarly, in a memorable (among policy wonks) article from 1992, Paul Krugman (1992 [2014]) clearly ties the political arguments over the Reagan-era tax policy with statistical arguments concerning inequality in the 1980s. Krugman opens his long essay with the following introduction:

> *During the mid-1980s, economists became aware* that something unexpected was happening to the distribution of income in the United States. *After three decades during which the income distribution had remained relatively stable, wages and incomes rapidly became more unequal.* Academic researchers soon began arguing vigorously about the causes of the growth in inequality.
>
> (Krugman 1992 [2014], emphasis added)

Our next quotation is also drawn from the same 1992 debate, and it comes from Sylvia Nasar's article in the *New York Times*:

> The broad pattern disclosed by the latest data is not in dispute, but the reasons for the shift are. Potential explanations range from the trend toward lower taxes on the wealthy to an explosion of executive pay to higher returns on capital.
>
> *It was not until economists started to analyze the figures that it became clear what a large share of the income gains in recent years was accounted for by the very rich.*

> "The number that no one had seen was how much of the growth went to a few people," said Mr. Krugman, who focused on the numbers in testimony before Congress several weeks ago.
>
> *That finding is already supplying fresh ammunition for those eager to reverse the upward tilt in income distribution or searching for new ways to raise Government revenue.*
>
> (Nasar 1992, emphasis added)

To provide a final example: Alan Reynolds was a participant in the 1992 debate that Krugman describes. In Reynolds (2006), he recounts some of the measurement issues under dispute. One major issue is the shift of income reporting by high earners into Subchapter-S corporations after the 1986 Tax Reform Act. Because of the sharp reduction in personal income tax rates relative to corporate tax rates, "a large amount of highest income on individual tax returns used to be reported as corporate profits" (Reynolds 2006: 81). This mere "bookkeeping change" had "nothing to do with the actual distribution of income" (p. 83).[2]

Yet beyond the arguments over measurement, Reynolds' discussion reflects the *political* nature of the battles. This is most obvious with the odd choice of dates used to describe what supposedly happened during "the 1980s." Reynolds notes a particularly humorous example:

> When asked . . . in 1992 to respond quickly to Ms. Nasar's piece, I complained about *the political gimmick of defining 1977 rather than 1980 as the start of the 1980s.*[3] *In a 1993 Clinton Administration report, the 1981–1989 term of the Reagan Administration was stretched to include the entire Carter term and the first Iraq War:* "Throughout the 1980s, slow growth in living standards was accompanied by growing inequality. . . . People at the bottom of the income scale actually lost ground: measured in inflation-adjusted dollars, their incomes fell between 1977 and 1991."
>
> (Reynolds 2006: 78, emphasis added)

As the block quotations in this section have illustrated, the debates about measurements of income inequality in America have tended to overlap with arguments about the tax rate reductions during the 1980s. And yet, even within this framework, we see that the particular choice of *income growth* statistics often pick a year in the 1970s as their start date.

An innocent explanation of this habit (offered in Krugman 1992) is that the income trends must be done on an apples-to-apples basis by comparing business cycle peaks. He castigates standard apologies for the Reagan years by writing, "The rise in median income from 1982 to 1989, Robert Bartley's 'seven fat years,'" – here Krugman refers to the title of Bartley's popular (1992) book written in defense of Reaganomics – "represented almost entirely a transitory business cycle recovery, which reached its inevitable limit at a level only 4 percent above the 1979 peak" (Krugman 1992). Furthermore, Krugman explains

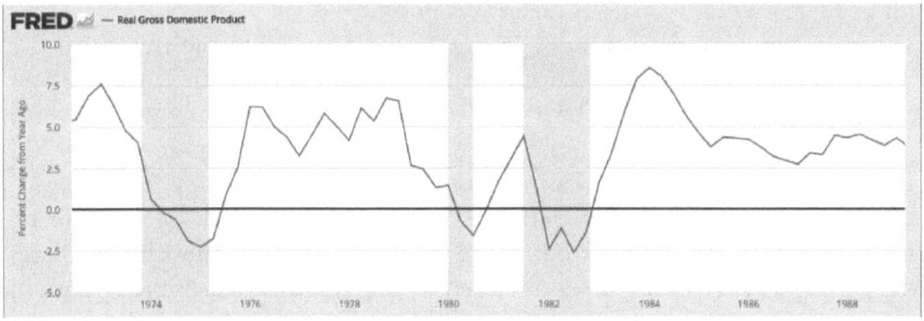

Figure 7.1 U.S. real GDP growth, 1973–1989 (percent change from previous year, quarterly, recession quarters shaded gray)

Source: St. Louis Federal Reserve (FRED)

that the statistics focusing on the period 1977–1989 are justified as a proxy for assessing "the 1980s" because the relevant CBO data were available for 1977 but not (the more appropriate) 1979.

A more cynical explanation, of course, is that a researcher who wishes to paint a bleak picture about allegedly stagnant income gains for low- and middle-income households can get a more provocative result if he or she picks the start date *before* the awful recession in the early 1980s. If one wants to discredit the "tax cuts for the rich" (which also included tax rate reductions across the board, for all income brackets), it would hardly work to start the analysis with (say) the inauguration of Ronald Reagan (in January 1981), let alone to compare U.S. economic growth just before and just after the 1982 rate cut actually went into effect. If such decisions were taken by the statistician, then the economy's rebound from the back-to-back recessions in the early 1980s would – rightly or wrongly – have vindicated the Reagan tax policies. Figure 7.1 shows economic growth during the 1970s and 1980s, to help the reader evaluate the choice of year analysts use when showing what happened to various groups.

II.I. Income concentration versus income growth

Another component of the explanation for the different time frames of analysis – in particular, referring to "the 1980s" for some claims but choosing a start date in the 1970s for other, related claims – is that standard measures of income concentration didn't show *large* upswings until the 1980s, and in particular the 1986 Tax Reform Act.

For example, consider the famous Piketty–Saez historical series for the share of income earned by the top 1%.

As Figure 7.2 illustrates, it is understandable how analysts who have a preconception that "tax cuts for the rich" were responsible for massive income inequality could look at the Piketty–Saez series and conclude that the major shift occurred when Ronald Reagan was in office.

Even so, we have used the dot in Figure 7.2 to indicate the trough in the Piketty–Saez series, which occurred in 1973. Even though the upswing was gentle, it is unmistakable that the post-1929 trend of a falling share of income for the top 1% reversed itself *not* in the 1980s but rather in the early- to mid-1970s.

Indeed, we can see the tension between the famous U-curve and the piggybacked policy narrative by quoting from the actual 2003 *QJE* article by Piketty and Saez. In their introduction, they write that in the United States "the period of falling inequality observed during the first half of the twentieth century [has been] succeeded by a very sharp reversal of the trend since the 1970s" (Piketty and Saez 2003: 1). Yet even though they acknowledge that their famous U-curve reversed in the 1970s, they seek to attribute the reversal to changes in fiscal policy and social norms, though they concede "we cannot prove that progressive taxation and social norms have indeed played the role we attribute to them" (p. 3). There is literally no mention of the gold standard or monetary policy in the paper.

To be clear, it is not my intention in this chapter to *endorse* the famous U-shaped curve popularized by Piketty and Saez. Indeed, other authors in this volume – not to mention the work of Alan Reynolds (2006), which I have already discussed – note several flaws with the famous result. Rather, my point is that *even if we stipulate the standard Piketty–Saez U-curve*, it makes little sense to explain the turnaround in income concentration by factors (CEO compensation, large tax rate reductions, hostility to unions, etc.) from the 1980s. The Piketty–Saez chart, taken at face value, suggests that if we are going to look to government policies to explain the changed fortunes of the 1%, then we should consider policies from the early 1970s. They themselves implicitly admit this

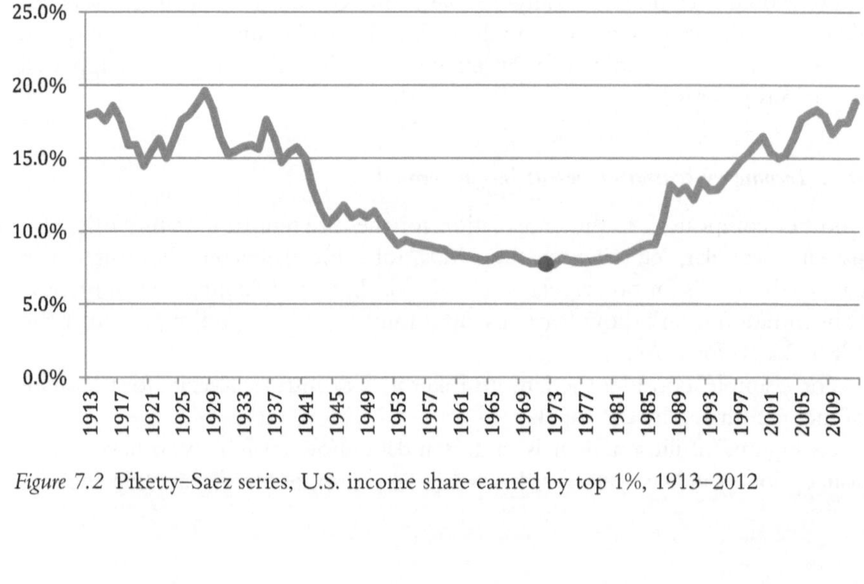

Figure 7.2 Piketty–Saez series, U.S. income share earned by top 1%, 1913–2012

when they introduce their statistics, even though they fail to follow through on the logical implications of their own charts.

To summarize, the Piketty–Saez measure of income concentration did not show a large jump until the 1980s, but the deceleration started much earlier and the actual turnaround occurred in the early 1970s. Furthermore, in this debate the statistics measuring income *growth* (not concentration) often start in the 1970s. In Figure 7.3 we see why.

With the particular measure used by the Census Bureau ("mean household income" expressed in CPI-U-RS 2015 dollars), one could use Figure 7.3 to argue that "From 1979 to 2015, the top 5 percent of households saw their real incomes jump almost 75 percent, while the bottom quintile only gained a total of 2.1 percent over the entire period." Including the 1979 data obviously makes the plight of the poor look worse (even though Ronald Reagan was not inaugurated until 1981), because the index fell sharply from 1979 to 1980. (Specifically, the real mean income of the bottom quintile fell by 3.2% in that year alone.) We gain perspective by going further back in time, as we do in Figure 7.4.

In Figure 7.4, we begin the series in 1967, and calibrate our index to 1973. As the chart indicates, there was strong income growth across the spectrum from 1967 (the furthest back the census data go) to 1973. Note that the NBER indicates a recession occurred from December 1969 through November 1970,[4] but that did not significantly reduce real incomes (as measured by this particular census definition).

In contrast, the recession that officially lasted from November 1973 through March 1975 took a much greater toll on real household incomes (across the board), such that real mean household income was roughly at the 1973 peak as of 1979 for the three lowest quintiles (only the bottom of which is charted

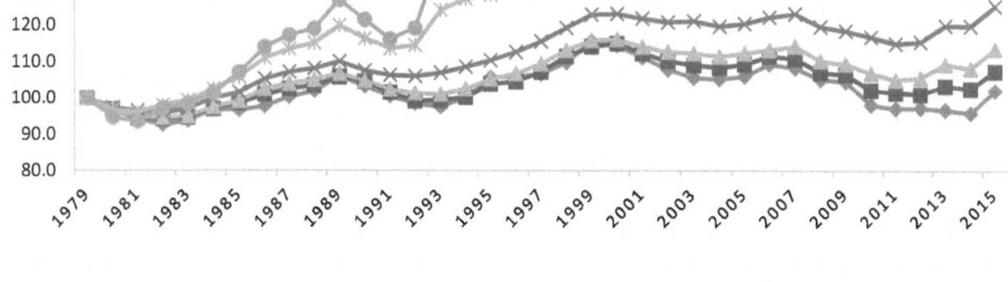

Figure 7.3 Mean household income by quintile and top 5%, 1979–2015 (Index 1979 = 100.0)

Source: U.S. Census Bureau

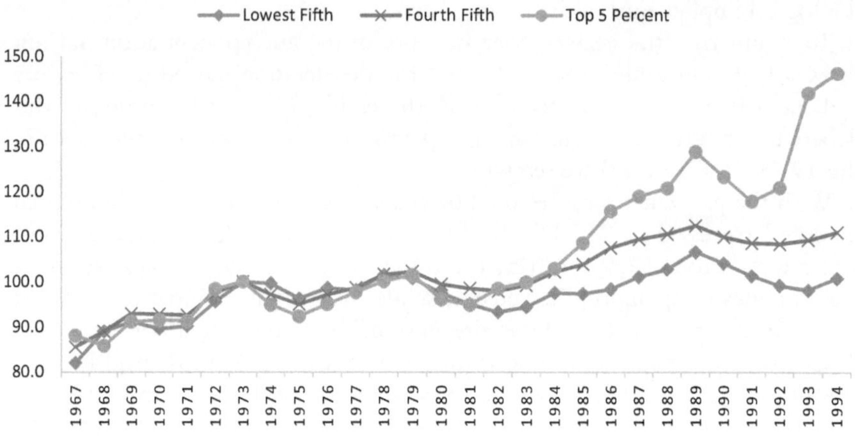

Figure 7.4 Mean household income by quintile and top 5%, 1967–1994 (Index 1973 = 100.0)
Source: U.S. Census Bureau

in Figure 7.4). Then, of course, the recessions in the early 1980s took an even bigger toll, especially on the poorest households.

To get a sense of the relative impact of the three recessionary periods, using our annual data from the census series: from 1969 to 1970, the real mean income of the bottom quintile fell 1.7%; from 1973 to 1975, it fell a cumulative 3.7%; and from 1979 to 1982 – in which we lump together the back-to-back recessions in this period – it fell a cumulative 7.4%.

So, it is true that the poorest were hit hard during the awful recessions occurring when Reagan first took office. Yet the story is clearly not just about "the 1980s": something apparently made the recession in 1973 particularly damaging, such that households had barely recovered by the time the worst recession since the Great Depression struck. (Specifically, in Figure 7.4, we see that all three lines are barely above 100% – chosen to indicate the 1973 peak – by 1979.)

As with the Piketty–Saez series, here too I do not mean to give blanket approval to the picture painted by the data in Figures 7.3 and 7.4. For example, according to Figure 7.4, it appears that the bottom 20% of U.S. households were worse off in real terms in 1993 than they were in 1973. This seems highly implausible, in the sense that surely very few people in 1993 – even among the poorest quintile – would want to switch places with their counterparts from 20 years earlier.

Other contributors to this book explain the various shortcomings with the type of census calculation exhibited in Figures 7.3 and 7.4. To reiterate, my purpose in this chapter is to stipulate such figures for the sake of argument.

Even on the typical redistributionist's own terms, it is not clear that the true culprit for the ostensibly troubling trends in income concentration is the flattening of the tax code in the 1980s. In particular, the tax rate reductions of 1982 and 1987–1988 can hardly explain why the census figures show the poorest households experienced a drop in real income of about 5% from 1973 to 1981.

To buttress my argument that the sharp increase in measures of inequality of the 1980s were anticipated by a reversal in income trends starting a decade earlier, we can quote from a 2016 survey of this literature put out by the Center on Budget and Policy Priorities. They summarize the trends in inequality this way:

The broad facts of income inequality over the past six decades are easily summarized:

- *The years from the end of World War II into the 1970s* were ones of substantial economic growth and broadly shared prosperity.
    - Incomes grew rapidly and at roughly the same rate up and down the income ladder, roughly doubling in inflation-adjusted terms *between the late 1940s and early 1970s.*
    - The income gap between those high up the income ladder and those on the middle and lower rungs – while substantial – did not change much during this period.
- *Beginning in the 1970s*, economic growth slowed, and the income gap widened.
    - Income growth for households in the middle and lower parts of the distribution slowed sharply, while incomes at the top continued to grow strongly.
    - The concentration of income at the very top of the distribution rose to levels last seen more than 80 years ago (during the "Roaring Twenties").
- Wealth – the value of a household's property and financial assets minus the value of its debts – is much more highly concentrated than income. The best survey data show that the top 3% of the distribution hold over half of all wealth. Other research suggests that most of that is held by an even smaller percentage at the *very* top, whose share has been rising over the last three decades.
- Data from a variety of sources contribute to *this broad picture of strong growth and shared prosperity for the early postwar period, followed by slower growth and growing inequality since the 1970s.* Within these broad trends, however, different data tell slightly different parts of the story (and no single source of data is better for all purposes than the others) (Stone et al. 2016, emphasis added)

The summary of Stone et al. confirms the assessment given here: Although the trends were accelerated in the 1980s, something else occurred a decade earlier that reversed the original postwar pattern.

III. The (alleged) "Productivity-Pay Gap"

As indicated in the introduction, I am ultimately going to argue that the reversal in income trends that so worries egalitarians is at least partially due to Nixon's closing of the gold window. Thus far, using two typical measures of income concentration and growth from this literature, I have shown that *whatever* the explanation, it must begin *earlier* than the 1980s.

In this section, I will come from the other side and argue that whatever the cause, it must begin *later* than the 1960s. Specifically, we can use two initially "shocking" charts that are typically deployed by those in favor of redistributionist policies, to hone in precisely on the early 1970s as the period when something fundamental changed.

The first chart is taken from a 2014 Pew Research Center article.

Again, I should acknowledge the caveats with data such as that presented in Figure 7.5. By only focusing on money wages, the chart ignores increased employer benefits (such as health insurance premiums, etc.). Furthermore, the adjustment to transform current into constant dollars surely leaves out important considerations: how many hours did a worker need to put in to buy a smartphone in 1965?

Even so, the data on "constant hourly wages" put out by the BLS affirm the narrative of this chapter: rank-and-file workers were on a general, upward trajectory, but things suddenly turned around in 1973. The recessions in the

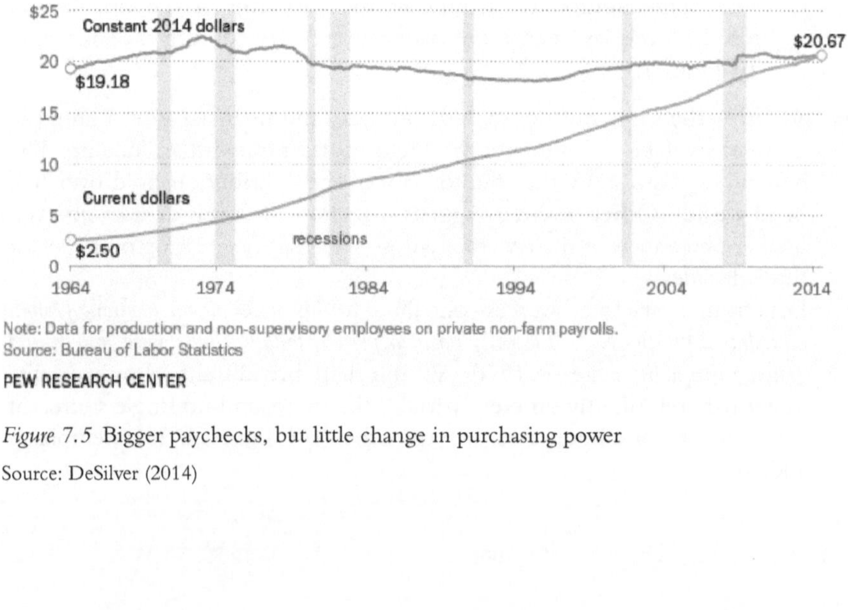

Figure 7.5 Bigger paychecks, but little change in purchasing power

Source: DeSilver (2014)

mid-1970s and early 1980s were devastating to real hourly wages, whereas the recession in 1969–1970 had not been. The general upward trajectory of the 1960s was mirrored by a general downward trajectory through the mid-1990s.

Next and most decisive, consider Figure 7.6, in which we reproduce a diagram of what we can call the "productivity-pay gap," with this particular version taken from a 2015 publication of the Economic Policy Institute (EPI).

The evidence presented in Figure 7.6 is typically used to clamor for "pro-worker" policies, including a more progressive income tax code, a higher minimum wage, etc. Yet the prima facie conclusion from Figure 7.6 is that *something very fundamental* changed and that it occurred *sharply* in the early 1970s. Indeed, note that although the EPI chart draws a line through 1973, the actual divergence between their two measures occurs a bit earlier.

The data presented in Figure 7.6 are my empirical smoking gun to place a large share of the blame (if the trend is considered problematic) for growing inequality on Richard Nixon's decision to officially end (what remained of) the U.S. gold standard on August 15, 1971. If my argument is correct, it means that the typical "camps" in the debate over U.S. inequality need to reexamine their positions. The advocates of government intervention into the economy should consider that it is more an activist *monetary* policy rather than a "neo-liberal" restraint in fiscal policy, which has caused the fundamental shift in the fortunes of the rich versus middle class and poor in the United States. On the other hand, the advocates of free markets should be

Note: Data are for compensation (wages and benefits) of production/nonsupervisory workers in the private sector and net productivity of the total economy. "Net productivity" is the growth of output of goods and services less depreciation per hour worked.

Source: EPI analysis of Bureau of Labor Statistics and Bureau of Economic Analysis data

Figure 7.6 Workers produced much more, but typical workers' pay lagged far behind

Source: Mishel et al. (2015)

more receptive to empirical claims that average households really *have* seen a significant decline in their economic standing since the early 1970s. Far from providing ammunition for their opponents, the evidence allows fans of the market economy to say, "Yet more proof that the classical liberals were correct to champion sound money."

In the remainder of this section, we will unpack the meaning of the ostensible productivity-pay gap illustrated in Figure 7.6. We will also critically examine the attempt by some libertarian and conservative analysts to dismiss such data as nonsense. Then, in Section IV, we will suggest theoretical mechanisms to explain how the switch from a gold standard to fiat money could give rise to a measured pay-productivity gap.

III.I. Understanding the alleged productivity-pay gap

The type of calculation exhibited in Figure 7.6 is an index showing *changes* in the two series from some initial starting point. (It is thus not a coincidence that the two series start out in 1948 at the same point; that occurs by construction.) The "productivity" measure is based on real GDP (nominal GDP adjusted by the GDP deflator) minus an allowance for depreciation, and then divided by the total number of hours worked. So, from one year to the next, the "(net) productivity" measure indicates the flow of new goods and services (net of capital depreciation) per hour of labor.

In contrast, the "pay" measure is based on total compensation per hour, which includes not just pay but also benefits, for private sector nonfarm workers who are not in supervisory roles. The nominal figure is made "real" by adjustments using changes in the CPI. So, from one year to the next, the "pay" measure indicates how much the average worker can buy in consumer goods and services with an hour's pay.

The apparent connection between these two measures over the period 1948–1972[5] does *not* mean that nonsupervisory workers in this period were being paid "enough to buy back the product"; workers' wages did not exhaust all of Net National Product during these decades. Rather, the EPI chart simply shows that the year-to-year *percentage increases* in their measure of (net) productivity fit very closely with such changes in their measure of real worker compensation. Again, we should stress that the initial starting point *by construction* is equal; it is not the case that nonsupervisory workers earned 100% of the nation's real income in the year 1948. The EPI authors themselves do not seem to fully appreciate this subtlety, when they write:

> From 1973 to 2013, hourly compensation of a typical (production/nonsupervisory) worker rose just 9 percent while productivity increased 74 percent. This breakdown of pay growth has been especially evident in the last decade, affecting both college- and non-college-educated workers as well as blue- and white-collar workers. *This means that workers have been*

> *producing far more than they receive in their paychecks and benefit packages from their employers.*
>
> (Mishel et al. 2015, emphasis added)

Strictly speaking, the statement I have placed in bold is a non sequitur. We need more information than the simple divergence in the two measures (i.e., productivity versus pay) before we can conclude that workers are not being paid fully for what they are producing. At first blush, it seems Mishel et al. are denying the marginal productivity theory of labor compensation, and indeed their chart plus the *tone* of their analysis implies that American workers by the year 2013 were at best being paid only *half* of what they were actually producing. Even if we stipulate models of "bargaining power," efficiency wages, and so forth, it surely can't be correct to claim that the U.S. labor market departs that drastically from the competitive model.

To anticipate the later argument of this chapter, I *am* going to offer a mechanism by which fiat money inflation *could* produce a divergence between the genuine marginal product of workers and the consumption they can afford in the marketplace. However, I want to acknowledge that the standard arguments in the inequality literature used to explain the empirical productivity-pay gap are often quite weak. To round out our discussion, in the next subsection I summarize objections to this approach.

III.II. Objections to the typical "Productivity-Pay Gap" argument

Rugy (2016) is a Mercatus paper that relies in turn on data from a Heritage Foundation study by Sherk (2016). Their conclusion is that the claims of a productivity-pay gap are spurious, and that a "more careful and comprehensive analysis of real worker pay and productivity data . . . shows that worker compensation is closely tied to worker productivity" (Rugy 2016). In Figure 7.7, we reproduce de Rugy's chart.

De Rugy summarizes Sherk's critique and refers to the aforementioned chart when she writes:

> Using data from the Bureau of Economic Analysis (NIPA tables) and the Bureau of Labor Statistics, Sherk points out that those stating that there is a large gap between productivity and wage growth have committed the following errors:
>
> - Compared the pay of only some workers to the productivity of all employees;
> - Counted productivity growth of the self-employed, but excluded their pay growth;
> - Measured inflation differently to calculate pay growth and productivity growth.

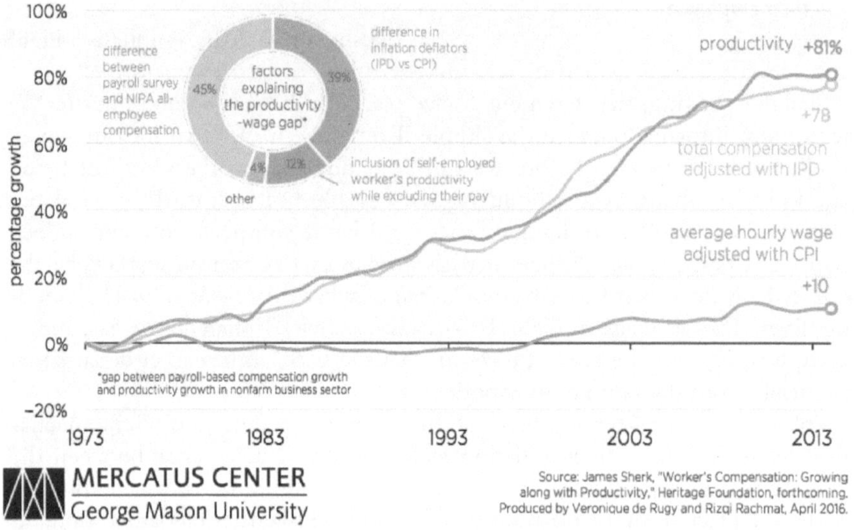

Figure 7.7 Total worker compensation and productivity since 1973

Source: de Rugy (2016)

> Employee compensation has in fact risen in step with productivity since 1973, both on average and across industries. The data show that since 1973, the average private sector employee's productivity has increased by 81 percent, while the average compensation has increased by 78.
>
> (Rugy 2016, emphasis added)

These are important issues and I do not want to detract from the analysis of de Rugy and Sherk; indeed, I have included their critique partly to be sure my own readers do not take the EPI chart at face value.

However, there is surely *still* something mysterious afoot. After all, if the EPI chart showed that *wherever* we start the analysis, we see a growing divergence between "productivity" and "pay," then de Rugy and Sherk's critique would be definitive. We would be assured that the EPI measures were leaving out something important, and that they hadn't put their finger on some fundamental flaw in the U.S. labor market.

Yet that's *not* what we see. Instead, notwithstanding the possible methodological flaws noted by de Rugy and Sherk, the EPI chart shows that from 1948–1972 there *was* a tight connection between the two series. Therefore, even if we ultimately agree with de Rugy and Sherk that there is nothing scandalous at work, economists should still be able to explain why the various complications these two authors bring up – such as the mismatch between the GDP deflator and CPI, the earnings of self-employed versus salaried and wage employees, etc. – for some reason began to mushroom in the early 1970s, but not before.

Finally, after I outline possible mechanisms in the following section that could generate a divergence between worker output and pay, the reader should review the arguments of de Rugy and Sherk. We will see that their various adjustments may certainly *explain* the size of the alleged gap, without necessarily *justifying* it.

IV. A brief history of the gold standard[6]

In this section, I review the history of the gold standard in the United States and the fateful decision President Richard Nixon made in 1971 when he closed the gold window, transforming the U.S. dollar into a pure fiat currency. This background is necessary to make sense of my suggestion that *this* policy shift – rather than changes in tax rates and attitudes toward workers – is a far more likely culprit for the data suggesting an increase in inequality.

Originally, the U.S. dollar was on a bimetallic standard, meaning that it could be redeemed for a specific weight of gold *or* silver. (Depending on the official redemption weights and the relative market price of gold versus silver, in practice this meant that the U.S. dollar was on a de facto gold or silver standard at a particular time.) During the Civil War, redemption was temporarily suspended, allowing the authorities to issue more paper currency to fund the war effort.

By 1879, the authorities had achieved their objective of returning "greenbacks" (paper currency) to the pre-Civil War parity with gold, so that this can be considered the year in which the United States had returned to the gold standard (Elwell 2011: 6). In conjunction with the other major powers that also pledged to redeem their respective national currencies (the British pound, the French franc, the German mark, etc.) in specified weights of gold, this system up until World War I is what economists mean by "the classical gold standard."

The rationale of the classical gold standard was to limit the discretion of monetary authorities. If any one country issued too much paper currency, it would experience domestic price inflation and a "worsening" balance of trade. It would become profitable for speculators to redeem the inflated currency for gold, and then ship the gold to the vaults of other countries where the authorities had been more cautious in printing up currency. Thus, the economists, business leaders, and statesmen before World War I understood the gold standard to provide stability in price levels across the major powers, giving a solid platform for the growth of international trade and investment (Bordo and Kydland 1995).

To quell fears of a resurgent silver standard, in the year 1900, the United States passed the Gold Standard Act, reassuring the world of the dollar's redeemability in gold (Elwell 2011: 8). Specifically, the Gold Standard Act declared:

> That the dollar consisting of twenty-five and eight-tenths grains of gold nine-tenths fine, as established by section thirty-five hundred and eleven of the Revised Statutes of the United States, shall be the standard unit of value, and all forms of money issued or coined by the United States shall be maintained at a parity of value with this standard, and it shall be the duty of the Secretary of the Treasury to maintain such parity.[7]

With the dollar so defined in terms of grains of gold, it worked out that one troy ounce of gold exchanged for about $20.67. Because the other major powers also had their currencies defined in various weights of gold, the classical gold standard implied a fixed exchange rate between the sovereign monies. For example, the Bank of England stood ready to redeem the British pound at the rate of £4.25 per ounce of gold. Because of the redemption weights adopted by the respective American and British authorities, the "anchor price" in the foreign exchange market worked out (with simple arithmetic) to be $4.86 for UK£1. (In day-to-day practice, there was nothing preventing currency traders from pushing the dollar price of a British pound above or below this amount, but if it strayed too far either way, then speculators could make a profit by presenting the weaker currency to its issuing government to obtain gold.) From the 1870s until 1913, much of the world economy was effectively operating with a single money: gold.

After the outbreak of World War I, most of the belligerents adopted various measures that made it difficult to redeem their respective currencies in gold. The U.S. government formally maintained the dollar's convertibility to gold at the official rate, though the Wilson Administration made it difficult to export gold out of the country from September 1917 through June 1919 (Crabbe 1989: 426). After the war, the major powers officially went back on the gold standard, though they only gradually began moving the redemption rate of their currencies back toward the prewar parity.

The first major blow to the U.S. gold standard occurred shortly after Franklin D. Roosevelt took office, during the depths of the Great Depression. Amidst a flurry of unprecedented interventions into the financial system, in 1933, FDR suspended the dollar's redeemability in gold and indeed required private citizens to turn in their monetary holdings of gold (in exchange for currency) under threat of heavy fines and up to ten years of imprisonment.[8] Freed from its redeemability requirement, the U.S. government promptly "devalued" the dollar, meaning that the dollar price of an ounce of gold increased. By 1934, the dollar had stabilized at a new value of $35 per ounce of gold.

From 1934 forward, including the international monetary arrangement known as "Bretton Woods," following World War II, the U.S. government agreed to redeem dollars at the rate of $35 per ounce of gold but *only* for other official entities (such as foreign governments and central banks). American citizens and foreign investors could *not* turn in their U.S. dollars for gold.

Eventually, even this limited redeemability proved too onerous for the U.S. government. The expenses of the Vietnam War and the so-called "War on Poverty" social programs of the 1960s put pressure on the Federal Reserve to create dollars with which to absorb the growing federal debt. Eventually, something had to give: Either the U.S. government needed to cut back its spending or it had to abandon the last remaining vestige of the gold standard.

On August 15, 1971, President Richard Nixon announced to the world that the U.S. government would no longer redeem the dollar for gold. This is the date that most commentators designate as the official end of the gold standard, and the conversion of the U.S. dollar into a true fiat currency. However, some purists argue that the process was more gradual, with a series of crises and fallback measures spreading out the conversion over the period of 1967–1973[9] (Elwell 2011: 13). However, even though at the time of his announcement Nixon wasn't indicating a formal, permanent move to fiat money, it is still the case that at no point *after* his announcement could anyone – even other central banks – redeem dollars for gold.

IV.I. Evidence of the importance of Nixon's decision

The historical record clearly demonstrates that the change in U.S. monetary policy had significant effects. First, we look at the growth of the "monetary base," a narrow definition of the stock of money that is entirely under the control of the Federal Reserve.

As Figure 7.8 indicates, in the postwar era, the Fed kept a tight leash on annual monetary base growth, with it only breaking through 5% briefly during the entire decade of the 1950s. Yet it steadily crept up during the 1960s, and after Nixon's actions in the early 1970s, the annual growth in monetary base was typically above 7.5%, and on several occasions broke through 10%. Note

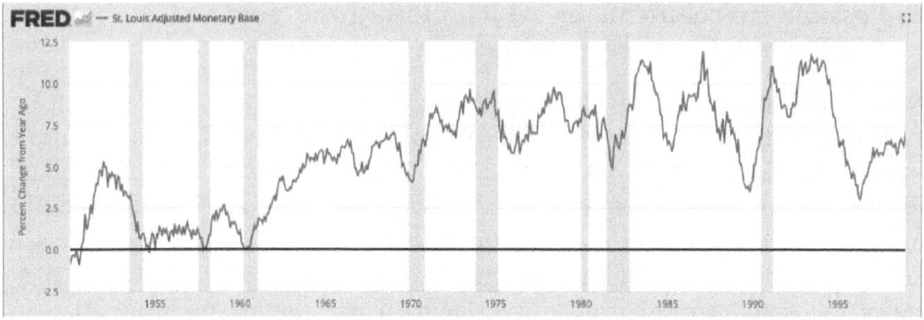

Figure 7.8 Yearly percentage growth in the monetary base, January 1950–January 1999 (monthly data, not seasonally adjusted)

Source: St. Louis Federal Reserve (FRED)

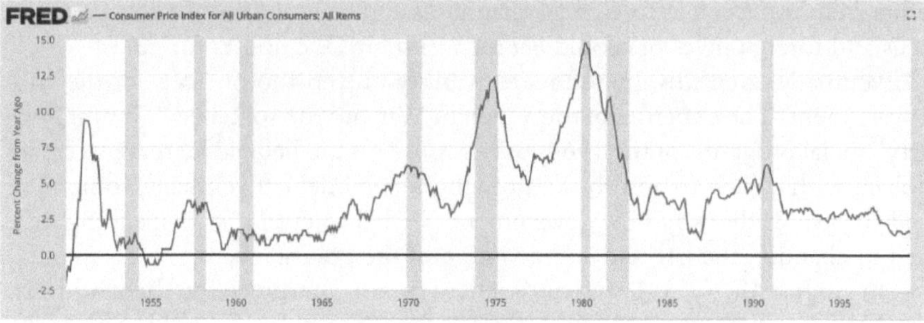

Figure 7.9 Yearly percentage growth in the Consumer Price Index, January 1950–January 1999 (monthly data, not seasonally adjusted)

Source: St. Louis Federal Reserve (FRED)

that we have stopped the chart in 1999 to leave out the wild swings due to Y2K fears, and of course had we included the enormous growth in the monetary base that occurred following the financial crisis in the fall of 2008, the variation we see currently in Figure 7.9 would have been completely drowned out. We see a similar pattern when we look at the behavior of the CPI.

Here again, we see that after a brief spike in the early 1950s, consumer price inflation was quite tame for a decade, before creeping up in the late 1960s. Then it took off in the early 1970s, giving rise to the famous "stagflation" of chronic unemployment amidst rising prices. It was only after the painful recessions of the early 1980s – associated with the relatively "tight money" policies of Fed chairman Paul Volcker – that consumer price inflation was brought back under (relative) control, though even here the annual rates of increase were typically higher in the 1980s and 1990s than they had been in the 1950s.

V. Possible mechanisms by which closing the gold window could exacerbate income inequality

Now that we have reviewed the history of U.S. monetary policy and the impact of dropping the dollar's convertibility to gold, in this section, I outline three possible mechanisms by which this drastic change in monetary policy could generate the divergence between "productivity" and "pay," as defined in the EPI and other such studies. In conjunction with the empirical evidence discussed so far, these theoretical mechanisms make a convincing case that the 1971 ending of the gold standard is at least *partly* to blame for the transformation in various inequality measures and should be included in future discussions about inequality.

V.I. Mechanism #1: seigniorage for the monetary authority

The first mechanism is straightforward: by having access to a printing press that can produce legal currency without external constraints, a government issuing a pure fiat currency is able to obtain real goods and services at virtually zero cost and must necessarily reduce the "real income" earned by the private sector.

The technical term in the literature for this is "seigniorage," defined as the difference in the face value of currency (or coinage) and the cost of producing it. For our purposes, we can illustrate the mechanism with a simple thought experiment. To isolate the role of seigniorage, we will assume all output is produced entirely by labor. Specifically, the only outputs in our simple economy are massages. There are 2,000 identical workers, as well as a king and his courtiers who perform no work.

To simplify the analysis, we assume that the workers operate seasonally: half of the workers give massages only from January to June, while the other half give massages from July to December. (We will label the first group the "Early Citizens" and the second group the "Late Citizens.") All massages are purchased in the spot market with cash.

In Year 1, from January to June, the 1,000 Early Citizens each give two massages to members of the Late Citizens. Then from July to December, the 1,000 Late Citizens reciprocate by each giving two massages to members from the former group. All massages in Year 1 occur at a price of $100. In the first half of the year, $200,000 in cash flows from the Late to the Early Citizens, while $200,000 in cash flows back again in the second half of the year. In Year 1, the king and his courtiers have no influence on the economy. With appropriate measures, we conclude that during Year 1, the 2,000 workers produced two massages and purchased with their wages two massages. (They are technically employed but their managers earn no pay; the revenues from the massages are fully passed on to the workers because there are no other inputs into this simple service.)

Year 2 begins the same way: $200,000 flows from the Late Citizens to the Early Citizens, in exchange for a total of 2,000 massages priced at $100 each. But then the king tells his finance minister to print an additional $200,000 in currency. The king hands out much of this new money to his courtiers. During the second half of Year 2, the price of massages doubles. The Late Citizens still provide a total of 2,000 massages, but now half of the massages are performed on the Early Citizens and the other half are given to the king and his courtiers.

Looking over Year 2 as a whole, we conclude that "real productivity" was the same: specifically, the workers produced 4,000 total massages; real GDP was therefore the same, the number of hours worked was the same, and so "real productivity" was the same. However, in Year 2, the citizens as a whole were only able to afford 3,000 massages with their wages. (Remember that in the second half of the year, 1,000 of the massages were given *not* to the ordinary citizens but to the king and his courtiers.)

Reacting to this new situation, a think tank concerned with labor issues produces an alarming study showing that real worker compensation in Year 2 has suddenly dropped 25% compared to the prior year, even though net worker productivity stayed constant. Think tanks that oppose minimum wage hikes and progressive income taxes dismiss the findings, arguing that adjustments based on "what price workers have to pay for a massage" are misleading, because in any given transaction, it is crystal clear that each massage therapist is being paid exactly what the massage parlor receives in revenue from the customer. Because no analyst can point to any "slippage" or "leakage" from the customer's payment to the worker's performance, the opponents of government intervention conclude that the labor market is working fine and the alleged mismatch between productivity and pay must be a statistical illusion.

Over several decades, the Early and Late Citizens became more proficient in their craft. A given massage is more soothing than before, and the workers become better at scheduling appointments so that they can produce more massages in a given block of time. As such, the properly measured "real productivity" of the workers rises significantly over the course of decades. At the same time, every year the king and his courtiers print new amounts of cash and enter the massage market to absorb some of the real output. Nominal wages and massage prices rise continually; yet after making their preferred adjustments, the pro-labor groups keep issuing studies showing that real worker compensation always lags behind increases in real net productivity. The pro-market groups, in contrast, continue to insist that these calculations are flawed and that workers are indeed receiving the full value of their correctly calculated marginal product.

To be clear, in my hypothetical scenario, the pro-market think tanks would be *wrong*. As I illustrated in the numerical example, if the king and his courtiers are able to receive massages merely by running the printing press, then there is a very real sense in which the workers are *not* receiving the "full value" of their output. (Remember in our example that in the first year of the inflation, the workers produced 4,000 massages total but received only – in their role as consumers – 3,000 massages.) This is true even though, by construction, a massage therapist directly pocketed the full revenue from any given massage. The solution to this "paradox" is that the regular citizens suffered a capital loss on the purchasing power of their cash balances when the king and his courtiers entered the massage market with newly printed currency. This is why the arguments of the hypothetical pro-market think tanks (in my contrived scenario) fall flat: even though there is nothing wrong with the competitive labor market, income is still effectively being transferred from the workers to the political elites through the inflationary process.

It should go without saying that in the real world, things are not nearly as stark as in my hypothetical economy, in which there are only massages. In particular, the objections that de Rugy and Sherk raise against the claims of a "productivity-pay gap" might be valid. However, my hypothetical example shows that their objections *could* be leaving out something important, and perhaps the statistical measures produced by groups such as EPI really *are* indicating something fundamental about the inability of workers to use their money wages to buy "real consumption" in the market.

V.II. Mechanism #2: severity of the business cycle

Another possible mechanism by which the move to a fiat money standard could have adversely impacted poorer workers is an increase in the severity of the business cycle.

As Figure 7.10 indicates, there have been 11 official recessions in the postwar period. If their impact on the poor is gauged by the height of the unemployment rate, then the three worst (by a wide margin) recessions occurred *after* the gold window was closed, and even the early 1990s recession was about tied with the worst recessions in the 1948–1971 period. (A similar pattern holds if we use "percentage drop in real GDP" as our metric for the severity of a recession.)

Using the Austrian business cycle theory (see, e.g., Garrison 2001), we can explain why the central bank with no gold constraint causes more violent fluctuations than a central bank *with* a (modest) gold constraint.[10] Specifically, under a fiat money standard, it is easier for the Federal Reserve to inflate, and therefore the distortion and duration of the "unsustainable boom period" can be increased.

In the previous section, we reviewed the evidence of increased monetary base growth, but we can also analyze how "artificially low" interest rates were in the pre- and post-Nixon period. In Figure 7.11, we provide one measure.

To be sure, our approach in Figure 7.11 is quite crude; we have taken the nominal effective funds rate and simply subtracted the (backward-looking) one-year increase in the CPI. It would be more appropriate (and strengthens

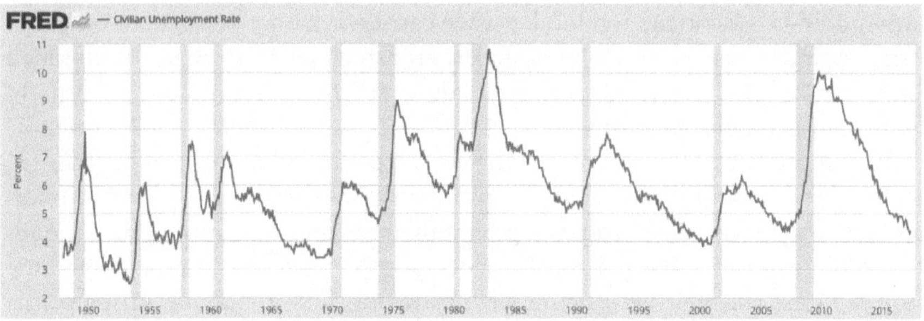

Figure 7.10 Civilian unemployment rate, January 1948–June 2017 (monthly, seasonally adjusted).

Source: St. Louis Federal Reserve (FRED)

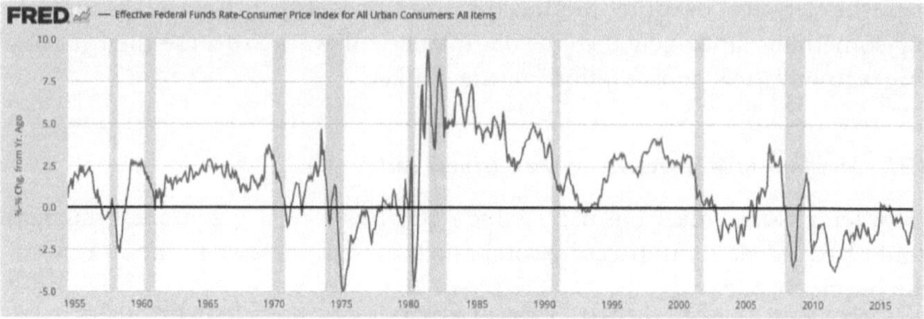

Figure 7.11 Real effective funds rate (nominal minus one-year increase in CPI), July 1954–June 2017 (monthly)

Source: St. Louis Federal Reserve (FRED)

my case[11]), though not as easy to chart in FRED, to take the *forward*-looking one-year increase in CPI. Even so, it is clear from the figure that *by far* the lowest "real" interest rates occurred after the closing of the gold window. Indeed, relying on the Austrian business cycle theory, I used a chart similar to the one in Figure 7.11 to conclude in the summer of 2007 (more than a year before the financial crisis) that the United States was headed for possibly the worst recession since the early 1980s.[12]

To summarize, various metrics indicate that the severity of the business cycle has increased in the postwar era since the closing of the gold window, especially if one subscribes to the Austrian theory of what generates booms and busts.

V.III. Mechanism #3: increased relative value of nonlabor factor inputs

Finally, we can discuss the mechanism that many casual observers suggest as a way for fiat money to hurt the common man while benefiting the rich: poor and middle-class workers tend to be wage earners who are dependent on long-term contracts that are only periodically updated, whereas richer individuals tend to have much more flexible arrangements where their income can more easily adjust to new information.

Part of the story here involves what the literature calls "Cantillon effects," named after the economist credited with first discussing it. Richard Cantillon (in 1755) explained that when the government creates new money and spends it into the economy, the prices of various goods rise step-by-step, as the new money filters through various merchants' hands. The sequence of recipients of the new money affects the relative impact that the inflation has on various individuals. The people who receive the new money early on tend to benefit, because they are able to spend the money before too many prices have risen (in response to the higher demand). But the people in the community who receive the money near the end of the process are the relative losers, because they have seen prices rising without enjoying an increase in their money income.

Related to this, we can mention the possibility that the "true" relative value of nonwage employees goes up when the government drops the gold standard. After all, a typical reaction from investors when they are plunged into a sea of unanchored money is to switch their assets into "inflation hedges" such as the precious metals, real estate, and equities, and away from historically standard assets such as savings bonds, savings accounts with commercial banks, and permanent life insurance policies. The "true" marginal product of speculators and hedge fund managers goes up in such an environment, and the owners of real estate (including farmland, oil deposits, and silver mines) also enjoy capital gains as the value of their property responds to the new situation. Horwitz (2003) discusses these more nuanced "costs of inflation" resulting from economic actors adjusting to an environment in which the purchasing power of the monetary unit falls at a steeper and less predictable rate.

In summary, the move from a hard money to a fiat money standard would presumably increase the share of real GDP accruing to land and capital owners, as well as managerial labor, and would presumably decrease the share of real GDP accruing to typical wage workers. Such an outcome would be consistent with the marginal productivity theory of factor payments. However, there would be some truth to complaints that "the system" had been rigged to transfer the physical output of the workers into the hands of the rich and powerful.

VI. Conclusion

The traditional debate over income inequality in the United States typically divides the factions into two sides that tend to come down similarly on two separate questions. Specifically, those analysts who favor government intervention (such as minimum wage hikes, a more progressive tax code, and higher unemployment benefits) tend to endorse the empirical estimates of very large income inequality. Likewise, those analysts who favor *laissez-faire* tend to downplay some of the popular measures of inequality, arguing that they overstate the disparity and paint a falsely bleak picture of the plight of the poor in America. Because there were significant tax changes in the United States and United Kingdom during the 1980s, the income inequality debate often centers on this decade.

In this chapter, I sought to overturn this usual pattern. I stipulated for the sake of argument the popular inequality measures (such as those of Piketty and Saez), and the statistics (such as those from the Census Bureau) that apparently show the poorest households have barely seen an improvement in real income in decades.

But rather than use these data to condemn the tax rate reductions of the 1980s, I instead argued that they make a prima facie case that something fundamental happened *in the early 1970s*. Especially, if we use the measures indicating the emergence of an apparent "productivity-pay gap," it becomes clear that our culprit was something around 1972.

I suggested that a much more plausible explanation is Richard Nixon's closing of the gold window on August 15, 1971. This fits the historical record much more cleanly. I then suggested three possible mechanisms through which the move to fiat money could cause a "productivity-pay gap." First, naïve seigniorage: government officials with access to the printing press can bid away real goods and services and necessarily reduce the consumption of those who actually produced them. Second, the severity of the business cycle: various measures show that the Federal Reserve set up the economy for harder crashes (in the sense of Austrian business cycle theory) after the removal of gold's fetters. Third, the change in relative value of factor inputs: speculators, land owners, and capitalists are more socially useful in a world of fiat money, and so it is "natural" that they would earn a larger share of the social product.

If my argument is correct, it should give pause to both fans and foes of the free market. Its fans should realize that they don't need to dispute the standard measures of inequality with such ferocity, because even if correct, those measures may simply indict the monetary activism of the central bank. On the other hand, foes of the free market should realize that if they truly want to help the most vulnerable members of society, they should seriously examine the actual role of central banking and fiat money in our economic history.

Notes

1 Tax rate history taken from the Tax Policy Center (Urban Institute and Brookings Institution). Available at www.taxpolicycenter.org/statistics/historical-highest-marginal-income-tax-rates. Accessed July 19, 2017.
2 Similar arguments appear in Slemrod (1996).
3 Although it is certainly true that the overall tone of Sylvia Nasar's (1992) article suggests that the new data she reports are a referendum on the Reagan years – after all, the very title the paper gave to the article is, "The 1980's: A Very Good Time for the Very Rich" – we should note that Nasar herself, in the article, refers to the 1977–1989 time frame as "the Carter-Reagan years."
4 The National Bureau of Economic Research's official dates for U.S. recessions are available at www.nber.org/cycles.html.
5 To repeat, even though the EPI authors drew the vertical line at 1973, their own chart shows that the connection between productivity had already broken down a year earlier.
6 There are several online articles giving brief histories of the gold (and silver) standard in U.S. history. See for example Elwell (2011).
7 Text of the Gold Standard Act. Available at www.historycentral.com/documents/Gold Standard.html. Accessed April 7, 2018.
8 The text of Executive Order 6102, issued on April 5, 1933. Available at www.presidency.ucsb.edu/ws/index.php?pid=14611&st=&st1=. Accessed April 7, 2018.
9 In 1973, for example, the U.S. government officially devalued the dollar to $42.22 per troy ounce of gold.
10 One complication with our suggested mechanism in this subsection is that the worst economic plight for Americans occurred during the Great Depression, when the United States was still on the gold standard. In this case, I would argue that the interventions of the Hoover and then Roosevelt Administrations – particularly their efforts to prop up

nominal wage rates in the face of massive deflation – were the immediate explanation. See Murphy (2016).

11 As it stands, Figure 7.11 makes it seem as if the "artificially low interest rates" only kick in *after* the recession starts. But if we more appropriately reduce the nominal fed funds rate by the CPI inflation rate that overlaps with the time period in question, then the series is effectively shifted back a year, such that the artificially low interest rates clearly kick in during the boom period.

12 My summer 2007 forecast (which included other elements that did *not* come to pass) was for a private consulting client. However, my worry about "the worst recession in 25 years" ran in an online article in October of that year; see Murphy (2007).

References

Alvaredo, Facundo, Atkinson, Anthony B., Piketty, Thomas, and Saez, Emmanuel. 2013. "The Top 1 Percent in International and Historical Perspective." *Journal of Economic Perspectives* 27 (3): 3–20, Summer. Available at https://eml.berkeley.edu/~saez/alvaredo-atkinson-piketty-saezJEP13top1percent.pdf.

Bartley, Robert L. 1992. *The Seven Fat Years: And How to Do It Again*. New York: Free Press.

Bordo, Michael D., and Finn E. Kydland. 1995 "The Gold Standard as a Rule." *Explorations in Economic History* 32 (4): 423–464, October.

Cantillon, Richard. 1755. *Essai sur la Nature du Commerce en Général.*

Crabbe, Leland. 1984 [1989]. "The International Gold Standard and U.S. Monetary Policy from World War I to the New Deal." *Federal Reserve Bulletin* 423–440, June. Available at https://fraser.stlouisfed.org/files/docs/meltzer/craint89.pdf.

DeSilver, Drew. 2014. *For Most Workers, Real Wages Have Barely Budged for Decades*. Pew Research Center, October 9. Available at www.pewresearch.org/fact-tank/2014/10/09/for-most-workers-real-wages-have-barely-budged-for-decades/.

Elwell, Craig K. 2011. *Brief History of the Gold Standard in the United States*. Congressional Research Service, June 23. Available at http://www.fas.org/sgp/crs/misc/R41887.pdf.

Garrison, Roger. 2001. *Time and Money: The Macroeconomics of Capital Structure*. London: Routledge.

Horwitz, Steven. 2003. "The Costs of Inflation Revisited." *The Review of Austrian Economics* 16 (1): 77–95.

Krugman, Paul. 1992 [2014]. "The Rich, the Right, and the Facts: Deconstructing the Income Distribution Debate." *The American Prospect* (Article originally appeared in print in the Fall 1992 issue, then posted online on June 4, 2014). Available at http://prospect.org/article/rich-right-and-facts-deconstructing-inequality-debate.

Mishel, Lawrence, Elise Gould, and Josh Bivens. 2015. *Wage Stagnation in Nine Charts*. Economic Policy Institute, Raising America's Pay, January 6. Available at www.epi.org/publication/charting-wage-stagnation/.

Murphy, Robert P. 2007. "The Worst Recession in 25 Years?" *Mises Daily Article*, October 1. Available at https://mises.org/library/worst-recession-25-years.

Murphy, Robert P. 2016. "Book Review of *The Midas Paradox: Financial Markets, Government Policy Shocks, and the Great Depression*." *The Quarterly Journal of Austrian Economics* 19 (1): 101–111, Spring. Available at https://mises.org/library/review-midas-paradox-financial-markets-government-policy-shocks-and-great-depression-scott.

Nasar, Sylvia. 1992. "The 1980's: A Very Good Time for the Very Rich." *New York Times*, March 5. Available at www.nytimes.com/1992/03/05/business/the-1980-s-a-very-good-time-for-the-very-rich.html.

Piketty, Thomas. 2014. *Capital in the Twenty-First Century*. Cambridge, MA: Harvard University Press.

Piketty, Thomas, and Emmanuel Saez. 2003. "Income Inequality in the United States: 1913–1998." *Quarterly Journal of Economics* CXVIII (1): 1–39, February. Available at https://eml.berkeley.edu/~saez/pikettyqje.pdf.

Reynolds, Alan. 2006. *Income and Wealth*. Westport, CT: Greenwood Press.

Rugy, Veronique de. 2016. *Contrary to White House Claim, Compensation Has Been in Line with Productivity*. Mercatus Center, April 14. Available at www.mercatus.org/publication/contrary-white-house-claim-compensation-has-been-line-productivity.

Sherk, James. 2016. *Workers' Compensation: Growing Along with Productivity*. Heritage Foundation Backgrounder No. 3088, May 31. Available at www.heritage.org/jobs-and-labor/report/workers-compensation-growing-along-productivity.

Slemrod, Joel. 1996. "High Income Families and the Tax Changes of the 1980s: The Anatomy of Behavioral Response." In M. Feldstein and J. Poterba, eds., *Empirical Foundations of Household Taxation*. Chicago: University of Chicago Press.

Stone, Chad, Trisi, Danilo, Sherman, Arloc, and Emily Horton. 2016. *A Guide to Statistics on Historical Trends in Income Inequality*. Center on Budget and Policy Priorities, November 7. Available at www.cbpp.org/research/poverty-and-inequality/a-guide-to-statistics-on-historical-trends-in-income-inequality.

8 Market liberalization and the poor in India

Measuring economic inequality through consumption

G.P. Manish

I. Introduction

The period between 1990 and 2010 was a time of historically high growth for the Indian economy. Following the market reforms of 1991, real per capita GDP grew at a rate of 3.7% per annum during the 1990s, and at a higher rate of 5.2% per annum in the following decade. While these impressive growth numbers of the post-reform period represent a continuation of the high growth rates recorded during the 1980s, when per capita GDP grew at the rate of 3.4% per annum, they are a significant improvement when compared to the first three decades under planning, when per capita GDP grew at a rate of merely 1.7% per annum.[1]

The impact that liberalization and the ensuing high rates of growth have had on the lives of the poor in India has been the topic of extensive and vigorous debate. Central to this debate has been the skepticism surrounding the official poverty estimates put out by the Planning Commission of India. As a result of this skepticism, several scholars have put forward their own independent estimates of poverty in India for the 1990s and the 2000s.

This welter of poverty estimates for the post-reform period has led to a lack of clarity regarding the extent to which poverty has declined during these years. While most estimates do conclude that the head count ratio of poverty[2] (HCR) in both rural and urban India did decline during the 1990s and the 2000s, there is little consensus regarding the extent of this decline. Moreover, there is also ambiguity about whether the rate of decline accelerated or decelerated as we move deeper into the post-reform period, with some estimates indicating that the rate of decline of poverty was higher in the 2000s as compared to that in the 1990s, and other estimates suggesting the contrary.

Estimates of the trend in inequality in India, while not as contentious, have also given rise to some debate. The estimates of most scholars indicate that the Gini coefficient of consumption expenditure[3] has increased during the post-reform years, especially in the urban areas. A few estimates, however, seem to suggest that this increase has been minimal at best, in both the rural and urban areas of the country.

Thus, when taken at face value, the various estimates of the decline in poverty and the trend in inequality do not provide a clear picture of how the lives of the poor in India have been affected due to the process of liberalization. At best, they lead to the conclusion that the introduction of market reforms did lead to a decline in the incidence of poverty, although this decline may have been lower than that recorded in the decade immediately prior to the onset of the reforms; and they lead one to conclude that consumption inequality has increased during the post-reform period, especially in the urban areas.

There is, however, a more fundamental problem with these measures of poverty and inequality. Due to their aggregative nature, they do not provide a clear or coherent picture of precisely how the lives of the poor have been affected by the reforms. Take, for instance, the case of the HCR. A decline in the HCR implies that a larger proportion of individuals can now avail of a consumption bundle that either yields a minimum amount of satisfaction or an amount of satisfaction that is higher than this minimum. Hiding behind a given decline in this measure, however, could be varying patterns of change in the consumption baskets of households.

Thus, a given decline in the HCR could take place because households now have the means to obtain a bundle of consumer goods that contains more of some or all the goods that they were consuming before, with there being no changes in the quality or in the range of the available goods. Or, this decline could be associated with a significant alteration in the consumption baskets of those who are now at or above the poverty line. These households might now be able to possess new goods that were not available before, along with goods of better quality than before. The gain in well-being associated with these differing patterns of change will necessarily be different for the households concerned.

A similar argument can be made regarding highly aggregative measures of inequality such as the Gini coefficient. To begin with, an increase in this measure might go hand in hand, not with an absolute decline in the real consumption (or income) of the relatively poor, but, instead, with an increase in the level of their real consumption (income). Moreover, assuming the latter to be the case, this increase in per capita consumption (income), might, just as in the case of the HCR, hide very different patterns of change in the actual consumption baskets of those in the lower reaches of the consumption expenditure (income) distribution.

This chapter attempts to provide a clearer picture of how the process of liberalization has affected the poor in India by analyzing changes in the pattern of ownership of four consumer durables across the various deciles of the distribution of consumption expenditure: televisions, electric fans, mobile phones, and two-wheelers. Given that each of these industries was liberalized as a result of the market reforms initiated in the 1990s, such an analysis helps paint a more coherent picture of how the consumption baskets and therefore the lives of the poor in India were touched by this process.

In adopting this approach to analyzing changes in standards of living, this chapter builds on other contributions that undertake a similar analysis of changes in the consumption baskets of American households in the post–World War II era in order to provide greater clarity to the analysis of trends in poverty and inequality in the United States (Rector and Sheffield 2011; Hassett and Mathur 2012; Horwitz 2015). Moreover, it also attempts to make a contribution to the literature that focuses on studying the qualitative changes, especially the changes in the consumption basket of the average consumer, that underlie episodes of economic growth as measured by increases in per capita GDP (Balassa 1959; Nutter 1962; Krueger 1975; Cox and Alm 1998, 1999; Manish 2013, 2014).

Thus, Nutter (1962), for example, analyzes the high growth rates recorded under central planning in the erstwhile Soviet Union. He examines disaggregated primary data in government documents across several consumer and capital goods industries and finds a marked deterioration in the quality of goods under the planned regime. Michael Cox and Richard Alm (1998, 1999), meanwhile, conduct a similar exercise for the United States during the 1980s and 1990s and find marked qualitative improvements in consumer goods over the two decades. In particular, they find that there was a sharp increase in product differentiation and in the variety of goods such as cars, houses, computers, and televisions, as well as a significant advance in the technology embodied in these goods.

The chapter is organized as follows: Section II provides a review of the literature on poverty and inequality in India in the 1990s and 2000s; Section III provides an outline of how the television, electric fan, mobile telecommunication, and two-wheeler industries were liberalized starting in the early 1990s; Section IV analyzes changes in the ownership patterns of these four goods while also providing some details on the qualitative improvements that took place in the television, mobile telecommunication, and two-wheeler industries in the post-reform period; Section V provides the conclusion.

II. Poverty and inequality in India in the post-reform period

II.I The debate over the official poverty estimates[4]

The erstwhile Planning Commission of India[5] made its calculations of poverty measures using data on consumption expenditure from household surveys conducted by the National Sample Survey Organization (NSSO). The NSSO conducts these surveys on a regular basis, albeit with differing sample sizes: those with smaller sample sizes, the "thin" surveys, are conducted every year, whereas those with the larger sample sizes, the "thick" surveys, are conducted once every five years. The official poverty statistics are calculated using the data from the thick, quinquennial surveys.

The first set of poverty estimates that proved to be controversial and provoked much debate were those for the period between 1993–1994 and 1999–2000. These estimates were calculated using data from the thick surveys conducted by the NSSO for these years: data that comprised the 50th and 55th rounds of surveys on consumer expenditure. The Planning Commission, in its official estimates, concluded that poverty had declined significantly during this period. These estimates had the HCR for rural India falling by 10 percentage points, from 37% to 27%; that of urban India declining by 9 percentage points, from 33% to 24%; and that of India as a whole falling by a full 10 percentage points, from 36% to 26% (Deaton and Kozel 2005: 186). Thus, according to the Commission, the annual rate of decline of the HCR over the period between 1993–1994 and 1999–2000 was 1.67% for rural India, 1.5% for urban India, and 1.67% for India as a whole.

These figures were, in due course, attacked for both underestimating as well as overestimating the decline in poverty during the years that followed the sweeping reforms of the early 1990s. Thus, Bhalla (2003) argues that the headcount ratio for India in 1999–2000 was no more than 15% (Bhalla 2003: 348). The implication, of course, is that the official estimates severely underestimate the decline in poverty during the 1990s. Assuming the official HCR for India is correct in 1993–1994, Bhalla's estimate implies that poverty fell by 3.5% per annum during the rest of the decade.

Sen and Himanshu (2004), meanwhile, present estimates to show that the headcount ratio for rural India fell by a mere 0.47% per year between 1993–1994 and 1999–2000, from a figure of 31.9% to 29.1%; while urban poverty declined only by 0.52% per year, falling from 29.2% to 26.1%. According to these authors, therefore, the poverty statistics put out by the Planning Commission overestimate the extent of the fall in poverty during the period between 1993–1994 and 1999–2000.

Deaton and Dreze (2002), meanwhile, present a separate set of estimates for the decline in poverty during the 1990s, which differ from those of Bhalla (2003) and Sen and Himanshu (2004). Their estimates indicate that the annual fall in the HCR during this period was 1.17% for rural India and 1% for urban India. The conclusions that follow from these figures is that the estimates of the Planning Commission considerably overstate the extent of the decline in poverty in both rural and urban areas.

Thus, while there is agreement about the fact that HCRs for rural and urban India did fall during the post-reform period in the 1990s, there is consensus on little else. There is, in fact, considerable disagreement regarding both the level of poverty at the end of the 1990s as well as the extent of the decline that took place immediately after the reforms of the early 1990s. As a result, there is considerable disagreement about the extent of the impact of liberalization on the poor during this decade.[6]

This debate about the extent of the decline in poverty during the post-reform period has also affected the official estimates of poverty for the decade of the 2000s. Key to the disagreements among scholars about the estimates of this decade was the Planning Commission's decision, in line with the recommendations of the Tendulkar Committee on the calculation of poverty estimates, headed by the economist Suresh Tendulkar, to change the official poverty lines used in its calculations of HCRs and other measures of poverty. The Committee, to correct certain defects in the then official estimates, largely involving the choice of price indices involved to update the lines, recommended raising the rural poverty line while also altering the urban line (Panagariya and Mukim 2013: 6).

These changes have meant that there are now multiple estimates of poverty incidence, and therefore of poverty decline, for the period between 2004–2005 and 2009–2010: one based on the new "Tendulkar poverty lines," and another based on the earlier official poverty lines, also known as the "Lakdawala poverty lines," as they were recommended in 1993 by the Lakdawala Committee headed by the economist D.T. Lakdawala. According to the former set of estimates, the annual rate of decline of the HCRs for rural, urban, and all areas are 1.60%, 0.96%, and 1.47%, respectively, for the period between 2004–2005 and 2009–2010. The Lakdawala estimates, on the other hand, are far lower, with corresponding figures of 0.43%, 0.34%, and 0.40% per annum (Himanshu and Sen 2014: 5).

Moreover, the Tendulkar Committee estimates show an increase in the rate of poverty decline during the 2004–2005 to 2009–2010 period as compared to the period between 1993–1994 and 2004–2005. In fact, according to this set of estimates, the rate of annual decline doubled in the latter half of the 2000s as compared to the previous 11 years. The estimates based on the Lakdawala lines, however, show the exact opposite. They show that poverty declined at a much faster rate between 1993–1994 and 2004–2005 than between 2004–2005 and 2009–2010. Indeed, they show that the rate of decline during the latter period was half that of the former (Himanshu and Sen 2014: 5).

II.II. Inequality after the reforms

Estimates of the trend in the inequality of consumption expenditure during the post-reform period are also calculated using data, usually from the thick rounds, of the surveys of consumption expenditure conducted by the NSSO. These estimates, while not as scattered and ambiguous as those of the incidence and decline in poverty during this period, are also, nevertheless, the subject of some debate.

The majority of scholars who calculate estimates of consumption inequality during the post-reform period in India conclude that there has been an increase in the Gini coefficients, especially for the urban areas.[7] Thus, Motiram and Vakulabharanam (2012), for instance, find that the Gini coefficient for India rose from 32.6% in 1993–1994 to 36.3% in 2004–2005, and further to 37% in 2009–2010. Moreover, they find that this increase was largely driven by rising urban inequality. The rural Gini coefficient rose only slightly, from

28.6% in 1993–1994 to 30.5% in 2004–2005, and thereafter stayed unchanged during the second half of the decade. The urban Gini coefficient, however, rose much more sharply: from 34.4% in 1993–1994 to 37.6% in 2004–2005, and then further to 39.3% in 2009–2010.

Himanshu and Sen (2014: 13) present estimates that show an even sharper increase in urban inequality. The all-India Gini coefficient, according to them, rose from 30.1% to 36.2% between 1993–1994 and 2009–2010, while the rural Gini during the same period rose only by 3 percentage points, from 25.8% to 28.8%. The urban Gini, however, increased by close to 7.5 percentage points, from 31.9% to 38.3%. Moreover, they also find a significant increase in the ratio of the average consumption expenditure of the top 10% of the population to that of the bottom 10% during this period in urban areas: with this ratio rising from 7.14 in 1993–1994 to 10.33 in 2009–2010. The increase in the rural areas for the same period is, however, only slight, with the ratio increasing from 5.06 to 5.94.

This picture of rising inequality in the post-reform era, especially in urban areas, has been questioned by Bhalla (2011). Citing the wide variations in prices observed between the different states and within the urban and rural sectors within the various states of India, Bhalla argues against relying on nominal measures of consumption inequality. Instead, he argues that more accurate measures of inequality will be given by calculating real Gini coefficients: calculations that must be made after deflating the nominal consumption expenditure figures by the appropriate price indices (Bhalla 2011: 8).

His estimates of real Gini coefficients, in stark contrast to the other aforementioned estimates, show much smaller increases in consumption inequality during the post-reform period. Moreover, this holds true for measures calculated using both the uniform recall period (URP) and the mixed recall period estimates (MRP) of consumption expenditure.[8] Thus, the real Gini for India, according to his calculations, using the URP estimates of nominal consumption expenditure, declined from 30.4% in 1993–1994 to 29% in 1999–2000, and then rose to 32.8% in 2004–2005. For the 11-year period between 1993–1994 and 2004–2005, therefore, the Gini rose only by a little more than 2 percentage points (Bhalla 2011: 9).

The estimates of the real Gini for India using the MRP consumption expenditure estimates tell a similar story. The Gini, in this case, rose slightly from 28.4% to 29.3% between 1993–1994 and 1999–2000, and then increased a little more to 31.2% in 2007–2008. The overall rise for the period between 1993–1994 and 2007–2008 was, therefore, only 2.8 percentage points (Bhalla 2011: 9).

III. The liberalization of the television, electric fan, mobile telecommunications and two-wheeler industries

III.I. The television industry

Television broadcasts in India began in 1959, when All-India Radio, the state-run radio company, began telecasting an hour-long program twice a week that was beamed to the residents of Delhi (Laurie 2006). The production of televisions in India, however, did not commence until 1970, when two public sector firms in the formal, organized sector, and two private firms in the small-scale sector were handed out licenses to produce 10,000 and 5,000 black and white televisions, respectively (Joseph 1992: 143; Guhathakurta 1994: 847).

The production of televisions in India during the 1970s was dominated by small-scale private firms and larger public sector firms: a result that reflected government policy and the way the central government chose to allocate the licenses that were necessary to commence production. Thus, by 1976, 71 out of the 81 firms producing black and white televisions were in the small-scale sector, with the rest in the public sector (Joseph 1992: 143).

Production was undertaken in a highly regulated environment. Over and above the need to acquire licenses to start or expand production, producers were also barred from importing any technology. They were forced, instead, to produce televisions using the home-grown, indigenous technology developed by the Central Engineering and Electronics Research Institute (CEERI) in Pilani (Guhathakurta 1994: 847). Moreover, the licensing system extended to the acquisition of inputs that had to be imported into the country.

The decade of the 1980s witnessed the first wave of liberalization. Between 1981 and 1987, several steps were taken to ease the various regulations and controls that had hitherto been placed on the sector. Most importantly, restrictions on entry into the sector were greatly eased, and large private sector firms were allowed to compete with the incumbent small-scale and public sector firms. The import of technology was also allowed, and firms could now enter into technical collaborations with foreign firms. Restrictions on the import of inputs were also eased, with firms now able to freely import inputs for which there was no significant indigenous capacity of production. This period also witnessed the introduction of color transmission. To promote the production of color televisions, licenses were given out freely to import kits from which such televisions were assembled (Guhathakurta 1994: 849).

This first wave of liberalization, however, was limited in scope. It left untouched the ban prohibiting foreign television producers from setting up shop in India. Moreover, it did not make it any easier to import televisions from abroad. In fact, the import of televisions into the country was still prohibited, except as part of a traveler's personal baggage; and in that case, it was subject to a hefty tariff of 240% (c.i.f.) (Guhathakurta 1994: 850). The more liberal import of foreign technology to produce black and white televisions and that of kits to assemble color televisions were also intended to be short-term measures; the goal in both cases was to expand indigenous manufacturing capacity and to then phase out the increased imports (Guhathakurta 1994: 849, 851).

The process of liberalization gained steam in the 1990s. In line with the New Industrial Policy of 1991 that did away with licensing in many industrial sectors, the production of consumer electronics, including televisions, was also completely delicensed by the late 1990s (Joseph 2012: 10). More importantly, the sector was thrown open to foreign competition: foreign companies were now free to invest in India and compete with the domestic television producers.

The 1990s also witnessed the dismantling of the foreign exchange licensing system. As a result, the import of inputs to produce televisions was no longer subject to licensing. Through the 1990s and the subsequent decade, a steady and significant liberalization of tariff and nontariff barriers inhibiting the import of various electronic components and equipment also took place. All physical controls on the import of these goods had been phased out by 2005 and the peak customs rate for these goods was gradually reduced to 25% as of 2004 (Joseph 2012: 12). The fact that India was a signatory of the WTO's Information Technology Agreement also resulted in a sizeable reduction in the tariff rates of various electronic components (Joseph 2012: 12). And perhaps most importantly, the import of televisions was also liberalized. First, such imports were allowed, and then gradually the tariff rates on them were also reduced.

III.II. The electric fan industry

The production of electric fans in India began in the colonial period, with the first fan produced in 1921. Notwithstanding this early start, the domestic fan industry failed to grow significantly prior to independence. Instead, the bulk of the fans sold in the country during this period consisted of imports (NRCD 2005: 2).

The attainment of independence and the ensuing adoption of central planning gave a boost to the fledgling industry. Soon after gaining independence in 1947, the central government banned the import of electric fans, thereby shielding the industry from foreign competition (NRCD 2005: 2). This was to continue all the way till the 1990s, ensuring that the growth of the industry during the period between the official adoption of central planning in 1950 and the reforms of 1991 took place in a sheltered environment.

Sheltered from foreign competition, the industry was subject to all the rigors of the industrial and foreign exchange licensing system that was foisted on domestic firms during the planning era. As per the Industrial Policy Resolution of 1956 (GOI 1956), the industry was effectively placed in schedule C, which consisted of all the industries that were to be left largely to private firms. Industries in these firms, however, were required to obtain all the necessary licenses prior to making decisions regarding production and the importation of inputs.

The years between 1950 and 1991 saw the gradual growth of fan output as well as a gradual increase in the number of organized sector firms participating in production. The first private firm to commence production in the organized sector was Jay Engineering Works, which started producing fans in 1947. This firm was gradually joined by others, such as Orient Fans in the early 1950s, Crompton-Greaves in the late 1950s, Khaitan and Rally Fans in the 1960s, and Polar Fans in the 1970s (NRCD 2005: 2). Along with these firms in the organized sector, there were firms in the small-scale sector that also produced fans.

The New Economic Policy of 1991 (GOI 1991) placed the electric fan sector among those that were not reserved exclusively for the public sector or subject to compulsory licensing. This decision, and the ensuing reforms of the early 1990s, ensured that the production of fans was gradually liberalized. Most importantly, domestic production was delicensed, and the cumbersome foreign exchange licensing system was dismantled, thereby facilitating the easier importation of inputs.

The post-reform period has thus witnessed a significant increase in the levels of competition in the sector. By 2010, there were as many as eight leading brands in the organized sector jostling for about 60% of the annual market. In addition, there were a hundred smaller, lesser known firms in the organized sector that accounted for about 25% of the market, while the remaining 15% was in the hands of producers in the small-scale sector (Singh, Barve and Sant 2010: 6).

In keeping with the increased competition, the output of fans produced in India has increased steadily during the post-reform era. In the initial period after liberalization, the second half of 1990s, however, the growth of output was relatively slow. The production of fans during this period increased from 8.6 million units per annum in 1994–1995 to 10.3 million units in 1999–2000, growing at close to 4% per annum (NRCD 2005: 3). The rate of growth of output, however, increased significantly in the following decade. Domestic fan production during the 2000s increased from the figure of 10.3 million units per year recorded for 1999–2000 to 40 million units per year in 2010, growing at a high rate of 14.5% per annum (Singh et al. 2010: 7).[9]

III.III. The gradual liberalization of the telecommunications sector

As per the Industrial Policy Resolutions (IPRs) of 1948 and 1956, the telecommunications sector was deemed to be of strategic and national importance and reserved for the public sector.[10] Accordingly, the Indian Telephone Industries (ITI) was set up in 1948 to produce telephone switches, transmission cables, and telephone instruments; this was soon followed by Hindustan Cables Limited, which was established in 1952 to manufacture a range of transmission cables, and Hindustan Teleprinters, established in 1956 to produce terminal equipment such as modems and teleprinters.

These public sector enterprises sold their output to the Ministry of Post and Telegraph, which had a monopoly on the provision of telecommunication services. The entire sector, including the producers of equipment as well as the lone service provider, was shielded from all forms of competition. As per the guidelines of the IPRs, they were shielded from all domestic competitors, with private players entirely barred from entering the sector. Moreover, they were also shielded from foreign competition via hefty tariff barriers as well as other quantitative import restrictions.

This situation remained more or less unchanged until the mid-1980s, when the New Telecom Policy (NTP) of 1984 resulted in a shake-up of the sector. The NTP, at long last, ended the public sector monopoly over the production of telecom equipment and allowed private firms to produce selected terminal equipment meant for subscriber premises, albeit under the restrictions imposed by the industrial licensing system.

In the following year, the Ministry of Post and Telegraphs was bifurcated. A separate Ministry of Communications was established, and within this a Department of Telecommunications (DOT), now responsible for managing and regulating the provision of telecom services, was set up. This was followed by the establishment of two new state-owned corporations: Mahanagar Telephone Nigam Limited (MTNL), set up to handle the distribution of services in Delhi and Mumbai, and the Videsh Sanchar Nigam Limited (VSNL), which was set up to provide international services. Telecom services to the rest of the country continued to be provided by the DOT as before.

The sector was buffeted by another round of more radical changes in the early 1990s. In line with the New Industrial Policy of 1991, which took the telecommunications sector off the list of industries reserved for the public sector, the production of all telecommunications equipment was delicensed and foreign capital was allowed to flow into the sector, albeit in partnership with a domestic firm and with foreign equity ownership of a maximum of 49%.

The reforms of the early 1990s touched not only the production of equipment but also the provision of telecommunications services.[11] In 1992, the government approved of private sector participation in the provision of wireless services, including fixed wireless and cellular wireless services. In addition, the NTP of 1994 allowed private sector participation in the provision of fixed wireline services.

The result of these decisions was a series of auctions of licenses for both cellular and fixed line services to private operators to provide telecom services in various parts of the country. The incumbent public sector providers, the DOT and MTNL, were not allowed to compete for the cellular licenses, but they would now have to compete with one fixed-line private service provider in their areas of operation.

This rash of reforms and the attendant influx of competition, although limited, were fought tooth and nail by the close to half a million employees of the DOT. Leery of having to compete and of having its monopoly disturbed, the DOT did everything in its power to scuttle the license auctioning process. Moreover, it took several steps in the aftermath of the auctions that all but drove the private service providers, especially the providers of cellular services, out of business. This, coupled with the rather unsuccessful entry of private providers of fixed line services, ensured that the public sector monopoly over the provision of telecom services remained, for all practical purposes, intact till the late 1990s.

The dam was finally breached with the introduction of the NTP of 1999, which resulted in a series of decisions that finally succeeding in breaking the stranglehold of the public sector over the provision of telecom services and really opened the sector up to competition. In the words of the erstwhile managing director of Idea Cellular, Sanjeev Aga, one of the leading providers of cellular services in the country, it was the "watershed event" that changed the face of the Indian telecom sector and ushered in the mobile revolution that swept the country in the following decade.

III.IV. Economic reforms and the two-wheeler industry

The Indian two-wheeler industry, which consists of scooters, motorcycles, and mopeds, first emerged in the mid-1950s as a result of government efforts to shelter indigenous production from foreign competition (George et al. 2002: 7). In 1949, imports of fully built vehicles were virtually eliminated due the imposition of a very high tariff. Subsequently, in 1953, requirements for the domestic production of automotive components were imposed on foreign assemblers of completely knocked down vehicles, which drove them out of the market (Tiwari et al. 2011: 29). Thus, due to these measures that effectively blocked out all foreign competition, Indian consumers, starting from the mid-1950s, could only purchase domestically produced vehicles.

The Indian two-wheeler industry that emerged in the mid-1950s was heavily constrained by the industrial and foreign exchange licensing systems. Any firm producing vehicles of any kind needed a license to start production as well as to expand production (George et al. 2002: 10). Moreover, the chronic shortage of foreign exchange that characterized the early years of planning, especially the period between 1955 and 1970, led the government to limit the imports of automotive components using both high tariff rates and quantitative restrictions (Tiwari et al. 2011: 31). This period did, however, witness significant collaboration between domestic and foreign producers of two-wheelers. Thus, the three domestic manufacturers of motorcycles during this period all had collaborations with foreign producers, as did the two domestic scooter manufacturers (George et al. 2002: 26).

This trend was reversed during the 1970s with the passage of the Foreign Exchange Regulation Act (FERA) in 1973, which greatly increased the controls placed on the import of raw material, technology, components, and equity by the automotive sector (Tiwari et al. 2011: 35). In fact, the 1970s witnessed no new foreign collaborations between domestic and foreign two-wheeler firms. This greatly hobbled the production of motorcycles, which was heavily dependent on foreign collaboration for technology: no new manufacturers or models entered this sector during this decade, resulting in technological stagnation. The production of scooters and mopeds, which were technologically more self-sufficient, was less affected: two new scooter producers entered the market in the 1970s, and the domestic production of mopeds commenced, with three new producers entering this sector (George et al. 2002: 11, 26).

The automotive sector and the two-wheeler industry were first touched by economic reforms and liberalization in the mid-1980s. There was, to begin with, an easing of some of the onerous industrial licensing requirements. The government, as part of its New Economic Policy of 1985, introduced the policy of broadbanding for the auto sector. Firms producing vehicles still had to obtain licenses to begin and to expand production, but these licenses were now more broadly defined, allowing for more flexible use of installed capacity (Tiwari et al. 2011: 41).[12] Moreover, the licenses issued allowed for a larger licensed capacity, which allowed producers to take greater advantage of economies of scale (George et al. 2002: 12). Along with this easing of licensing requirements, there was also an easing of the controls placed on foreign collaborations. This allowed incumbent producers, especially in the motorcycle segment, to launch new products and to upgrade their technology.

These measures of liberalization resulted in the entry of several new producers into the motorcycle and scooter segments of the two-wheeler industry during the 1980s, and especially in the period between 1985 and 1990. As many as four new motorcycle producers, for example, entered the industry during this period, all of them with technical collaborations with foreign producers, whereas two new producers of scooters, also armed with foreign technical collaborations, commenced production during this period (George et al. 2002: 11, 26).

The trickle of reforms turned into a flood over the course of the next two decades. In July 1991, for instance, the entire automotive components sector as well as the manufacturing of all vehicles (with the exception of passenger car producers) was completely delicensed (Tiwari et al. 2011: 45). Domestic producers in the two-wheeler industry were, therefore, free to make production decisions, not based on the edicts and decrees of the government but based on their assessment of market conditions. There was also an easing of rules governing foreign direct investment (FDI) in 1991. FDI up to a limit of 51% of equity was allowed without government approval; and a greater share of foreign investment up to a limit of a 100% was also allowed but subject to government approval (Tiwari et al. 2011: 45). The latter regulation was also removed in 2002, and up to 100% FDI was allowed in the automotive components and all vehicle manufacturing sectors.

Moreover, beginning in the early 1990s, there was also a gradual liberalization of import restrictions. Quantitative restrictions on the import of components were removed in 1997 (Tiwari et al. 2011: 47) and the tariffs placed on them were also gradually reduced, reaching a low of 10% in 2008–2009 (Tiwari et al. 2011: 48). Similarly, quantitative restrictions on the import of vehicles in a semi- or completely knocked down state (SKD/CKD) and in completely built form (CBU) were removed in 2001, while tariff rates on CKD units was reduced to 10% by 2008–2009 (Tiwari et al. 2011: 48). The tariff rates on SKD and CBU units, however, remained high throughout the 1990s and the 2000s, and were as high as 60% for some and 100% for others by the end of the latter decade (Tiwari et al. 2011: 48, 50).

IV. Televisions, electric fans, mobile phones and two-wheelers: analysis of ownership patterns in the post-reform period

IV.I.I. The patterns of television ownership

Tables 8.1 and 8.2 provide data on the rate of television ownership across households in various deciles of the distribution of consumption expenditure

Table 8.1 Ownership of televisions per 1,000 rural households

Deciles	*1993–1994*	*2009–2010*	*CAGR*
I	3	94	24%
II	7	160	22%
III	11	235	21%
IV	20	294	18%
V	29	353	17%
VI	37	398	16%
VII	58	471	14%
VIII	83	565	13%
IX	127	612	10%
X	246	702	7%

Source: NSSO (1997: A-1, A-2, 2012: A-938)

Table 8.2 Ownership of televisions per 1,000 urban households

Deciles	*1993–1994*	*2009–2010*	*CAGR*
I	79	429	11%
II	166	597	8%
III	236	691	7%
IV	292	768	6%
V	372	830	5%
VI	439	827	4%
VII	480	823	3%
VIII	530	818	3%
IX	562	839	3%
X	592	778	2%

Source: NSSO (1997: A-51, A-52, 2012: A-956)

for rural and urban India. The data were obtained from the 50th and 66th rounds of the consumer expenditure survey conducted by the National Sample Survey Organization (NSSO 1993–94, 2009–10). As the data show, the years between 1993–1994 and 2009–2010 saw a robust increase in the ownership rate of televisions across all deciles of the consumption expenditure distribution in both rural and urban areas, with households at the lower end of the distribution increasing their rates of ownership at a higher rate than those at the upper end of the distribution.

As is evident from Table 8.3, the robust growth in the ownership of televisions during this period meant a significant increase in the average rates of ownership across the distribution of consumption expenditure in rural India. The average ownership rate in the two lowest deciles, for example, increased from a meager 0.5% of households in 1993–1994 to 12.7% of households in 2009–2010, whereas across the bottom four deciles the corresponding figures were 1% and 19.6%, respectively. Meanwhile, in the middle of the distribution, only 3.3% of households possessed a television set in 1993–1994, and

Table 8.3 Average ownership rate of televisions in rural households (percentage)

Deciles	*1993–1994*	*2009–2010*
I and II	0.5	12.7
I through IV	1	19.6
V and VI	3.3	37.6
IX and X	18.7	65.7

Source: Author's Calculations from NSSO (1997: A-1, A-2, 2012: A-938)

Table 8.4 Average ownership rate of televisions in urban households (percentage)

Deciles	*1993–1994*	*2009–2010*
I and II	12.3	51.3
I through IV	19.3	62.1
V and VI	40.6	82.9
IX and X	57.7	80.9

Source: Author's Calculations from NSSO (1997: A-51, A-52, 2012: A-956)

the corresponding figure for 2009–2010 was much healthier, 37.6% of the households. It is interesting to note that the average ownership rate of the top two deciles in 1993–1994 was lower than that of the bottom four deciles in 2009–2010.

Table 8.4 presents similar trends for urban India. Whereas only 12.3% of households in deciles I and II possessed a television in 1993–1994, a much higher percentage, 51.3%, did so in 2009–2010. Similarly, the average ownership rate of television across the four lowest deciles increased from 19.3% in 1993–1994 to 62.1% of households in 2009–2010. It is interesting to note that the average ownership rate for both the two lowest deciles and across the four lowest deciles were higher in 2009–2010 than the corresponding figure for the two middle deciles in 1993–1994. Moreover, whereas 62.1% of households in the four lowest deciles enjoyed the services of a television in 2009–2010 in urban India, only 57.7% of households in the top two deciles did so in 1993–1994.

Tables 8.5 and 8.6 provide data on the percentage gaps of ownership across deciles for rural and urban India for the years 1993–1994 and 2009–2010, calculated from the data presented in Tables 8.1 and 8.3. The percentage gap G_1 measures the difference between the average ownership rate of televisions of the top two deciles, IX and X, and that of deciles I and II. G_2, meanwhile, shows the difference between the average ownership rate of deciles IX and X and deciles I through IV, whereas G_3 shows the corresponding difference

Table 8.5 Percentage gaps in television ownership (rural)

Measure	*1993–1994*	*2009–2010*
G_1	18%	53%
G_2	18%	46%
G_3	15%	28%

Source: Author's Calculations from NSSO (1997: A-1, A-2, 2012: A-938)

Table 8.6 Percentage gaps in television ownership (urban)

Measure	*1993–1994*	*2009–2010*
G_1	45%	30%
G_2	38%	19%
G_3	17%	-2%

Source: Author's Calculations from NSSO (1997: A-51, A-52, 2012: A-956)

between the former and the average ownership rate of televisions of deciles V and VI.

As is evident from the tables, these measures evolved very differently for rural as compared to urban India during this period. Thus, whereas all three measures show an increase in the case of rural India, they all show a decline for the urban part of the country. In rural India, the value of $G_{2,}$ for example, increased from 18% in 1993–1994 to 46% in 2009–2010. Thus, whereas the average rate of television ownership by households in the top two deciles of the consumption expenditure distribution exceeded that of the lowest four deciles by 18% in 1993–1994, this figure had shot up to 46% by 2009–2010. Similarly, the value of G_3 rose from 15% to 28%.

In urban India, however, the differences in average ownership rates between the top two deciles and other deciles lower in the distribution narrowed. The value of $G_{2,}$ for example, fell from 38% in 1993–1994 to 19% in 2009–2010. Thus, whereas the average ownership rate of televisions of households in deciles IX and X had been a full 38% higher than that of households in the four lowest deciles in 1993–1994, it was only 19% higher in 2009–2010. Similarly, G_3 also fell from 17% to −2% during the same period.

IV.I.II. Televisions and television broadcasts: qualitative improvements

When the production of televisions first began in India in the 1970s, only black and white televisions were produced. This was the result of government policy and not of television producers catering to the preferences of consumers. During this period, the government simply refused to give out any licenses to produce color televisions. Moreover, the production of such televisions would have been an exercise in futility in any case, because the Indian government had a monopoly over the transmission of television signals and had chosen to transmit only black and white signals.

The situation changed in the 1980s, when the government decided to allow color transmission. By now, it is important to note that black and white transmission and televisions were more or less obsolete in many parts of the world. Color televisions and transmission had, indeed, already made their way, not only into the homes of the average television viewer in the developed part of the world but had also been introduced in other developing nations such as Nigeria, Sri Lanka, and China (Reeves 1994: 3).

The introduction of color transmission and the modest liberalization in the production of televisions in the 1980s, however, failed to significantly alter the product mix on offer. In fact, the production of black and white televisions increased rapidly during this decade, rising from 369,000 units in 1980 to 3.6 million units in 1990 (Joseph 1997: 110). And while the production of color televisions did increase significantly from zero units in 1980 to 1.2 million units in 1990, by the end of the 1980s, black and white televisions still accounted for 75% of the annual production (Joseph 1997: 110). Moreover, things did not change much in the early 1990s as well, and as of 1995 color televisions accounted only for 24% of the annual television output (Joseph 1997: 110).

The changes started to take effect only after the production of televisions was delicensed in 1996–1997, and the sector was thrown open to foreign competitors. The second half of the 1990s and the following decade witnessed a significant and rapid transformation in the product mix available to consumers. The production of color televisions grew quickly, while that of black and white televisions declined. Thus, by 2001–2002, the share of black and white televisions in annual production had declined to 37.5% (Indian MIT 2005: 8), and by 2004, this share had fallen further to just 20% (Laurie 2006: 19). This period also witnessed the entry of several foreign producers into the Indian television market. By the early 2000s, multinational giants such as Phillips, LG, Sony, Samsung, and Panasonic had begun producing televisions in India and were competing against Chinese companies such as Haier, TCL, and Konka, and with domestic firms like BPL, Videocon, and Onida (Laurie 2006: 8).

Moreover, there were constant improvements in quality within the color television sector. As the decade of the 2000s progressed, flat screen color televisions started taking the place of traditional color televisions using the cathode ray technology (CRT). The market share of flat screen televisions increased rapidly during this period, climbing from a mere 2.7% in 2001–2002 to 47% in 2005–2006 (Gupta 2006: 216). The second half of the decade also saw increased production and imports of LCD televisions.

The most far-reaching qualitative improvement as far as the television sector is concerned, however, relates not so much to the quality of the televisions themselves as to the quality of the television broadcasts. During the 1980s, despite the advent of color transmission and color televisions, television broadcasts were still monopolized by the Indian government. As a result, the possessors of televisions had only one channel, Doordarshan, the public service broadcaster, to watch during this decade.

The following decade brought with it not only the liberalization of the production of televisions but also the setting free of the airwaves, with the government allowing private participation in broadcasting. The number of broadcasters quickly grew from the one public sector monopolist in 1991 to 24 by the end of 2011. This was accompanied by a steady increase in the number of channels available to view, from the one beamed by Doordarshan in 1991 to 161 pay channels by 2011 (TRAI 2012a: 80–82).[13] The growing list of available channels – featuring prominent international channels such as ESPN, CNN, BBC, HBO, TLC, and VH1, as well as a host of Bollywood movie channels and news and entertainment channels in Hindi and many regional languages – catered to many different groups of consumers (TRAI 2012a: 127–142).

IV.II Electric fans: ownership patterns in the post-reform period

Tables 8.7 and 8.8 provide data on the rates of ownership of electric fans across the deciles of the consumption expenditure distribution for households in rural India for the years 1993–1994 and 2009–2010. These data, like those on the ownership rates of televisions, are drawn from the consumer expenditure surveys conducted by the National Sample Survey Organization (NSSO) in the years 1993–1994 and 2009–2010 (NSSO 1997, 2012). As is evident from the tables, the growth of the ownership rates of fans in the lower deciles of the distribution outstripped that of households in the middle and upper deciles in both rural and urban areas during this period.

As Table 8.9 shows, the years between 1993–1994 and 2009–2010 also witnessed a significant increase in the average ownership rates of fans for households in all deciles of the distribution in rural India. Thus, focusing on the

Table 8.7 Ownership of electric fans per 1,000 rural households

Deciles	*1993–1994*	*2009–2010*	*CAGR*
I	14	205	18%
II	36	289	14%
III	46	357	14%
IV	73	440	12%
V	94	511	11%
VI	120	550	10%
VII	163	629	9%
VIII	213	684	8%
IX	286	737	6%
X	416	825	4%

Source: NSSO (1997: A-1, A-2, 2012: A-938)

Table 8.8 Ownership of electric fans per 1,000 urban households

Deciles	*1993–1994*	*2009–2010*	*CAGR*
I	181	664	8%
II	339	822	6%
III	432	831	4%
IV	489	902	4%
V	569	922	3%
VI	613	938	3%
VII	646	946	2%
VIII	676	943	2%
IX	704	966	2%
X	733	970	2%

Source: NSSO (1997: A-51, A-52, 2012: A-956)

Table 8.9 Average ownership rate of electric fans in rural households (percentage)

Deciles	*1993–1994*	*2009–2010*
I and II	2.5	24.7
I through IV	4.2	32.3
V and VI	10.7	53.1
IX and X	35.1	78.1

Source: Author's Calculations from NSSO (1997: A-1, A-2, 2012: A-938)

lower ends of the distribution, in 1993–1994 a mere 2.5% of households in the two lowest deciles owned an electric fan, whereas 24.7% of households in these deciles did so in 2009–2010. And across deciles I through IV, the corresponding figures were 4.2% and 32.3% of households, respectively. It is interesting to note that the average rate of ownership across these deciles in 2009–2010 was almost as high as that in the top two deciles of the distribution in 1993–1994.

There were similar increases in the average ownership rates of fans for households throughout the consumption expenditure distribution in urban India. As is evident from the data presented in Table 8.10, these increases in average rates of ownership were especially pronounced for households in the lower ends of the distribution. Thus, in 1993–1994, whereas only 26% of households possessed an electric fan in the two lowest deciles of the consumption expenditure distribution, a much greater 74.3% of households did so in 2009–2010, a figure that is higher than that of the top two deciles in 1993–1994. The extent of the increase in ownership was similar when measured across the lowest four deciles of the distribution. Thus, whereas 36% of households in deciles I through IV owned an electric fan in 1993–1994, a full 80.5% of households did so in 2009–2010.

Table 8.10 Average ownership rate of electric fans in urban households (percentage)

Deciles	*1993–1994*	*2009–2010*
I and II	26	74.3
I through IV	36	80.5
V and VI	59.1	93
IX and X	71.9	96.8

Source: Author's Calculations from NSSO (1997: A-51, A-52, 2012: A-956)

Table 8.11 Percentage gaps in electric fan ownership (rural)

Measure	*1993–1994*	*2009–2010*
G_1	33%	53%
G_2	31%	46%
G_3	24%	25%

Source: Author's Calculations from NSSO (1997: A-1, A-2, 2012: A-938)

Table 8.12 Percentage gaps in electric fan ownership (urban)

Measure	*1993–1994*	*2009–2010*
G_1	46%	23%
G_2	36%	16%
G_3	13%	4%

Source: Author's Calculations from NSSO (1997: A-51, A-52, 2012: A-956)

Tables 8.11 and 8.12 provide data on three measures of the gap in ownership rates for households across the deciles of the consumption expenditure distribution. The trends in these measures were different for rural and urban India. In the former, the increase in average ownership rates of fans across the distribution analyzed earlier went hand in hand with an increase in the difference between ownership rates across the various deciles.

In sharp contrast to these trends in rural India, the ownership gap measures in urban India decreased between 1993–1994 and 2009–2010. G_1, for instance, recorded a steep decline from 46% to 23%, as did G_2 from 36% to 16%. G_3, meanwhile, declined from 13% to 4%. These decreases in the ownership gap measures indicate that the robust increases in the average rates of ownership of fans in urban India across the consumption expenditure distribution was associated with a decline in the difference in the ownership rates for households in the different deciles of the distribution.

IV.III.I. Mobile phones and mobile subscriptions: the explosion in ownership post-reforms

During the period between 1980 and 2010, telephone subscriptions in India grew at a high and increasing rate. During the 1980s, when there was limited liberalization in the production of telecom equipment and a public sector monopoly over the provision of telecom services, the number of telephone subscriptions grew at a rate close to 9% per annum.[14] Because cellular services were not available to customers during this period, this growth was driven entirely by an increase in the number of fixed line subscriptions, which grew from 2,149,470 to 5,074,734.

In the 1990s, when greater liberalization in the production of telecom equipment was accompanied by a largely futile attempt to break the monopoly of the public sector over the provision of telecom services, total telephone subscriptions grew at the higher rate of close to 22% per annum. Given the emergence of the first mobile phone subscriptions in 1995, this growth was driven by an increase in both these subscriptions and an increase in fixed line subscriptions. Whereas the former grew from 76,680 lines in 1995 to 3,577,095 lines in 2000, the latter increased from 5,074,737 lines in 1990 to 32,436,134 lines in 2000. Total subscriptions, therefore, went up from 5,074,737 to 36,013,229 over the course of the decade.

The decade of the 2000s, when there was private participation in the provision of both fixed line and mobile telecom services, saw the growth rate of total subscriptions rise to an annual rate of 36%. This high growth was fuelled, almost exclusively, by a veritable explosion in the number of mobile subscriptions. The number of fixed line subscriptions, after initially increasing from 32,436,134 lines in 2000 to 50,176,509 lines in 2005, declined thereafter to 35,090,000 lines by 2010. Mobile phone subscriptions, on the other hand, shot up from 3,577,095 lines in 2000 to 752,190,000 lines in 2010, growing at close to 71% per annum. Total subscriptions, meanwhile, rose from 36,013,229 to 787,280,000 lines during this decade.

The growth of 9% per annum during the previous decade notwithstanding, the average ownership rate of telephone subscriptions in India was a very low 0.59% as of 1990. Thus, at the start of the 1990s, less than 1 out of every 100 households in India had a telephone subscription. Over the course of the 1990s, this rate increased but marginally, rising to nearly 3.5% by the year 2000. Given this very low rate of average ownership of telephone subscriptions, it would be safe to conclude that, as of 2000, the bulk of telephone subscriptions in India were in the hands of households in the top deciles of the distribution of consumption expenditure.

Further evidence for this conclusion comes from the fact that, throughout the 1990s, it was very difficult to get a fixed line telephone subscription. In fact, a subscription was not available on demand. Instead, the prospective consumer had to wait, on average, for a period of 49 months to obtain a subscription in 1991 (Noll and Wallsten 2011: 16). While the size of this waiting list shrank over the course of the decade, a waiting period of two years was still involved with obtaining a fixed line subscription in 1995. The waiting list only disappeared in 1999, when a fixed line subscription was finally available on demand (Noll and Wallsten 2011: 18–19). Given the existence of a waiting list to obtain a new subscription and the length of the wait involved, it would be fair to surmise that a rich individual with political connections would be more likely to obtain a fixed line subscription than one who was poor.

In stark contrast, the ten-year period between 2000 and 2010 witnessed a very impressive and significant increase in the average ownership rate of telephone subscriptions. Indeed, as of 2010, this rate stood at just over 65%, with 65 out of every 100 Indian households in possession of a telephone subscription. This increase in the average ownership rate during the 2000s was driven, as the figures on the growth of subscriptions analyzed earlier would suggest, entirely by an increase in the number of mobile subscriptions. In 2000, the number of mobile subscriptions per 100 households stood at a paltry 0.34, but by the end of the decade, this figure had increased to a little over 62. In line with the decline in the number of fixed line subscriptions during this period, the number of these subscriptions per 100 Indian households actually fell from 3.11 in 2000 to 2.91 in 2010.

Table 8.13 presents data on the ownership rates of mobile phones for households across the deciles of the distribution of consumption expenditure in rural and urban India in 2009–2010. As the data shows, the impressive growth in the number of mobile phone subscriptions over the course of the period between 2000 and 2010 was not restricted only to households in the upper deciles of the distribution. Instead, households in the middle and lower deciles also shared in this growth, both in rural and urban India.

Table 8.13 Ownership of mobile phones per 1,000 households

Deciles	*Rural*	*Urban*
I	167	378
II	245	576
III	336	672
IV	382	754
V	475	827
VI	516	839
VII	582	835
VIII	628	886
IX	683	902
X	764	910

Source: NSSO (2012: A-938, A-956)

Table 8.14 Average ownership rate of mobile phones in 2009–2010 (percentage)

Deciles	*Rural*	*Urban*
I and II	20.6	47.7
I through IV	28.3	59.5
V and VI	49.6	83.3
IX and X	72.4	90.6

Source: Author's Calculations from NSSO (2012: A-938, A-956)

Further evidence to this effect is provided in Table 8.14, which shows the average rate of ownership of mobile phones across deciles of the distribution of consumption expenditure for both rural and urban India in 2009–2010. As the data clearly show, the rate of ownership is significant even for households in the lower and middle deciles of the distribution. This holds true especially for households in urban India.

Thus, when looking at the two lowest deciles in the distribution, the average rate of ownership of mobile phones was 20.6% and 47.7% in rural and urban India, respectively. Or, stated differently, nearly 21 out of every 100 households in the two lowest deciles owned a mobile phone in rural India, while close to 48 out of every 100 households in the corresponding deciles in urban India did so. When looking at households within the bottom four deciles, 28 out of every 100 households and nearly 60 out of every 100 households owned a phone in rural and urban India, respectively. And as for the two deciles in the middle of the distribution, i.e., deciles V and VI, the average rate of ownership of phones stood at 49.6% in rural India and 83.3% in urban India.

IV.III.II. Mobile phones and cellular services: qualitative improvements

This increase in ownership across the deciles of the distribution of consumption expenditure was accompanied by a steady increase in the number of mobile phone handsets available for purchase. From a scenario where the choice in handsets was limited to a few, the number of different models of phones available for purchase in 2011 stood at 296 (TRAI 2012b: 15). Along with greater choice in the type of handset that they could purchase, consumers also had to pay less for mobile phone services in 2010 as compared to earlier in the decade. Thus, in March 2007, the average cost incurred (including both rental and call charges) on an outgoing call per minute for prepaid customers was more than Rs. 1.10 per minute. By March 2010, this figure had declined to less than Rs. 0.60. Similarly, for postpaid customers, the average cost incurred on an outgoing call per minute was more than Rs. 0.90 in March 2007 – a figure that fell below Rs. 0.80 by March 2010 (TRAI 2012b: 26).

Moreover, there was also an improvement in the quality of the cellular services available to consumers. In 2003, the average call drop rate for phone calls made from mobile phones in the four metropolitan telecom circles (serving Chennai, Delhi, Kolkata, and Mumbai) stood at 1.41%, whereas the corresponding figure for the other telecom circles (those serving, roughly, the various states) was 2.53% of all phone calls. These figures fell through the decade so that in 2010, the figure for the metropolitan areas was 0.78%, whereas that for the states was 1.02% (TRAI 2012b: 33).

A similar improvement was seen in the percentage of phone connections with good voice quality. In 2003, this figure for the metro areas stood at 81.9% and that for the states was 97.1%. By 2010, these figures had risen to 98.5% for the metro areas and 97.7% for the states (TRAI 2012b: 33).

IV.IV.I. Motorcycles and scooters: ownership patterns after liberalization

Tables 8.15 and 8.16 provide data on the rates of ownership of motorcycles and scooters across the deciles of the consumption expenditure distribution for households in rural India for the years 1993–1994 and 2009–2010. These data, like those on the ownership rates of televisions, electric fans, and mobile phones, are drawn from the consumer expenditure surveys conducted by the National Sample Survey Organization (NSSO) in the years 1993–1994 and 2009–2010 (NSSO 1997, 2012).

As is evident from these tables, despite households across the distribution recording increases in the ownership rates of these goods over this period, the average ownership rates of motorcycles and scooters in 2009–2010 in rural India was still extremely low for all but the households in the top two deciles of the distribution. This is shown, especially, in Table 8.16, where the average ownership rate for these goods in households in the bottom two deciles is an extremely low 1.5% in 2009–2010, whereas average ownership rates for deciles III and IV also did not exceed a low 4% of households. The corresponding rate for households in the middle two deciles, meanwhile, was also a very low 8.4% in 2009–2010. Based on these numbers, one can conclude that motorcycles

Table 8.15 Ownership of motorcycles and scooters per 1,000 rural households

Deciles	*1993–1994*	*2009–2010*	*CAGR*
I	2	7	9%
II	2	22	17%
III	3	28	16%
IV	4	50	18%
V	5	64	19%
VI	7	104	20%
VII	12	126	17%
VIII	18	188	17%
IX	35	256	14%
X	95	363	9%

Source: NSSO (1997: A-1, A-2, 2012: A-938)

Table 8.16 Average ownership rate of motorcycles and scooters in rural households (percentage)

Deciles	*1993–1994*	*2009–2010*
I and II	0.2	1.5
III and IV	0.4	3.9
I through IV	0.3	2.7
V and VI	0.6	8.4
IX and X	6.5	31

Source: Author's Calculations from NSSO (1997: A-1, A-2, 2012: A-938)

Table 8.17 Ownership of motorcycles and scooters per 1,000 urban households

Deciles	*1993–1994*	*2009–2010*	*CAGR*
I	3	32	17%
II	11	88	15%
III	13	127	16%
IV	32	201	13%
V	61	302	11%
VI	83	330	10%
VII	122	400	8%
VIII	154	452	7%
IX	213	551	7%
X	285	477	3%

Source: NSSO (1997: A-51, A-52, 2012: A-956)

and scooters did not enter in a significant manner into the consumption baskets of households in both the lower and the middle deciles of the consumption expenditure distribution in rural India and that these goods, therefore, did not significantly affect the welfare of these households even after two decades of liberalization.

The data on ownership rates for these goods for households in the urban areas, presented in Tables 8.17 and 8.18, however tell a different story. In the urban areas, the period between 1993–1994 and 2009–2010 not only witnessed increases in ownership rates for households across the consumption expenditure distribution, with the rate of growth of ownership of households in the lower and middle reaches of the distribution being higher than that of households in the top two deciles. It also saw meaningful and significant increases in rates of ownership for households in the lower and middle deciles, as shown by the average ownership rates depicted in Table 8.18. The average ownership rate for households in the middle two deciles of the distribution had, for example, reached a figure of 31.6% by 2009–2010. The corresponding rate for households in the third and fourth deciles, meanwhile, was also a not insignificant 16.4%. Thus, unlike in the case of the rural India, motorcycles and scooters did

Table 8.18 Average ownership rate of motorcycles and scooters in urban households (percentage)

Deciles	*1993–1994*	*2009–2010*
I and II	0.7	6
III and IV	2.3	16.4
I through IV	1.5	11.2
V and VI	7.2	31.6
IX and X	24.9	51.4

Source: Author's Calculations from NSSO (1997: A-51, A-52, 2012: A-956)

play a reasonably significant role in the consumption baskets of households in these deciles of the distribution after two decades of liberalization.

IV.IV.II. Motorcycles and scooters: qualitative improvements

The first signs of qualitative improvements in the motorcycles and scooters available to Indian consumers emerged soon after the first wave of liberalization in the mid-1980s. In the motorcycles segment, this period saw the introduction of new models for the first time in over 20 years (George et al. 2002: 26). Seven new models were quickly introduced (George et al. 2002: 26), all of them produced by Indian firms in collaboration with foreign manufacturers, and signs of competition began to emerge for the first time in the sector. The sales of the old models, which suffered from the twin drawbacks of low fuel efficiency and high weight, declined as consumers switched over to the new models that were much lighter as well as more fuel efficient (George et al. 2002: 12).

This pattern of product differentiation continued into the 1990s and the 2000s, as the pace of reforms gathered steam. In fact, the rate at which new models of motorcycles were introduced increased to such an extent that by 2012, the entry-level segment of the sector, featuring the cheapest motorcycles with an engine capacity between 75 cc and 110 cc, alone had as many as 12 models, more than the entire motorcycle segment put together in the late 1980s (Ray and Makkar 2012: 7). Moreover, there were other models in the more expensive segments of the sector. Thus, there were as many as eight models in the segment with slightly more expensive motorcycles with an engine capacity between 110 cc and 125 cc (Ray and Makkar 2012: 9), and 20 models vying for the attention of consumers in the segment with the most expensive motorcycles with an engine capacity between 150 cc and 220 cc (Ray and Makkar 2012: 10).

The scooter sector of the two-wheeler industry tells a similar story. With the first wave of liberalization in the 1980s, two new scooter models were introduced into the market (George et al. 2002: 26), with features such as automatic transmission and gearless riding that were missing from the older models (George et al. 2002: 12). And like the motorcycle sector, the rate of product differentiation increased significantly in the 1990s and the 2000s. Thus, by 2012, there were ten scooter models (Ray and Makkar 2012: 12), and these new models had pushed out the old models of the pre-liberalization era from the marketplace.

V. Conclusion

The 20-year period after the commencement of market reforms and liberalization, between 1990 and 2010, was a time of historically high growth for the Indian economy. The impact that liberalization and the ensuing high rates of growth have had on the lives of the poor in India, however, has been the topic of extensive and vigorous debate.

The various estimates of the decline in poverty and the trend in inequality do not provide a clear picture of how the lives of the poor in India have been affected due to the process of liberalization. At best, they lead to the conclusion that the introduction of market reforms did lead to a decline in the incidence of poverty, although this decline may have been lower than that recorded in the decade immediately prior to the onset of the reforms; and they lead one to conclude that consumption inequality has increased during the post-reform period, especially in the urban areas.

This chapter first notes that, due to their aggregative nature, these measures of poverty and inequality do not provide a clear or coherent picture of precisely how the lives of the poor have been affected by the reforms. Specifically, they do not provide any information about whether or not there was a significant alteration in the consumption baskets of those who are now at or above the poverty line.

The chapter then attempts to provide a clearer picture of how the process of liberalization has affected the poor in India by analyzing changes in the pattern of ownership of four consumer durables: televisions, electric fans, mobile phones, and two-wheelers across the distribution of consumption expenditure between 1993–1994 and 2009–2010. For three of these goods, i.e., televisions, mobile phones, and two-wheelers, it also analyzes if there were significant qualitative improvements during this post-reform period. Given that each of these industries was liberalized as a result of the market reforms initiated in the 1990s, such an analysis helps paint a more coherent picture of how the consumption baskets and, therefore, the lives of the poor in India were touched by this process.

It is seen that, for all four goods, there was a significant increase in the average ownership rate among households in the lower and middle deciles of the distribution, with the increase being especially pronounced in the urban areas. The chapter also finds significant qualitative improvements in the televisions, mobile phones, and two-wheelers available during the period under consideration. Based on this evidence, the chapter concludes that, especially in urban India, market reforms have generated a significant improvement in the consumption baskets of Indians in the lower and middle deciles of the distribution of consumption expenditure.

Notes

1 The growth rates for the 1980s, 1990s, and 2000s represent compound annual growth rates calculated by the author from the World Development Indicators data set made available by the World Bank. The growth figure for the period between 1950 and 1980, which constitutes the first three decades under planning, is from Rodrik and Subramaniam (2005: 194).

2 The head count ratio of poverty measures the proportion of the population that lives below the poverty line in a specified region.

3 As explained in greater detail in Section II, most estimates of inequality in India are of consumption and not of income inequality. This is a result of the fact that they are usually constructed using the data of consumption expenditure that are generated by the surveys conducted by the National Sample Survey Organization.

4 For a summary of the debate surrounding the official poverty figures for the 1990s, see Datt and Ravallion (2002) and Deaton and Kozel (2005). For the debate surrounding the official figures for the 2000s, see Panagariya and Mukim (2013) and Himanshu and Sen (2014).

5 The Planning Commission, which was created in 1950, was replaced by the Niti Aayog in 2014.

6 This confusion and lack of consensus stem from three broad issues with the data underlying the various estimates. First, there is the widening gap between estimates of average per capita consumption expenditure obtained from the NSSO surveys and the National Accounts statistics, with the latter increasing at a far higher rate than the former. Second, there is the issue of survey design. In all rounds prior to the 55th round of surveys undertaken in 1999–2000, the NSSO had adopted a uniform 30-day recall period for consumption expenditure estimates on all items. In the questionnaire sent out as part of the 55th round, the NSSO decided to use two recall periods for the high-frequency items: one asked respondents to estimate expenses incurred on these items over the past 7 days, and another that asked them to do the same for the past 30 days. Meanwhile, for the low-frequency items, the NSSO decided to change the recall period from the usual 30 days to 365 days. The third issue, pioneered by Angus Deaton in particular (Deaton and Dreze 2002; Deaton 2003; Deaton and Tarozzi 2005), questions the legitimacy of the poverty lines used in calculating the official estimates. Integral to this argument are misgivings regarding the price indices used to revise the poverty lines. For a more detailed overview and analysis of all three of these issues, see Deaton and Kozel (2005) and the sources cited therein.

7 For a sampling of this literature, see Deaton and Dreze (2002), Himanshu and Sen (2004), Banerjee and Piketty (2005), Pal and Ghosh (2007), Motiram and Vakulabharanam (2012), and Basole 2014.

8 As mentioned in footnote 4, in all rounds of surveys prior to the 55th round conducted in 1999–2000, the NSSO had used a uniform recall period of 30 days for consumption expenditure estimates for all items. The controversy generated by the introduction of both the 7-day and the 30-day recall periods for items purchased frequently and the sudden lengthening of the recall period to 365 days for items purchased infrequently in the 55th round, however, forced the NSSO to change track. In the following thick rounds (round 61 in 2004–2005 onward), the NSSO decided to use two different sets of questionnaires during its surveys. One of them went back to using the 30-day recall periods for all items, whereas the other used a 30-day recall period for items purchased frequently and a 365-day recall period for those bought infrequently. Estimates of consumption expenditure generated using the first set of questionnaires, featuring a 30-day recall period for all items, are called uniform recall period (URP) estimates in the literature. Estimates generated using the second set of questionnaires, with both the 30-day and the 365-day recall periods, meanwhile, are referred to as mixed recall period (MRP) estimates.

9 Growth rates represent compound annual growth rates calculated by the author.
10 This paragraph and the four that follow are based on information provided in Mani (1989, 2000) and Noll and Wallsten (2011).
11 The rest of this section is based on information provided in Noll and Wallsten (2011) and Panagariya (2008: ch 17).
12 Thus, licenses were now given out not for the production of specific products like motorcycles or scooters but for the much broader category of vehicles with two- or three-wheels in general. Producers could now use their installed capacity to switch between the production of motorcycles, scooters, mopeds, and three-wheelers, allowing them greater flexibility (Panagariya 2008: 165).
13 Two points should be noted regarding these statistics on TV channels. First, although many of the 161 pay channels were available nationwide, some of them were broadcast only regionally. Second, the total number of channels (free and pay) registered with the Ministry of Information and Broadcasting was as high 762 as of December 2011. There is, however, no information provided in TRAI 2012 regarding how many of these channels were actually being broadcast
14 All growth rates in this section are compound annual growth rates, calculated by the author using data from the World Development Indicators data set of the World Bank. All data on the number of telephone subscribers (fixe line and mobile) as well as the data on average ownership rate of telephone subscriptions (both fixed line and mobile) in 1990 and 2000 are also from the same source.

References

Balassa, Bela. 1959. *The Hungarian Experience in Economic Planning: A Theoretical and Empirical Study*. New Haven, CT: Yale University Press.

Banerjee, A., and T. Piketty 2005. "Top Indian Incomes, 1922–2000." *World Bank Economic Review* 19 (1): 1–20.

Basole, A. 2014. "Dynamics of Income Inequality in India: Insight for Top World Incomes Database." *Economic and Political Weekly* 49 (40): 14–17.

Bhalla, S. 2003. "Recounting the Poor: Poverty in India, 1983–1999." *Economic and Political Weekly* 37 (4): 338–349.

Bhalla, S. 2011. *Inclusion and Growth in India: Some Facts, Some Conclusions*. Working Paper 39. London: School of Economics Asia Research Center.

Cox, W. Michael, and Richard Alm. 1998. *The Right Stuff: America's Move to Mass Customization*. Annual Report. Dallas: Federal Reserve Bank of Dallas.

Cox, W. Michael, and Richard Alm. 1999. *Myths of Rich and Poor*. New York: Basic Books.

Datt, G., and M. Ravallion. 2002. "Is India's Economic Growth Leaving the Poor Behind?" *Journal of Economic Perspectives*, 16 (3): 89–108.

Deaton, A. 2003. "Prices and Poverty in India, 1987–2000." *Economic and Political Weekly* 37 (4): 362–368.

Deaton, A., and J. Dreze. 2002. "Poverty and Inequality in India: A Re-Examination." *Economic and Political Weekly*: 3729–3748, September 7.

Deaton, A., and V. Kozel. 2005. "Data and Dogma: The Great Indian Poverty Debate." *The World Bank Research Observer* 20 (2): 177–199.

Deaton, A., and A. Tarozzi. 2005. "Prices and Poverty in India." In Angus Deaton and Valerie Kozel, eds., *The Great Indian Poverty Debate*. New Delhi: Macmillan.

George, S., Jha, R., and H. Natarajan. 2002. *The Evolution and Structure of the Two-Wheeler Industry in India*. Working Paper. New Delhi: IGIDR.

Government of India (GOI). 1956. *Industrial Policy Resolution*. New Delhi: Government of India Publications.

Government of India (GOI). 1991. *Industrial Policy Resolution*. New Delhi: Government of India Publications.

Guhathakurta, S. 1994. "Electronics Policy and Television Manufacturing Industry: Lessons from India's Liberalization Efforts." *Economic Development and Cultural Change* 42 (4): 845–868.

Gupta, S. 2006. "Indian Television Industry: A Strategic Analysis." *Vilakshan: XIMB Journal of Management* XX: 195–216.

Hassett, K., and A. Mathur. 2012. *A New Measure of Consumption Inequality*. Washington, DC: American Enterprise Institute.

Himanshu, and K. Sen. 2014. *Revisiting the Great Indian Poverty Debate: Measurements, Patterns and Determinants*. Working Paper 203. Manchester: Brooks World Poverty Institute Working Paper.

Horwitz, S. 2015. "Inequality, Mobility and Being Poor in America." *Social Philosophy and Policy* 31 (2): 70–91.

Joseph, K. J. 1992. "Market Segmentation and Performance of Firms: Case Study of Indian Television Industry in 80s." *Economic and Political Weekly*: 141–148, November 28.

Joseph, K. J. 1997. *Industry Under Economic Liberalization: The Case of Indian Electronics*. London: Sage Publications.

Joseph, K. J. 2012. *Strategic Approach to Strengthening the International Competitiveness in Knowledge Based Industries: Electronics Industry*. Discussion Paper 88. New Delhi: Research and Information System for the Non-Aligned and Other Developing Countries (RIS).

Krueger, Anne. 1975. *The Benefits and Costs of Import Substitution in India: A Microeconomic Study*. Minneapolis: University of Minnesota Press.

Laurie, J. 2006. *The Changing Face of the Indian Television Industry: 2006*. Hong Kong: The Asia Case Research Center, The University of Hong Kong.

Mani, S. 1989. "Technology Development and Acquisition: Case of Telecom Switching Equipment." *Economic and Political Weekly* 24 (47): 181–191.

Mani, S. 2000. "Deregulation and Reform in India's Telecommunications Industry." In Mutsuhiro Kagami and Masatsugu Tsuji, eds., *Privatization, Deregulation and Economic Efficiency: A Comparative Analysis of Asia, Europe and the Americas*. Cheltenham: Edward Elgar.

Manish, G.P. 2013. "Market Reforms in India and the Quality of Economic Growth." *The Independent Review* 18 (2), Fall.

Manish, G. P. 2014. "Qualitative Aspects of the Indian Growth Spurt of the 1980s." *Review of Austrian Economics* 27 (3): 325–340, September.

Ministry of Communications and Information Technology (MIT). 2005. *Information Technology: Annual Report, 2004–05*. New Delhi: Government of India Publications.

Motiram, S., and V. Vakulabharanam. 2012. "Indian Inequality: Patterns and Changes, 1993–2010." In M. Dev, ed., *India Development Report*. New Delhi: Oxford University Press.

National Resource Center for Cluster Development (NRCD). 2005. *Diagnostic Study Report of Fan Industry Cluster in Hyderabad*. New Delhi: National Industry of Small Industry Extension Training.

National Sample Survey Organization (NSSO). 1997. *Use of Durable Goods by Indian Households: NSS 50th Round, 1993–94*. Report No. 426. New Delhi: Department of Statistics, Ministry of Statistics and Program Implementation, Government of India.

National Sample Survey Organization (NSSO). 2012. *Household Consumption of Various Goods and Services: NSS 66th Round, 2009–10*. Report No. 541. New Delhi: Department of Statistics, Ministry of Statistics and Program Implementation, Government of India.

Noll, R., and S. Wallsten. 2011. *An Assessment of Indian Telecommunications Reform*. Working Paper 434. Stanford: Stanford Center for International Development.

Nutter, G. Warren. 1962. *The Growth of Industrial Production in the Soviet Union*. Princeton, NJ: Princeton University Press.

Pal, P., and J. Ghosh. 2007. *Inequality in India: A Survey of Recent Trends*. Working Paper 45. Washington, DC: Department of Economic and Social Affairs, United Nations.

Panagariya, A. 2008. *India: The Emerging Giant*. New York: Oxford University Press.

Panagariya, A., and M. Mukim. 2013. *A Comprehensive Analysis of Poverty in India*. Policy Research Working Paper 6714. Washington, DC: The World Bank.

Ray, S., and J. Makkar. 2012. *Indian Two Wheeler Industry*. New Delhi: ICRA Limited.

Rector, R., and R. Sheffield. 2011. *Air Conditioning, Cable TV and an Xbox: What Is Poverty in the United States Today?* Backgrounder No. 2575. Washington, DC: The Heritage Foundation.

Reeves, G. 1994. *Indian Television: The State, Privatization and the Struggle for Media Autonomy*. Perth: Center for Asian Communication, Media Studies and Cultural Studies, Edith Cowan University.

Rodrik, D., and A. Subramaniam. 2005. "From 'Hindu Growth' to Productivity Surge: The Mystery of the Indian Growth Transition." *IMF Staff Papers* 52 (2): 193–228.

Sen, A., and Himanshu. 2004. "Poverty and Inequality in India: Getting Closer to the Truth." *Economic and Political Weekly* 39 (38): 4247–4263.

Singh, D., Barve, A., and G. Sant. 2010. *Ceiling Fan: The Overlooked Appliance in Energy Efficiency Discussions*. Working Paper. Pune: Prayas Energy Group.

Telecom Regulatory Authority of India (TRAI). 2012a. *The Indian Telecom Services Performance Indicators, July to September 2011*. New Delhi: Government of India Publications.

Telecom Regulatory Authority of India (TRAI). 2012b. *Telecom Sector in India: A Decadal Profile*. Report Prepared by the National Council of Applied Economic Research. New Delhi: Government of India Publications.

Tiwari, R., Herstatt, C., and M. Ranawat. 2011. *Benevolent Benefactor or Insensitive Regulator? Tracing the Role of Government Policies in the Development of India's Automobile Industry*. Policy Study 58. Honolulu: East West Center.

9 The economic history of taxation and inequality in the United States

Phillip W. Magness

I. Introduction: a causal claim

In recent decades, the study of inequality in the United States has been defined by strong claims about historical patterns in the distribution of income and wealth. The most prominent example presents a U-curve narrative (UCN) spanning the 20th century, in which persistent high inequality in the late Gilded Age gives way to a mid-century leveling, followed by a sharp rebound after 1980. This inequality U is fundamentally empirical in nature, with its shape emerging from attempts to measure the top distributional shares of income and wealth holdings over the last century. Its uses are simultaneously theoretical and prescriptive. Proponents of the UCN diagnose the causes of changing inequality over time and link them not only to historical events but also to specific tax policies. Based on this diagnosis of the causes of the inequality U, they turn next to fiscal policy and recommend tax increases to alleviate the depicted rebound of income and wealth concentrations over the past 40 years as well as a host of associated social ills that are said to derive from this pattern (Piketty 2014; Saez and Zucman 2016; Atkinson 2015; Stiglitz 2012).

In some areas of the vast literature on inequality, depictions of the UCN approach the level of a stylized fact of American economic history (Krugman 2014a, 2014b). As Emmanuel Saez and Gabriel Zucman (2014) contend, "There is no dispute that income inequality has been on the rise in the US for the past four decades." Presenting this observation as the culmination of "a spectacular U-shaped evolution" over the century, they call upon policymakers to adopt sweeping and highly progressive tax measures aimed at reducing top income and wealth shares to their depicted mid-20th-century levels.

The precedent of historical income tax regimes weighs heavily upon this recommendation, particularly since the mid-century trough of the U-curve coincided with periods of high statutory marginal income tax rates that, at points, exceeded 90% for the top income brackets. In making this assertion, scholars such as Saez and Zucman as well as their frequent collaborator Thomas Piketty (2014) assert a strong causal mechanism that links historical tax policies to their own distributional measurements of wealth and income. Their tax recommendations are thus essentially an attempt to replicate, extend, and improve upon the policies that, according to them, caused the mid-century leveling depicted in their distributional estimates.

In this chapter, I argue that Piketty, Saez, and Zucman's prescriptive tax proposals are built upon a serious misreading of the history of income taxation in the United States and the accompanying empirical products of its operation. While these authors have made significant contributions to the measurement of inequality over time, their findings are limited by both a highly imperfect source of data and the ensuing uncertainties about what the U-curve actually captures. I propose an alternative explanation wherein both the Piketty and Saez (2003) income share estimate and the Saez and Zucman (2016) wealth share estimate are shown to be highly sensitive to historical modifications to the federal tax code. Thus, we cannot rule out the possibility that the results of tax-derived distributional estimates simply depict the tax code's effects upon tax incidence and tax eligibility, as opposed to actual distributional outcomes.

As an alternative explanation to the causal claims of the UCN, I investigate the possibility that the most prominent features of the depicted U-curve are simply statistical relics of changes to federal income tax liability and the overall federal tax base as distinct from their actual effects upon income or wealth. This distinction is important for the measurement debate, because taxpayers alter their reporting behavior in direct response to the incentives and structures of the tax code with the purpose of minimizing their overall tax burdens. Reported income is therefore itself dependent upon how the tax code classifies and assesses its burdens, and it may be expected to shift in response to both legal avoidance and illegal evasion strategies.

While these findings do not necessarily negate the existence of historical changes in top distributional shares or even rising inequality in recent years, they severely undermine the claimed causal link between high progressive taxation and inequality reduction. One immediate implication of this finding is that it may help to explain the divergence between the income tax-derived estimates of Piketty, Saez, and Zucman and those based on alternative wealth estimation techniques (e.g., surveys) in recent years, the latter being less responsive to changes in tax incidence. The findings presented here also introduce substantial ambiguity into our understanding of the measurement of wealth and income distributions, suggesting a need for greater caution when using historical claims about inequality to justify policy responses.

II. The Piketty prescription

The clearest empirical depictions of the century-long UCN appear in the top income share estimates of Piketty and Saez (2003) and the top wealth share estimates of Saez and Zucman (2016). These two series are derived from a common source in the Internal Revenue Service's annual *Statistics of Income* (SOI) report from 1916 to the present, and supplemented after 1960 with the availability of micro-data files.[1] The income series uses SOI data to estimate distributions directly, while the more recent wealth series builds upon the income series as a foundation while attempting to capitalize from reported income to

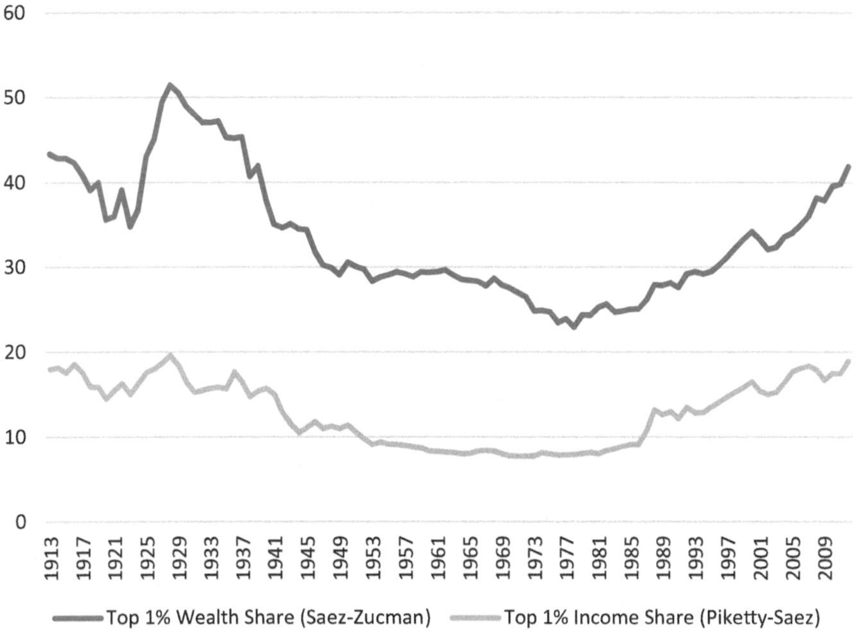

Figure 9.1 Top 1% income and wealth shares, 1913–2013
Sources: Piketty and Saez (2003); Saez and Zucman (2016)

wealth.[2] The corresponding top 1% shares for both series are depicted in Figure 9.1, displaying a U-curve in both cases.

In presenting and explaining these series, their authors attach a strong historical interpretation that causally links the observed shape of the U to a combination of global events and tax policies. Briefly summarized, the outset of the 20th century corresponds to a period of high inequality that persists, with modest fluctuation, until the late 1920s. While the Great Depression initiates a leveling of top income and wealth shares, the largest drop occurs during World War II. Scholars differ somewhat in what they emphasize as the leveling mechanism at play, settling upon some combination of effects from the Depression, war, and fiscal policy. Piketty, Saez, and Zucman, in particular, attribute the post-leveling trough between World War II and the 1980s to that period's highly progressive tax system. After 1980, they enlist tax cuts to explain the depicted inequality rise now that the claimed leveling mechanism from the mid-century is removed.

Piketty (2017) offers a standard synopsis of this claim, applied generally to Western countries:

> The central role of politics and the changing representations of the economy is particularly evident when studying the evolution of the distribution of income and wealth throughout the twentieth century. The reduction of

> inequality observed in Western countries between the 1900s–1910s and the 1950s–1960s is largely explained by the wars and revolutions that marked this period, as well as by the new social and institutional compromise that emerged following such upheaval. Similarly, the rise in inequality observed since the 1970s–1980s owes much to the political and institutional reversal of recent decades, notably in fiscal and financial matters.

The case of the United States is subject to a further caveat as it largely spared the physical destruction of the two world wars, although Piketty also attributes the decline in the first half of the U to the effects of the Depression.[3] The "social and institutional compromise" he refers to in this excerpt is the advent of high confiscatory income tax rates upon the wealthiest earners – a practice he further dubs "an American invention" and credits as something of a precedent behind his own preferred global wealth tax proposal (Piketty 2014: 505).

Income taxes assume the role of a primary causal mechanism behind reducing inequality in Piketty's depiction (or at least the primary policy tool, as economic disasters and warfare are still held to exert similar effects). Piketty (2014) directly credits the decline in top income shares from their late 1920s peak to the moment "[Franklin] Roosevelt came to power in 1933" and shepherded through a "sharp increase in the top income tax rate, which had been decreased to 25% in the late 1920s and again under [Herbert] Hoover's disastrous presidency" (p. 507). The upswing in the second half of the U is similarly credited to income tax policy, beginning with Ronald Reagan's reductions of top federal income tax rates in the early 1980s. Per Piketty's assessment, "the size of the decrease in the top marginal income tax rate between 1980 and the present is closely related to the size of the increase in the top centile's share of national income over the same period" (p. 509). Summarizing the role of taxation throughout, Piketty similarly attributes the downswing and trough of the U between roughly 1932 and 1980 to a period when "the top federal income tax rate in the United States averaged 81 percent" (p. 507). Even as a casual historical depiction, there is much to take issue with in Piketty's historical account. His attributed dates and political history do not align with the actual tax changes he describes, particularly in the interwar period.[4] As presented though, they attempt an explanation for the UCN displayed in Piketty and Saez's empirical results.

A postulated causal link between progressive taxation and inequality reduction is a recurring feature of other works pointing toward a century-long distributional U-curve. While conceding that they could not prove this relationship from their time series alone beyond informal observation, Piketty and Saez (2003: 3) speculated that top income shares never recovered from the pre-Depression peak "because of the dynamic effects of progressive taxation on capital accumulation and wealth inequality." Saez extends this argument in a further investigation of wealth dynamics with Wojciech Kopczuk (2004: 447), offering the tentative claim "that steep progressive income and estate taxation, by reducing the rate of wealth accumulation of the rich, may have been the most important factor preventing large fortunes to be reconstituted after the shocks of the 1929–1945 period."

Recent works by some of the same authors have pressed this causal claim with greater force, shedding the cautious qualifications of their earlier articles. As Saez and Zucman (2016: 544) now assert, "The most likely explanation [for the mid-century inequality trough] is the drastic policy changes of the New Deal. The development of progressive income and estate taxation made it difficult to accumulate and pass on large fortunes." An accompanying policy brief advanced this claim even more aggressively, touting taxes as "key tools that reduced the concentration of wealth after the Great Depression." "The same proven tools are needed again today," they conclude (Saez and Zucman 2014). Piketty (2014: 495) concurs, crediting progressive taxation for holding down the concentration of wealth in the United States after World War II. A purported "spectacular decrease in the progressivity of the income tax in the United States," he continues, "probably explains much of the increase in the very highest earned incomes." This observation leads him to espouse a return to high levels of taxation "not to raise additional revenue" but to "put an end to such incomes and large estates, which lawmakers have for one reason or another come to regard as socially unacceptable and economically unproductive."

A recent assessment by Heather Boushey, Bradford DeLong, and Marshall Steinbaum (2017) even assigns a name to this claimed causal relationship in the last century, dubbing the UCN's trough the "Social Democratic Age." Summarizing Piketty's work in *Capital in the 21st Century*, they attribute this pattern to a series of allegedly "egalitarian" economic policies between 1945 and 1980, foremost among them being high progressive tax rates. Pointing to the reversal of these policies, they raise the possibility that "we are being driven into a second Gilded Age." Krugman (2014a, 2014b) offers a similar assessment, endorsing the effectiveness of progressive taxation as an inequality ameliorating tool and deriding skeptics of these same policies as "inequality deniers."

Although these assessments are by no means universal, they represent a strong and growing belief in two concurrent claims: (1) inequality is on the rise and (2) this rise is directly attributable to a post-1980 retreat away from high progressive taxation. Both claims are empirical in nature, although as we shall see that elements of each are also difficult to reliably measure. They nonetheless warrant detailed consideration in conjunction with their respective implications for a historical interpretation of the income tax.

III. Revisiting 20th-century income tax history

Before assessing the empirical validity of the arguments made by Piketty, Saez, Zucman, and others, I will propose an alternative interpretation of the history of income taxation in the United States over the period that coincides with the UCN. As per Geoffrey Brennan and James Buchanan (1980), a tax system may be assessed by two distinctive features of its constitutional design and implementation. The first consideration is the tax rate a government imposes, encompassing the realized level of a tax assessment upon a given activity or source of earnings. The second consideration is the tax base, entailing the scope of the assessment's reach upon the populace or its tax-eligible portions. The mechanisms governing both the rates and the federal tax base were constitutionally expanded in the United States by the adoption of the income tax amendment in 1913. Subsequent modifications have followed in the form of statutory changes to the tax code.

Few historians have explored these implications in depth in relation to inequality, but the periods of claimed leveling and rebound in the UCN also directly coincide with substantial modifications to the federal tax rate and tax base. Broadly considered, World War II marked a turning point between income tax regimes with very different features, affecting both aspects of Brennan and Buchanan's conceptual model. It helps to view the 20th-century history of the income tax as falling into two distinct phases, assessing the characteristics of the tax base and tax rates in each.

During the first phase, lasting from 1913 to roughly 1940, the federal income tax was narrowly assessed on an intentionally small tax base of income earners who sat almost exclusively in the upper ranges of the income earnings distribution. In some years, less than 10% of U.S. households were even eligible for income taxation. Tax rates in this period included two distinct bouts with high marginal rates on the wealthiest earners. The top marginal rate exceeded 70% during World War I and was raised again to this level in a series of steps involving both Hoover and Roosevelt during the Great Depression, although an extended reduction to 25% in the mid-1920s counterbalanced this pattern. Congress modified the tax schedule over a dozen times in this first phase, including instances that introduced double digit rate changes in a single year. Table 9.1 depicts the major tax legislation from 1913 to 1943 (the year that legislation mandating automatic payroll deduction was adopted), along with the minimum eligibility brackets as well as the top marginal tax rate.

Lax and inconsistent enforcement in this period also led to recurring issues of tax evasion and avoidance, and a number of eligible deductions as well as low audit risk almost certainly reduced or eliminated tax liabilities for the vast majority of households at the lower end of the income ladder. Taken together, the initial phase of income taxation imposed a rate structure that was often, though not exclusively, steeply progressive. The more pronounced feature of this system, though, was its application to a very narrow tax base consisting of very few persons outside of the country's highest income decile.

The revenue measures of World War II transformed the original income tax regime almost overnight, initiating the second phase of mass income taxation that began in 1941 and persists to the present day. Executing one of the largest tax base expansions in history, a succession of wartime revenue measures pushed the tax eligibility threshold downward to include the majority of U.S. households at a low and simple but also more vigorously enforced rate structure. The base expansion further included the introduction of automatic

Table 9.1 Timeline of tax legislation and rates, 1913–1943

Year	*Tax Statute*	*Personal Exemption (Single Filer)*	*Top Bracket*	*Top Marginal Rate (%)*	*% of Tax Units Required to File Federal Returns*
1913	Underwood Act (1st Income Tax)	$3,000	$500,000	7	0.95
1914		$3,000	$500,000	7	0.93
1915		$3,000	$500,000	7	0.86
1916	Revenue Act of 1916	$3,000	$2,000,000	15	1.10
1917	War Revenue Act	$3,000	$2,000,000	67	8.60
1918	Revenue Act of 1918	$1,000	$1,000,000	77	10.94
1919		$1,000	$1,000,000	73	12.99
1920		$1,000	$1,000,000	73	17.32
1921	Revenue Act of 1921	$1,000	$1,000,000	73	15.55
1922		$1,000	$200,000	58	15.59
1923		$1,000	$200,000	58	17.33
1924	Mellon Act	$1,000	$500,000	46	16.24
1925		$1,500	$100,000	25	9.03
1926	Revenue Act of 1926	$1,500	$100,000	25	8.82
1927		$1,500	$100,000	25	8.60
1928		$1,500	$100,000	25	8.40
1929		$1,500	$100,000	25	8.24
1930		$1,500	$100,000	25	7.45
1931		$1,500	$100,000	25	6.39
1932	Revenue Act of 1932	$1,000	$1,000,000	63	7.58
1933		$1,000	$1,000,000	63	7.20
1934	Revenue Act of 1934	$1,000	$1,000,000	63	7.81
1935	Revenue Act of 1935	$1,000	$5,000,000	79	8.61
1936	Revenue Act of 1936	$1,000	$5,000,000	79	10.05
1937		$1,000	$5,000,000	79	11.64
1938		$1,000	$5,000,000	79	11.21
1939		$1,000	$5,000,000	79	13.59
1940	Revenue Act of 1940	$800	$5,000,000	79	25.68
1941	Revenue Act of 1941	$750	$5,000,000	81	45.05
1942	Revenue Act of 1942	$500	$200,000	88	63.28
1943	Current Tax Payment Act	$500	$200,000	88	74.85

Sources: Tax Foundation, Federal Individual Income Tax Rates (1913–2013); Tax unit filing percentages estimated by Piketty and Saez (2003)

payroll withholding after 1943. This practice armed the IRS with an important tool for ensuring tax compliance – particularly at the bottom of the income ladder where earners who sat on or near the eligibility threshold could previously evade their tax obligations due to a low risk of audit. These features have been retained and expanded upon in the modern income tax system, which remains a broadly applicable institution with nearly universal filing requirements for all income earners.

Tax rates in the post-1941 phase initially preserved the highly progressive New Deal era structure for the wealthiest earners, even while the rest of the tax base expanded downward. Successive measures stabilized this schedule and tended to favor modest adjustments from the status quo over the rapid rate fluctuations seen in the 1910s, 1920s, and 1930s. Significantly, the Internal Revenue Act of 1954 retained the postwar rate structure as a baseline for the next three decades (subject to rate revisions), although it also expanded and standardized deductions. The United States entered the postwar period by retaining multiple elements of a wartime schedule in which the top marginal rate exceeded 90% on the highest income earners. Successive measures reduced this statutory rate, with a significant tax cut in 1964 and further cuts in the Reagan era. Congress increased top rates again in 1993, and the two decades since have produced modest rate fluctuations owing to successive fiscal stimulus measures. The top statutory rate sits at 37% on the highest earning bracket as of 2019. Progressivity has remained a consistent feature of this system throughout, although with variation in its application and severity. Table 9.2 depicts the revenue measures from the end of World War II through 2000, along with accompanying rates and tax base statistics.

Table 9.2 Timeline of tax legislation and rates, 1944–2000

Year	*Tax Statute*	*Personal Exemption (Single Filer)*	*Top Bracket*	*Top Marginal Rate (%)*	*% of Tax Units Required to File Federal Returns*
1944	Individual Income Tax Act of 1944	$500	$200,000	94	79.99
1945	Revenue Act of 1945	$500	$200,000	94	84.64
1946		$500	$200,000	91	89.07
1947		$500	$200,000	91	91.65
1948	Revenue Act of 1948	$600	$200,000	91	85.61
1949		$600	$200,000	91	84.20
1950	Revenue Act of 1950	$600	$200,000	91	84.97
1951	Revenue Act of 1951	$600	$200,000	91	87.93
1952		$600	$200,000	92	88.76
1953		$600	$200,000	92	89.99
1954	Internal Revenue Act of 1954	$600	$200,000	91	87.40
1955		$600	$200,000	91	88.81
1956		$600	$200,000	91	89.34
1957		$600	$200,000	91	89.36
1958		$600	$200,000	91	87.47
1959		$600	$200,000	91	88.45
1960		$600	$200,000	91	88.86
1961		$600	$200,000	91	87.86
1962		$600	$200,000	91	88.01
1963		$600	$200,000	91	88.24
1964	Tax Reduction Act (Kennedy Act)	$600	$200,000	77	88.75
1965		$600	$100,000	70	90.40
1966		$600	$100,000	70	92.52

Year	*Tax Statute*	*Personal Exemption (Single Filer)*	*Top Bracket*	*Top Marginal Rate (%)*	*% of Tax Units Required to File Federal Returns*
1967		$600	$100,000	70	93.23
1968		$600	$100,000	70	94.74
1969		$600	$100,000	70	96.24
1970		$625	$100,000	70	92.94
1971		$675	$100,000	70	91.11
1972		$750	$100,000	70	92.71
1973		$750	$100,000	70	94.44
1974		$750	$100,000	70	95.54
1975		$750	$100,000	70	92.26
1976		$750	$100,000	70	92.99
1977		$750	$102,200	70	93.08
1978		$750	$102,200	70	94.28
1979		$1,000	$102,200	70	95.11
1980		$1,000	$108,300	70	94.26
1981	Kemp–Roth Act	$1,000	$108,300	70	94.05
1982		$1,000	$41,500	50	92.34
1983		$1,000	$55,300	50	91.68
1984		$1,000	$81,800	50	93.05
1985		$1,040	$85,130	50	93.49
1986	Tax Reform Act of 1986	$1,080	$88,270	50	93.10
1987		$1,900	$54,000	38.5	94.99
1988		$1,950	$17,850	28	95.68
1989		$2,000	$18,550	28	96.04
1990	OBRA 1991	$2,050	$19,450	28	95.52
1991		$2,150	$49,300	31	95.25
1992		$2,300	$51,900	31	93.16
1993	OBRA 1993	$2,350	$250,000	39.6	92.89
1994		$2,450	$250,000	39.6	92.97
1995		$2,500	$256,500	39.6	93.81
1996		$2,550	$263,750	39.6	94.30
1997		$2,650	$271,050	39.6	94.68
1998		$2,700	$278,450	39.6	95.29
1999		$2,750	$283,150	39.6	96.07
2000		$2,800	$288,350	39.6	96.77

Sources: Tax Foundation, Federal Individual Income Tax Rates (1913–2013); Tax filing household percentages estimated by Piketty and Saez (2003)

When contextualized historically against the income tax system's operation and examined empirically, the UCN's presumptive link between tax rates and levels of inequality runs into several complications. The first stems from a pronounced divergence between the top statutory marginal rate – emphasized as the causal mechanism by Piketty (2014: Figure 14.1) – with the average tax rate that was actually paid by top earners, beginning at the tail of World War II. Note that top marginal rates here are used as a proxy for the overall height of the tax schedule, but also reflect the extreme statutory progressivity that also existed at the mid-century mark. A single filer in the million dollar bracket would face a top marginal rate of 91% on all income above $200,000. The relatively low thresholds of this period (for example, the 50% marginal rate for this same earner kicked in at $18,000) meant that the hypothetical millionaire's overall statutory tax rate exceeded 80% of his or her income – barring any deductions to reduce that burden.

Yet deductions and other legal tax shelter devices were extremely generous at the mid-century mark, and intentionally so to incentivize charitable giving, investment in municipal bonds, certain property and real estate investments, and numerous other categories of income use with preferential tax treatment under law. By taking advantage of legal loopholes and tax-planning, the same millionaire in 1960 actually paid an effective overall tax rate of just above 40%. The conspicuous generosity of the mid-century tax code's loopholes created a large divergence between the top marginal rates on the statute books and the actual tax obligations of persons theoretically subject to those rates.

This divergence is unique to the mid-century period. It is depicted for the highest income brackets in Figure 9.2 and persists until the tax reforms of the 1980s eliminated a number of loopholes and exemptions for the highest earners, returning the two measures to the closer trajectories experienced before World War II. While top statutory rates in the mid-century period consistently averaged over 81% as Piketty is keen to emphasize, the actual effective tax rate was consistently much lower during this frequently idealized "Social Democratic Age." The average year's effective tax rate on million-dollar earners across the 1945–1980 period, or the depicted trough of the UCN, was only 49.6% by comparison – certainly higher than today, but much less so than that the statutory rate suggests and also much lower than the average "sticker price" tax rate such earners would have paid without the benefit of generous legal loopholes. These patterns suggest that Piketty et al. have misdiagnosed the mid-century tax regime's actual burdens, substantially overstating its mid-century progressivity and thus exaggerating its causal role in the claimed inequality leveling.

As with the pronounced divergence between statutory and effective tax rates, proponents of the UCN have largely missed the effects of World War II tax base expansion upon tax eligible households. Far from functioning as a leveling mechanism operating through the top of the distribution alone, the mid-century tax regime severely penalized households in the lowest income brackets. The postwar rates and ramped-up enforcement dramatically *increased* the federal tax burden upon large swaths of people who previously paid little or no income tax. Furthermore, they did so at a time when realized tax burdens upon the wealthiest earners were actually declining slightly in relation to other tax brackets due to the workings of the effective, as opposed to statutory, rate.

A glimpse of these effects may be seen in Figure 9.3, which displays a shift in the focal point of income tax liabilities directly coinciding with the UCN's mid-century trough. This pattern may be seen in the overall income tax liability paid by the top 1% and top 10% of eligible tax filers. During the interwar period lasting until 1941, the top 1% of tax filers consistently paid over 70% of federal income tax revenues. With the tax base expansions of World War II, the tax liability shifted downward such that the top 1% of filers paid only 20%

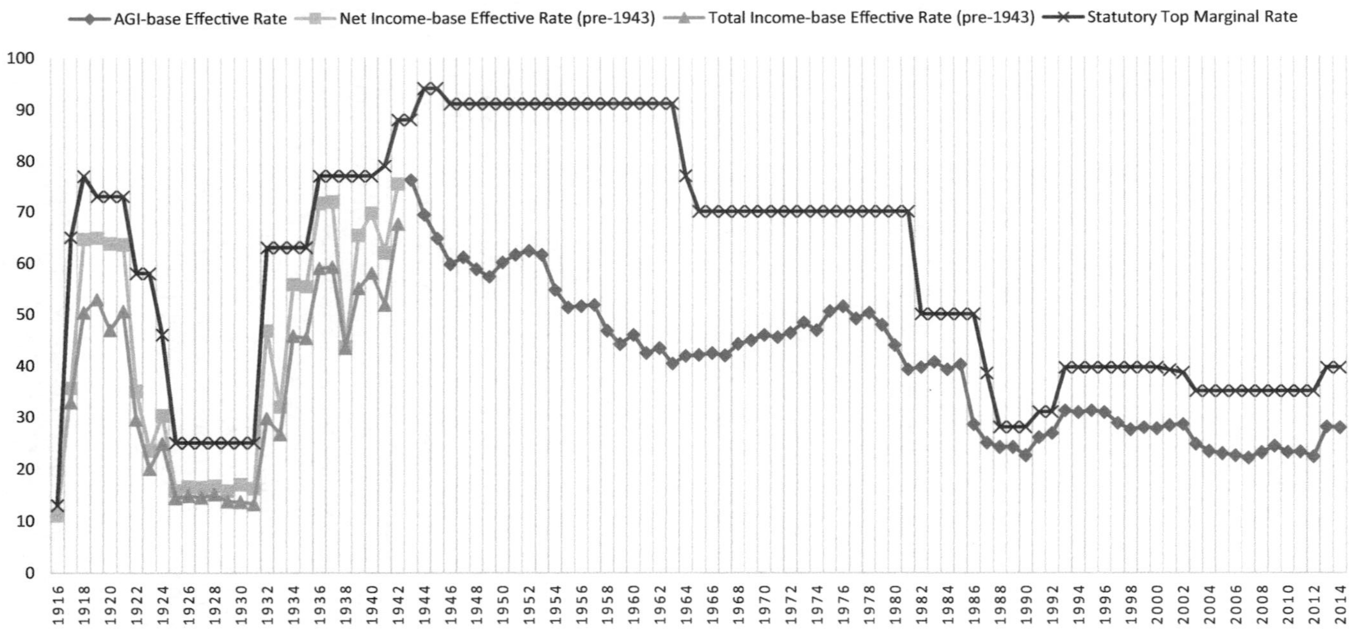

Figure 9.2 Statutory versus effective tax rate on >$1 million income bracket

Sources: Internal Revenue Service 1916–2012. Effective Tax Rate is calculated by taking taxes paid within the designated bracket as a percentage of Adjusted Gross Income (AGI). Effective rates prior to 1943 reflect the IRS's pre-AGI accounting practices and are given here using Net Income and unadjusted Total Income (or gross) as a baseline, and approximate the boundaries in which an AGI-based effective rate would have fallen. Statutory tax brackets are held constant using the million dollar level in this series, as IRS tax brackets were not indexed to inflation until the last two decades of the 20th century.

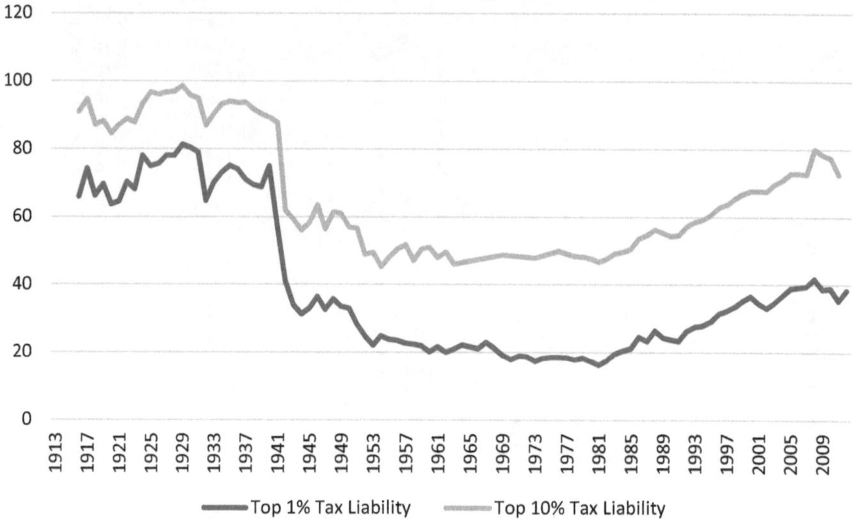

Figure 9.3 Federal income tax liability of top filers, 1916–2013

Sources: Percentages reflect top filer tax liability as a share of total tax liability. Top 1% for 1916–1962 and top 10% for 1916–1978 calculated from Statistics of Income. Both the series from 1979 to present as reported by the Congressional Budget Office. Top 1% figures from 1963 to 1978 utilize the top 0.5% estimates by Feenberg and Poterba (1995), as harmonized with both the SOI and CBO series in years of overlap.

of the federal income tax burden by mid-century. Similar patterns may be seen in the tax liability of the top 10% of eligible filers. Thus, both of these metrics reinforce the fact that the proponents of the UCN overstate the extent of the progressivity of the tax system in the post–World War II years. Notably, both metrics also display a pronounced rebound after 1980, further confirming the overall *increase* in income tax progressivity seen in this same period from two Congressional Budget Office indexes (Harris and Sammartino 2007).[5]

It is difficult not to notice that this direct measure of federal income tax incidence shows remarkable similarities to the two inequality U-curves of the Piketty–Saez and Saez–Zucman series for income and wealth. While they are presented as distinctly different metrics, each displays a sharp drop during World War II, a relatively flat mid-century trough, and a rebound after 1980. This similarity is telling as it may resolve a number of methodological questions about the reliability of the main estimates behind the UCN, as will be discussed in further detail below.

IV. Reconciling individual income tax return data with the UCN

On a more general level, the examination of tax base and tax rate considerations illustrates a number of areas where the UCN is inattentive to pertinent

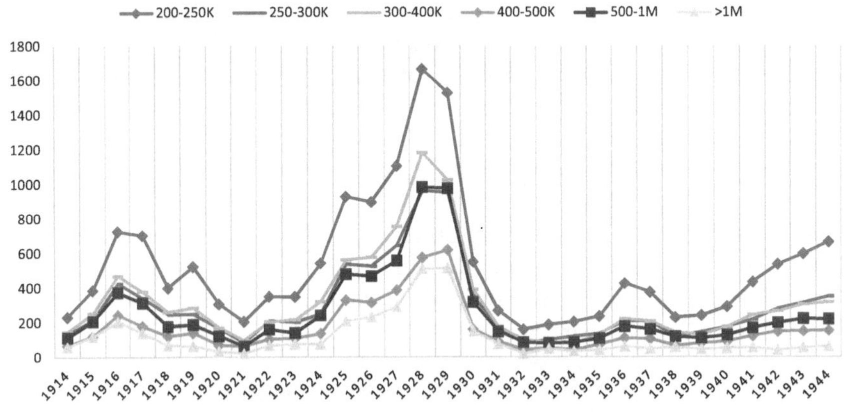

Figure 9.4 Total number of tax returns filed, high-income brackets

Sources: Internal Revenue Service 1916–2012.

details concerning the historical development of income tax regimes, and particularly the effects of policy changes upon the quality of the underlying data they generate from tax collection. An illustrative example may be seen in Figure 9.4, which shows the number of tax filers per income bracket among the extreme wealthy end of the income distribution prior to World War II. The number of filers reporting incomes of greater than $200,000 fluctuated wildly in this period, often directly coinciding with changes to top marginal tax rates.

These fluctuations consistently track each other across multiple high-income brackets, suggesting that they cannot be accounted for by the ultra-wealthy simply shifting between brackets from year to year (or, in the slightly longer term, the effects of inflation since the patterns are sustained).[6] Rather, the number of recorded "millionaires" tends to rise and decline directly with the tax code in this period. For example, the number of million-dollar filers skyrocketed from 75 to 207 in 1924–1925, and again from 290 to 511 in 1927–1928, before evaporating at the onset of the Great Depression. The appearance of high-end tax filers tends to correspond inversely with top-end tax rate changes, such as the war finance hikes of 1917 and 1918, the Mellon tax cuts of 1921 and 1924, and the Depression era tax hikes of both Hoover and Roosevelt (see Table 9.1). While income swings of this type are, to some degree, the products of corresponding business cycle events, their sheer size and frequency also suggests an acute responsiveness to tax policy changes.

Neither are these changes a likely effect of taxation ameliorating inequality, as both appearance and disappearance of ultra-wealthy earners are almost instantaneous in each swing. Put differently, the wealthiest earners in this era appear to have been adept at successfully shifting their incomes to legally avoid extreme progressivity in the tax code's highest rates over short periods of time. These strategies effectively obscure their true income levels and derivative wealth from the data that may be reliably gleaned from income tax records.

In periods of lower rates – especially 1925–1931 when the top marginal rate was 25% – the wealthiest earners appear to have been more likely to report a closer approximation of their actual earnings as tax-eligible income than in years when high rates penalized this level of earnings and other legal tax devices could mitigate the statutory burden.

This pattern is consistent with a developed literature on tax avoidance in the 1920s by Eugene Smiley and Richard Keehn (1995) and notably coincides with the predictions of Andrew Mellon (1924) during his term as Secretary of the Treasury. As these authors all observed, high tax rates adopted during World War I inadvertently incentivized the wealthiest earners of the period to shift their earnings into tax-insulated holdings, such as exempt municipal bonds. By lowering top marginal rates in a succession of steps in the 1920s, the federal government actually reduced tax avoidance. Smiley's (2000) extension of this research through 1929 found that adopting an adjustment for shifting tax avoidance patterns had the effect of lowering the levels of inequality depicted for this period in the earlier works of Simon Kuznets (1953). While these findings were available at the time that Piketty and Saez constructed their own groundbreaking estimates for U.S. income inequality in 2003, they were not incorporated into the series they constructed. As a result, the problems highlighted by these findings – especially for the interwar years of the 1920s and 1930s – remain largely unaddressed in the empirical literature.

A related responsiveness to tax code changes may be seen in Figure 9.5, which tracks the number of tax filings in the lowest brackets over time. Here, a very different pattern is apparent for all filing brackets under $5,000. The rapid expansion of the federal tax base after 1940 appears in the visible – indeed

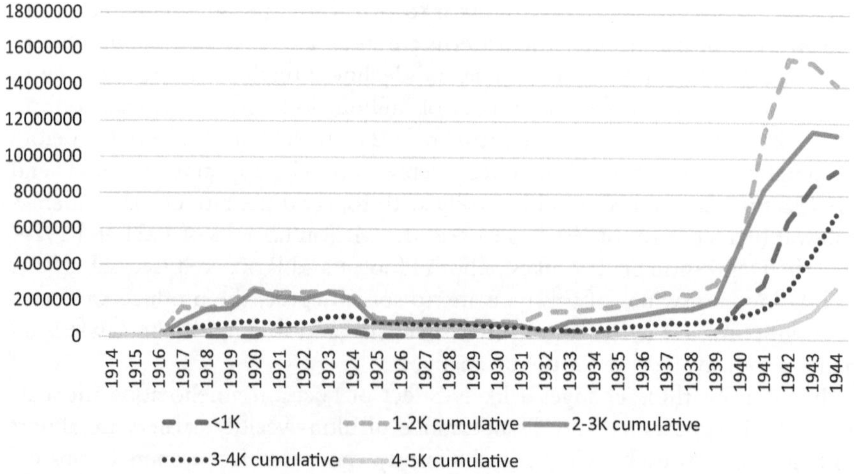

Figure 9.5 Total number of tax returns filed, lower income brackets

Sources: Internal Revenue Service 1916–2012.

astronomical – increase in the number of filers in the lowest income brackets. Between 1940 and 1942 alone, the number of filers in the $1,000–$2,000 bracket tripled – a product of reduced exemption levels and the introduction of the 1040A filing form, intended to expand the federal tax eligibility of lower-income earners. This pattern continued through the introduction of payroll withholding in 1944.

Acknowledging that inflationary considerations can and do affect income levels even as statutory brackets remain fixed by law, the observed growth in lower-to-middle-income filers is consistent across all brackets in this range. Even after crediting the boost to employment that occurred during the war, the instantaneous tripling or quadrupling of the number of filers in these categories suggests an alternative explanation: income earners at or near the minimum tax eligibility threshold were likely underreporting their actual earnings prior to the wartime tax base expansion. After 1940, a combination of increased tax rates, a lower tax eligibility threshold, more aggressive enforcement (including automatic payroll deductions after 1943), and a higher audit risk dramatically increased tax compliance in these same categories.

A cumulative implication of Figures 9.4 and 9.5 is that distributional estimates derived from income tax data such as the SOI were likely plagued by severe data quality issues prior to World War II, one of which comes from the strategic behavior by taxpayers to lessen their tax liabilities. If the wealthiest earners are able to shift their income streams and assets into various tax shelters (e.g., tax exempt municipal bonds and corporate income, taxed at different rates), then it follows that IRS records in years with high top marginal tax rates will understate the actual realized income earnings of these filers. Specifically, wealthy individuals may be able to shelter some of their income streams during years with high personal income tax rates by shifting them into a multitude of corporate tax structures subject to lower rates. A shift in the opposite direction might be expected if the top individual rates were to drop below applicable corporate rates. Several scholars have noted the potential distortive effects of this problem in both the pre-Depression period (Smiley and Keehn 1995) and in the wake of the Tax Reform Act of 1986 (Reynolds 2007; Auten and Splinter 2017).

A similar and less-discussed problem may also occur at the bottom of the income ladder, particularly in the early 20th century when the tax eligibility threshold was high and annual income earnings were self-reported. If income earners in lower brackets are able to avoid filing due to a combination of exemptions and lax enforcement practices, then it follows that IRS records will fail to capture a large segment of lower income-earning households entirely. Tax enforcement of this type was a recurring problem for the IRS for the first three decades of the income tax's existence.

Both omissions have the statistical effect of augmenting the patterns of the UCN, ceteris paribus. Shifted income among top earners for purposes of tax avoidance would reduce their reported income levels on paper relative to the rest of society, giving the illusion of lower inequality in high-tax years and higher inequality in low-tax years. Missing returns among lower-income earners would remove them from the distributional calculations entirely, giving the illusion of higher inequality at times of lax enforcement or a high minimum tax eligibility threshold.[7] Furthermore, the rapid addition of previously "missing" lower-income earners to the tax base would create the illusion of a pronounced leveling effect, as we see during World War II just as the tax base is expanded.

Each of these factors presents a substantial complication to the posited link between fiscal policy and the "great levelling" of the early 20th century. The severe downward shift in distributional shares between 1941 and 1945 in the Piketty–Saez estimates would appear to be a statistical relic of the drastic changes to the federal tax code in these years, as distinct from an unusually acute reduction of inequality in a very short period of time. This period witnessed a large and almost exclusively downward tax base expansion onto lower income earners, coupled with aggressive reforms to increase tax compliance. As such, a number of earners who underreported or were missing entirely from the prewar tax system suddenly appeared on the tax rolls, inducing a dramatic shift in the amounts and distributional locations of reported income.[8] Holding all else equal and keeping existing top marginal rates in place, a downward tax base expansion through eligibility changes and more aggressive enforcement should unambiguously increase the tax liability of lower income earners relative to the rich.[9]

That the acute 1941–1945 shift is primarily a feature of tax collection, and not changing distributional outcomes itself, is attested in both the observed patterns of filing across income brackets and the near-identical downward shift in federal tax incidence in the same four-year period. These patterns further speak to the overall unreliability of wartime tax data for estimating distributional outcomes during the precise period of the leveling displayed by Piketty and Saez. A more cautious examination of these data might accordingly expect to find a much more gradual and modest leveling pattern beginning with the stock market crash of 1929, and thus preceding the reintroduction of high progressivity to the top marginal tax rate structure.

A somewhat more developed literature applies a similar line of argument to the more recent Tax Reform Act of 1986 (TRA86), suggesting that data-reporting distortions occur due to income-shifting strategies among the wealthy in response to this measure. Alan Reynolds (2007) first raised this line of criticism about Piketty and Saez's distributional estimate, noting that the rate reductions and loophole closures of TRA86 induced wealthier individuals to shift portions of their income streams from corporate to individual returns to take advantage of the new rates. If so, this practice implies that the witnessed rebound of the UCN is also a statistical by-product of the tax code changes. The closing of tax loopholes, more stringent enforcement measures such as documentation for claimed dependents, and tax-shifting responses to the declining difference between personal and corporate income tax rates (Gordon and Slemrod 1998) all suggest extensive tax reporting complications from the 1986 act.

Mechling et al. (2017) adopt a similar line of reasoning but work backward in time from TRA86 to the mid-century trough. If wealthy individuals shifted their income streams to other tax categories in order to avoid extremely high top marginal rates on individual income, it stands to reason that the distributional estimates for the bottom of the U-curve are likely too low for the corresponding years. In either case, the proposed revisions of each have a flattening effect on the overall time series relative to the patterns depicted in the UCN.

Further proposed revisions by Auten and Splinter (2017) expand the definition of income to account for sources not included in individual tax return data, as well as government transfers, with the cumulative effect of substantially reducing the magnitude of the post-1980 inequality rebound depicted in the UCN. These and other recent findings suggest that individual income tax returns, taken alone, provide a highly incomplete picture of income that skews toward the incentive structures of individual income tax reporting.

V. The challenges of measuring wealth inequality

Inequality is difficult to measure, and particularly so over long periods of time. The biggest challenge by far is the paucity of data as most countries simply do not possess sufficient records prior to the last few decades of the 20th century, if at all. The United States benefits in this regard by having a number of related metrics that permit empirical investigations going back more than a century, but even here the data quality worsens as one moves further back in time. Recognition of this problem is crucial to our historical understanding of inequality, as many of the most significant economic and political events in the UCN account occurred before the advances in data collection and reporting that have taken place between the 1960s and the present.

To better conceptualize the issues at stake, it helps to examine the primary methods and data sources for calculating distributional shares of both income and wealth. Figure 9.6 depicts the top 1% wealth share as measured by three distinct estimation techniques (one of which is displayed in both its raw form and subject to a harmonizing adjustment). Notably, only one of these series depicts an unambiguous U-curve. The strengths and weaknesses of each estimation method will be discussed in detail.

The first approach, and the one that is most supportive of the UCN, is to utilize income tax data from the IRS to derive estimates of top distributional shares. For top income shares, the calculations are done directly using a Pareto interpolation technique developed by Piketty and Saez (2003). The data complications of this approach are numerous due to some of the reasons we have discussed in the overview of federal income tax history. Briefly, tax-derived estimates are only as good as their underlying data source. In the case of income tax returns, there are reasons to believe that historical IRS records are highly sensitive to (1) strategic tax avoidance and evasion behaviors by taxpayers, particularly in response to high rate changes, (2) inconsistent and sometimes lax

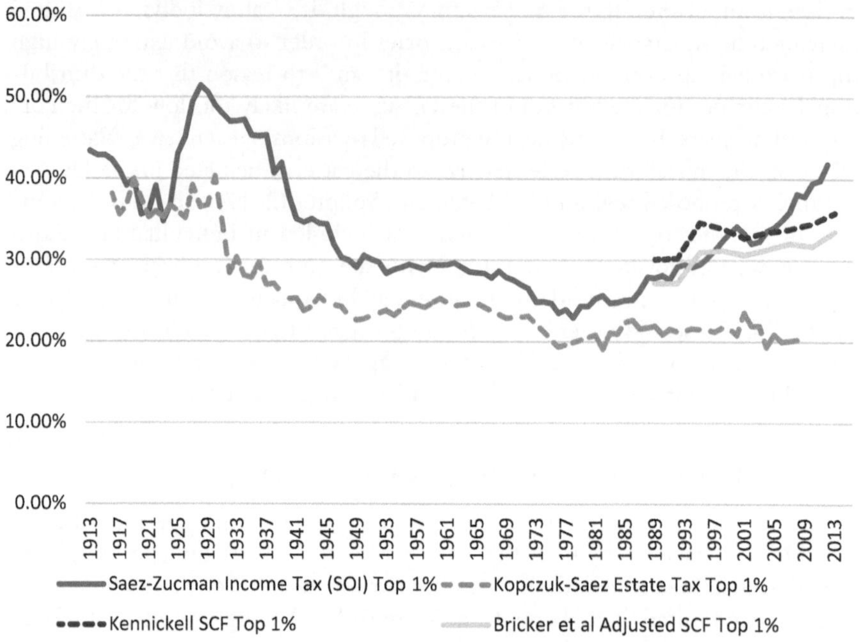

Figure 9.6 Top 1% U.S. wealth share: comparison of measures

Sources: Kopczuk and Saez (2004); Saez and Zucman (2016); Kennickell (2009); Bricker et al. (2016)

enforcement practices, as were common before World War II, (3) administrative features of tax collection such as the introduction of payroll withholding, and (4) changes to the tax base that dramatically altered the number of households that were required to file returns. Nor are these problems a new concern for economists, most of them having been noted by Milton Friedman (Stewart et al. 1939) in response to two early attempts to derive distributional estimates from IRS records. While these and other related problems appear to be quite pronounced at times in U.S. tax return statistics, income tax records form the basis of the Piketty and Saez (2003) income series and are a core building block of the Saez and Zucman (2016) wealth series, which uses capitalization estimates taken from the same data source. Both depict a pronounced U-curve.

A second tax-based estimation technique has proven more suitable for calculating wealth shares, owing to its own functional operation as a snapshot measure of an individual's cumulative wealth holdings. In this approach, estate tax returns are used to estimate the size and overall distribution of estate filings for decedents in a given year. Using population-wide mortality rates as a control, it is possible to calculate an estate tax multiplier that yields a distributional estimate for wealth holdings. This approach is used in the century-long wealth distribution series of Kopczuk and Saez (2004). The estate tax method has certain advantages over income tax data. Specifically, the federal estate tax was historically less prone to legislative tinkering and drastic rate changes in the 20th century than the dozens of modifications and overhauls affecting the income tax system. It is nonetheless sensitive to the mortality rate adjustment, with some debate emerging in recent years about the most appropriate figures to use here (Kopczuk 2015).

A notable feature of the resulting estate tax series is its divergence from the UCN. To be sure, the estate tax series shows a pronounced decline in top wealth shares since the early 20th century. It differs from the UCN in two ways though. First, the most pronounced drop in the estate tax series occurs almost a decade prior to the income tax-derived U-Curve. As noted in the previous section, the income tax series displays a marked decline after 1940, coinciding with the wartime income tax base expansions. The estate tax multiplier shows the largest drop occurring between 1929 and 1932, likely reflecting the Great Depression's devastation of stock and capital asset holdings among the wealthy in those years. By contrast, the estate tax multiplier shows a far more modest pattern between 1941 and 1945, consistent with routine year-to-year fluctuations.

Second and equally notable, the estate tax series shows no evidence of a post-1980 rebound in inequality, and thus the posited rise that constitutes the second half of the U shape. A pronounced divergence actually emerges between the two series in 1986, the year of the tax reform. After this point, the income capitalization series shows a rapid increase in top wealth shares to the present. The estate tax measure remains essentially flat for the same years, outside of a few minor year-to-year fluctuations.

Saez and Zucman (2016) speculate that this divergence derives from a growing mortality gradient between wealthy and nonwealthy persons since the 1980s, thereby skewing the mortality adjustment of the estate tax method and obscuring the inequality upswing. Kopczuk (2014, 2015) notes that the evidence for this skew is weak though and is likely subject to its own data limitations. Saez and Zucman show only a weak magnitude mortality gradient through income tax-derived mortality data – a source that excludes the crucial category of nontaxpaying retirees. More comprehensive mortality measures, such as Social Security records, do not appear to display the hypothesized gradient. Assuming that Kopczuk's (2015: 555) critiques of the mortality gradient issues in Saez and Zucman hold true, the drawbacks of the estate tax approach are still comparatively minor in relation to the extensive underlying data problems with capitalizing wealth from income tax returns.[10] In addition to its aforementioned dependence upon imputation for nontaxable capital assets, the income tax series suffers from several clearly identifiable historical events that altered the data reported therein in fundamental ways. The aforementioned World War II shift chafes with the tax base expansion and rising tax progressivity of those years, though it is entirely consistent with the tax incidence shift depicted in Figure 9.3. Based upon Reynolds' argument and the subsequent empirical work of Mechling et al., the income shifting behavior surrounding

TRA86 appears to be a more likely explanation for the divergence between the estate tax series and the income capitalization series behind the UCN.

In recent years, a number of scholars have turned to a third approach to estimating top distributional shares for wealth and income: survey data. Modern statistical sampling techniques allow the estimation of top distributional shares by surveying the income and assets of a given country's population at large. Several dozen governments around the world have begun administering surveys to this end on a regular basis. The main U.S. series derives from the Federal Reserve's periodic Survey of Consumer Finances (SCF), and is actually something of a methodological leader in survey design for this purpose and is recognized for its high level of accuracy (Vermeulen 2014).

The survey approach has both benefits and drawbacks. Since survey data derive from a source that is independent of the tax system, their results are not sensitive to the potential distortions of tax policy. This includes income-shifting strategies and similar complications that arise from changes to tax rates and tax administration over time. They thus avoid many of the aforementioned problems with the income tax estimation and its derivative capitalization approach for wealth, as well as the uncertainties over the appropriate mortality adjustment for the estate tax multiplier.

Two distinct limitations warrant mention though. First, the survey approach runs into an acknowledged complication with the measurement of incomes and assets on the extreme upper tail of the distribution. The measurement of ultra-wealthy individuals entails both nonrandom sampling and privacy concerns, given that information from the survey could be used to identify a Bill Gates or another high-profile figure with extreme wealth. In order to accurately measure the top tail effects, special steps must be taken in the survey design to account for these issues. In the case of the SCF, privacy restrictions necessitate the exclusion of the extreme upper tail – usually the Forbes 400 list – from the survey's reported results. The survey's designers work around the resulting distortions from this omission by intentionally oversampling earners that fall just outside of the Forbes 400 list, and by sampling families that fall within the Forbes 400 range but do not register individual wealth as per the Forbes ranking (Kennickell 2008). While some inequality studies have attempted to augment the SCF with data from the Forbes list, this practice carries a substantial risk of overcounting top earners due to differences in methodology between the lists and what appears to be an upward bias in the Forbes measurement. Unaddressed, a merger of this type would likely result in an artificial increase of depicted wealth concentration.[11]

The second limitation from the survey approach is a simple matter of available data over time. A consistently administered SCF exists only from 1989 until the present. These results are sometimes augmented by predecessor surveys that the Federal Reserve administered on an ad hoc schedule, though with the substantial caveat that these earlier measures lacked the empirical sophistication of the modern survey's upper tail design. At most, predecessor surveys may be used to imperfectly extend this series to the 1950s or 1960s, depending on the data used. While some attempts at producing a harmonized survey series exist (Wolff 1994; Roine and Waldenström 2013; Kuhn et al. 2017), they extend no further than the mid-century trough, and they require substantial interpolation to account for multiyear data gaps in addition to the aforementioned survey design differences. As a result, survey estimates are of limited value as an external check upon either the estate tax or income tax capitalization estimates prior to 1989. We may nonetheless see the comparative patterns of these extended estimates, along with the estate tax multiplier and the Saez and Zucman (2016) tax data series in Figure 9.7.

This comparison, much like Figure 9.6, further illustrates that a dramatic post-1980 upswing in wealth inequality is apparent only when using the SOI-derived capitalization method. Here, the SCF displays its own gentle increase in top wealth shares that exceeds the essentially flat estate tax multiplier but also falls far short of the pronounced rebound in the income tax capitalization series.

The comparative attempts to measure economic distributions over time do not speak strongly for the UCN in the United States. The U-curve is a distinctive feature of only one of the three main estimation methods – that which uses income tax returns from the IRS's SOI series, either directly in the case of income or as a statistical foundation for capitalizing wealth from the same source. The estate tax multiplier shows an earlier drop in the first part of the 20th century, followed by a stabilization that persists to this day. The SCF

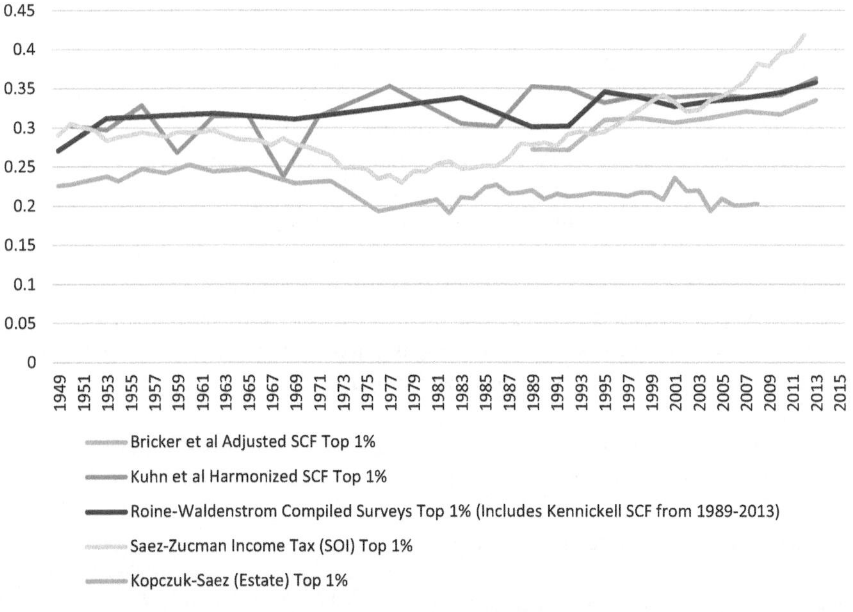

Figure 9.7 Estimates of top 1% wealth share, 1949–2013

shows only a modest increase in recent years that falls short of surging inequality levels and, importantly, is measured independent of tax code changes. In this sense, it is also a more direct measure. Capitalized income after all is a flow used to approximate a measure; it does not attempt to directly measure the stock of wealth as seen in the other methods, and indeed its foundational baseline is contingent upon also accepting the Piketty and Saez (2003) income series in constructing the metric. The comparative stability in the estate and survey methods therefore supports the previous section's suggestion that SOI-derived tax capitalization estimates are primarily capturing a proxy for income tax incidence.

Given the discussion of the preceding section, substantial reasons exist to scrutinize the reliability of income tax data as a source for deriving distributional estimates. Curiously, two of the most problematic periods for income tax data – the tax base expansion of World War II and the tax system overhaul of TRA86 – are also the two main turning points for the U-curve's downswing and later rebound. Taken in sum, these factors provide multiple strong reasons to exercise caution in attributing strong claims of empirical support to the UCN.

VI. Conclusion

The cumulative effect of these historical insights suggests that we should no longer expect a pronounced century-long U-curve for the United States but a substantially flatter pattern – perhaps resembling a tea saucer with much more subdued movements on both ends of the century (Geloso et al. 2019; Auten and Splinter 2017). A flatter century-long trend is still subject to localized peaks and troughs, and likely displays leveling periods of its own, as likely happened between the 1929 crash and the end of the Great Depression. Its overall shape though is probably more consistent with the estate tax series, or perhaps the modestly rising SCF series for recent decades.

The strong correlation between tax liability and the tax-derived distributional series further suggests a circularity to the causal argument behind using income taxes as an inequality-alleviation device. Piketty et al. have essentially constructed an argument where an empirical product of their preferred policy simultaneously justifies its own implementation and validates its own effectiveness when implemented. The implications of this causal claim are effectively unfalsifiable as a result. Piketty (2015: 84) in particular appears not only susceptible but also approving of this condition, writing:

> In my view, one main benefit of a progressive wealth tax is that it would produce better information regarding the size and evolution of different wealth groups such that the wealth tax could be adapted in the future on the basis of this better information.

Progressive taxation thus becomes quite literally the means of proving its own claimed objective. This position is certainly consistent with a particular ideological worldview, as well as an expressed confidence in the efficacy of a particular type of high taxation as a policy tool to shape social outcomes. It is not a particularly convincing historical account, though, and its evidence suffers from a certain preferential credulity for the promised outcome. All considered, the evidence of the UCN as a historical explanation for inequality appears to rest on a tautological assumption about its relation to a specific preferred tax regime.

A more robust historical account likely requires revisiting several fundamental questions of how distributional shares may be measured over time. The three specific techniques discussed here each show elements of promise, but at present the lack of consistent replication of a common pattern through independent metrics remains a substantial drawback. In a more general sense, economists who study inequality would do well to pay closer attention to the complex historical intricacies of tax policy in the 20th century. The extent to which historical tax regime changes alter the reliability of the metrics used to calculate distributional shares has been neglected amidst a zeal to demonstrate the effectiveness of preferred tax policies as tools to shape distributional outcomes.

It may be time to revisit fundamental questions of measurement, including whether distributional outcomes can even be explained by a single cohesive century-long narrative. The nuances of economic history intuitively caution against sweeping theorems of this type. As we have seen from an examination of the evidence behind the UCN, its measurement cannot be reliably differentiated from the statistical relics of tax liability over time. This circumstance warrants extreme caution in assigning any further determinative claim to the efficacy of taxation premised upon the U-curve pattern or its promised amelioration of distributional inequality.

Notes

1 Since 1960, the IRS has released an annual sample of approximately 100,000 individual income tax returns, stripped of individual identifiers and intended for scholarly study. Most estimates of income distributions in the modern era use these files as a supplement to the aggregate SOI reports, as well as a means of verifying the accuracy of SOI-derived distributional estimates.

2 The capitalization technique uses reported capital income from individual tax returns to estimate the present value of a tax unit's capital assets from their expected rate of return over time. When aggregated across all asset classes, this yields a measure of wealth. One limitation of this approach is that it requires the authors to make strong assumptions that affect the measure in aggregate. Asset classes that do not directly generate tax-reported income – a grouping that may encompass as much as two-thirds of all returns to capital – must be imputed instead. Furthermore, capitalization requires the estimator to make assumptions about the expected rate of return on capital assets and to assign that rate across a widely disparate range of asset classes. The estimation challenges presented by this approach are discussed at length in Kopczuk (2014).

3 Somewhat curiously, Piketty's claims about the Depression's effects in the United States are not in evidence in the Piketty and Saez (2003) income series. Piketty's top 10% income share estimate declines by less than 3 percentage points between 1929 and 1940, followed by a sharp and precipitous 10 percentage point drop concentrated entirely during World War II.

4 Specifically, Piketty errs in assigning credit for the 1932 income tax hike to Roosevelt when in fact it was a revenue measure of his predecessor Herbert Hoover. In the same passage, he dates the Mellon tax plan to several years after its actual implementation under the 1921 and 1924 Revenue Acts and imagines a nonexistent top rate reduction during Hoover's term. In further elaborations from the same chapter, he continues to misreport basic historical information about top marginal rates and their corresponding dates and presidencies (Magness and Murphy 2015). The stated 81% average for the UCN trough period is similarly misleading as it only describes the top statutory marginal tax rate and not the realized effective tax rate on top earners, which was consistently much lower. While these and other recurring errors of fact evince a larger unfamiliarity with American tax legislation and its accompanying political history, they remain a prominent feature of Piketty's inequality narrative. Piketty was made aware of these errors in a 2015 correspondence with the author of this chapter. He dismissed the erroneous dates and tax rates as "typos" of little consequence to be corrected in future editions. As of this writing, he has not corrected these errors and has repeated them in subsequent published works.

5 The first CBO measure evaluates progressivity by comparing the Gini indexes of before-tax and after-tax income. The second measure evaluates tax payments by household income shares, ranked by income. Both measures display an increase in overall individual income tax progressivity between 1979 and 2007 (Harris and Sammartino 2007: Figure 19). Both indexes reflect only individual income taxes. The inclusion of separately assessed payroll taxes somewhat counteracts this rise in progressivity for the same years. These data likely reflect the relative positions of the tax burdens on lower and higher income brackets after the post-1980 rate cuts and tax system overhaul. Notably, they also belie the claim by Piketty et al. that individual income tax progressivity has decreased since 1980.

6 The practice of adjusting tax brackets and accompanying standard deductions to account for inflation did not begin until the implementation of tax indexing between 1981 and 1985. Tax bracket statistics prior to this period accordingly reflect current year dollars, although Congress generally retained the characteristics of top bracket levels. An inflation adjustment in these years might accordingly re-rank certain returns near the statutory threshold into a higher or lower bracket; however, at the extreme upper end of the distribution, the general trajectory of filing trends closely aligns across all brackets above $100,000.

7 Piketty and Saez (2003) acknowledge, for example, that reported SOI statistics for some years are insufficient to reach even the top 10% threshold for tax units. They attempt to address this problem by estimating an expanded income filer base using known ratios of married to single tax filers, thereby swelling the bottom end of the top 10% of filers. The necessary guesswork of this step is indicative of both the problem of data quality in prewar years and the number of discretionary adjustments that must be made to reach even a basic distributional estimate.

8 These "missing incomes" almost certainly exceed the modest adjustments that Piketty & Saez (2003) make to their series to account for the high personal exemption threshold in most prewar years. Given their apparent concentration in lower-level tax brackets, they also likely diverge from the universally upward direction of the Piketty–Saez adjustments in the pre–World War II period. One further distortion to prewar income data that has largely escaped attention is the historical treatment of state and local public sector employees, a large number of whom were legally exempt from federal income tax payments prior to 1939 due to an unresolved conflict between constitutional case law on the taxation of states and the enacting statutes of the 1913 income tax system. Although the number of affected persons remains unknown in most years, a 1937 study by the IRS estimated that some 2.6 million state and local government employees accounted for $3.6 billion in untaxed income earnings that were not reflected on federal income

tax rolls. The effect of this unaccounted income is potentially sizable considering that the IRS received 6.3 million tax returns totaling $23 billion in the same year. See *Tax-Exempt Salaries Hearings before the Committee on Ways and Means*. U.S. House of Representatives, Seventy-Sixth Congress, First Session. (Government Printing Office, 1939), p. 26.

9 As an added complication, the combination of more aggressive enforcement and a broader tax base would be expected to induce a diversion of a greater amount of potentially productive resources into accounting and tax planning services.

10 Kopczuk (2014) argues that the estate tax method carries certain advantages over capitalization from income tax data, owing to the large number of assumptions and imputations that must be made for the latter. Saez, in contrast, has moved away from his earlier work on the estate tax approach and currently presents the IRS-derived capitalization series as a more accurate reflection.

11 Saez and Zucman (2016) contend that the Federal Reserve's adjustments are insufficient, and accordingly propose adding the Forbes 400 list into the SCF series to reconcile it with the post-1980 upswing of the UCN. Doing so almost certainly double-counts some individuals though due to different methodologies employed by the two measures. It also introduces an unrealistic assumption about the SCF, namely, that its upper tail issues have gotten systematically worse over time despite improvements to the SCF survey design. This scenario is highly unlikely due to the trajectory of refinements to the SCF methodology, including greater attentiveness to the intricacies of tail sampling in recent years spurred by an awareness of the problem. A further refinement by the SCF survey designers (Bricker et al. 2016) includes their own Forbes 400 adjustment but also an adjustment to account for the effects of defined benefit pension income, which were omitted from both the raw SCF and the proposed modifications of Saez and Zucman. These adjustments largely counteract each other, with the resulting adjusted SCF series still diverging from the Saez–Zucman U-curve after the late 1980s, as well as displaying an overall lower level of inequality and more modest rate of growth. A further reason to doubt the practice of augmenting or "filling in" survey data with the Forbes 400 list may be found in the work of Raub et al. (2010), which illustrates a sustained pattern of overestimation of wealth by the magazine's methodology when compared to estate records of deceased persons who formerly belonged to the list. Anecdotally, numerous examples also attest to Forbes list members intentionally overvaluing their own worth in an attempt to improve their rankings for status reasons, the most famous being Donald Trump. See Jonathan Greenberg, "Trump Lied to Me About His Wealth to Get onto the Forbes 400," *Washington Post,* April 20, 2018.

References

Atkinson, Anthony B. 2015. *Inequality*. Cambridge, MA: Harvard University Press.

Auten, Gerald, and David Splinter. 2017. *Income Inequality in the United States: Using Tax Data to Measure Long-Term Trends*. Mimeo. Washington, DC: US Department of the Treasury, Office of Tax Analysis.

Boushey, Heather, J. Bradford DeLong, and Marshall Steinbaum, eds. 2017. *After Piketty: The Agenda for Economics and Inequality*. Cambridge, MA: Harvard University Press.

Brennan, Geoffrey, and James M. Buchanan. 1980. *The Power to Tax: Analytic Foundations of a Fiscal Constitution*. Cambridge: Cambridge University Press.

Bricker, Jesse, et al. 2016. "Measuring Income and Wealth at the Top Using Administrative and Survey Data." *Brookings Papers on Economic Activity* 2016 (1): 261–331.

Feenberg, Daniel R., and James M. Poterba. 2000. "The Income and Tax Share of Very High-Income Households, 1960–1995." *The American Economic Review* 90 (2): 264–270.

Geloso, Vincent, Magness, Phillip, Moore, John, and Philip Schlosser. 2019. "How Pronounced Is the U-Curve? Revisiting Income Inequality in the United States, 1917–60." Working Paper. SSRN. Available at https://ssrn.com/abstract=2985234

Gordon, Roger H., and Joel Slemrod. 1998. *Are 'Real' Responses to Taxes Simply Income Shifting Between Corporate and Personal Tax Bases?* Working Paper No. w6576. Cambridge: National Bureau of Economic Research.

Harris, Edward, and Frank Sammartino. 2011. *Trends in the Distribution of Household Income Between 1979 and 2007*. Washington, DC: Congressional Budget Office.

Internal Revenue Service. 1916–2012. *Statistics of Income*. Annual Reports. Washington, DC: Government Printing Office.

Kennickell, Arthur B. 2008. "The Role of Over-Sampling of the Wealthy in the Survey of Consumer Finances." *Irving Fisher Committee Bulletin* 28: 403–408.

Kennickell, Arthur B. 2009. *Ponds and Streams: Wealth and Income in the US, 1989 to 2007*. Washington, DC: Divisions of Research & Statistics and Monetary Affairs, Federal Reserve Board.

Kopczuk, Wojciech. 2014. "Recent Evolution of Income and Wealth Inequality: Comments on Piketty's Capital in the Twenty-First Century." *Tax Law Review* 68: 545.

Kopczuk, Wojciech. 2015. "What Do We Know About the Evolution of Top Wealth Shares in the United States?." *The Journal of Economic Perspectives* 29 (1): 47–66.

Kopczuk, Wojciech, and Emmanuel Saez. 2004. *Top Wealth Shares in the United States: 1916–2000: Evidence from Estate Tax Returns*. No. w10399. National Bureau of Economic Research.

Krugman, Paul. 2014a. "The Piketty Panic." *New York Times*, April 25.

Krugman, Paul. 2014b. "On Inequality Denial." *New York Times*, June 1.

Kuhn, Moritz, Schularick, Moritz, and Ulrike I. Steins. 2017. *Income and Wealth Inequality in America, 1949–2013*. London: Centre for Economic Policy Research.

Kuznets, Simon. 1953. *Shares of Upper Income Groups in Income and Savings*. Washington, DC: National Bureau of Economic Research.

Magness, Phillip W., and Robert P. Murphy. 2015. "Challenging the Empirical Contribution of Thomas Piketty's Capital in the Twenty-First Century." *Journal of Private Enterprise* 30 (1).

Mechling, George, Stephen Miller, and Ron Konecny. 2017. "Do Piketty and Saez Misstate Income Inequality? Critiquing the Critiques." *Review of Political Economy* 29 (1): 30–46.

Mellon, Andrew W. 1924. *Taxation: The People's Business*. New York: Macmillan.

Piketty, Thomas. 2014. *Capital in Twenty-First Century*. Cambridge, MA: Harvard University Press.

Piketty, Thomas. 2015. "Putting Distribution Back at the Center of Economics: Reflections on Capital in the Twenty-First Century." *The Journal of Economic Perspectives* 29 (1): 67–88.

Piketty, Thomas. 2017. "Toward a Reconciliation Between Economics and the Social Sciences." In H. Boushey, et al., eds., *After Piketty: The Agenda for Economics and Inequality*. Cambridge, MA: Harvard University Press.

Piketty, Thomas, and Emmanuel Saez. 2003. "Income Inequality in the United States, 1913–1998." *The Quarterly Journal of Economics* 118 (1): 1–41.

Raub, Brian, Johnson, Barry, and Joseph Newcomb. 2010. "A Comparison of Wealth Estimates for America's Wealthiest Decedents Using Tax Data and Data from the Forbes 400." National Tax Association Proceedings, 103rd Annual Conference on Taxation.

Reynolds, Alan. 2007. *Has US Income Inequality Really Increased?* Washington, DC: Cato Institute Policy Analysis.

Roine, Jesper, and Daniel Waldenström. 2013. *Long-Run Trends in the Distribution of Income and Wealth*. IZA Discussion Paper No. 8157. Uppsala: Uppsala University, April.

Saez, Emmanuel, and Gabriel Zucman. 2014. *Exploding wealth inequality in the United States. Washington*, DC: Washington Center for Equitable Growth, October 20.

Saez, Emmanuel, and Gabriel Zucman. 2016. "Wealth Inequality in the United States Since 1913: Evidence from Capitalized Income Tax Data." *The Quarterly Journal of Economics* 131 (2): 519–578.

Smiley, Gene. 2000. "A Note on New Estimates of the Distribution of Income in the 1920s." *The Journal of Economic History* 60 (4): 1120–1128.

Smiley, Gene, and Richard H. Keehn. 1995. "Federal Personal Income Tax Policy in the 1920s." *The Journal of Economic History* 55 (2): 285–303.

Stewart, Charles. 1939. "Income Capitalization as a Method of Estimating the Distribution of Wealth By Size Groups." Comments by Fritz Lehman and Milton Friedman. *Studies in Income and Wealth* 3: 95–146.

Stiglitz, Joseph E. 2012. *The Price of Inequality: How Today's Divided Society Endangers Our Future*. New York: Norton.

Vermeulen, Philip. 2014. *How Fat Is the Top Tail of the Wealth Distribution?* European Central Bank Working Paper No. 1692. Available at www.ecb.europa.eu/pub/pdf/scpwps/ecbwp1692.pdf

Wolff, Edward N. 1994. "Trends in Household Wealth in the United States, 1962–83 and 1983–89." *Review of Income and Wealth* 40 (2): 143–174.

10 The measurement of income distribution and the measurement of inequality

A critical analysis

Stephen C. Miller

I. Introduction

I.I. Economic inequality as a concept

Intuitively, economic inequality is the gap in living standards between individuals or between groups of people within a polity or geographic area. Since an individual's standard of living primarily depends on his or her income and wealth, the extent of the income and wealth inequality between them, i.e., the gap between the income and the wealth of individuals, usually provides an accurate picture of the degree of economic inequality between them. Thus, to say that economic inequality has increased is to say that the gap between the income and the wealth of certain individuals or groups of people has grown in a meaningful way. And similarly, if economic inequality is said to be decreasing, then the income, wealth, and living standards of individuals have become more similar than they were in the past.

When social scientists seek to measure economic inequality, they are trying to capture the meaningful gaps between the rich and the poor. The premise behind inequality research is that growing or shrinking gaps in living standards should be captured in income, wealth, and mobility data. The reason so many researchers look at income distribution data, for example, is that income is an important driver of living standards. The presumption is that if the data show disproportionate income or wealth changes, then inequality has increased. Similarly, if the data show no change in economic mobility, or even a slight decline, then it appears that some social or political barrier is likely preventing people from moving up and down the economic ladder.

In order to measure changes in inequality, researchers rely on income and wealth distribution data. Different measures, namely, Gini coefficients or Income Shares, are used to determine the level of inequality within an economy. The change in inequality is then measured by the changes in distribution levels. Mobility data often use the same data sources as distribution data but are designed to answer a different question: How easy or difficult is it for people to move across the distribution?

However, the intuition that greater economic equality means a greater equality of living standards can conflict with trends in measured income distribution, wealth distribution, and mobility. Because of the way distribution and mobility are measured, their changes can run counter to an intuitive notion of inequality. For example, it is possible for meaningful gaps in living standards to close while the income distribution data make it seem like inequality is increasing. Similarly, mobility can appear flat, while at the same time a growing portion of people are seeing real income increase.

I.II. How economic inequality is measured

There are three common types of measures of economic inequality: Gini coefficients of income or wealth, Income or Wealth Shares, and measures of Income or Wealth Mobility. This chapter will focus on how these measures are used to understand income inequality specifically, but both the descriptions of how the statistical measures are constructed and the critical analysis of the measures that follow apply not only to measures of income inequality but also to those of wealth inequality. Gini coefficients and Income or Wealth Shares are distribution measures, i.e., measures of how income or wealth are distributed among percentile groups or quantiles of the distribution. Mobility measures, meanwhile, look at the extent to which the incomes and wealth of individuals within an economy rise or fall over a period of time.

Income distribution is measured either as the extent of the dispersion of income, typically with Gini coefficients, or as a specific quantiles' share of the national income, typically shares of the top 10%, top 1%, top 0.1%, or top 0.01%. The data sources for distribution measures vary depending on available data. In the United States, multiple data sources are used, with the most common sources being U.S. Census Bureau Current Population Survey (CPS) data and Internal Revenue Service Statistics of Income (SOI) data. The Federal Reserve Board also has historical data on income and wealth in its Survey of Consumer Finances.

Mobility data in the United States typically rely on the same sources, especially the CPS (or older Census Bureau data for years before the CPS existed) and the SOI. Mobility data are examined in different ways, with two key distinctions: mobility is either examined intragenerationally or intergenerationally and can be either presented as a relative or absolute measure. Relative income mobility, for example, looks at movement across the income distribution. Absolute income mobility simply looks at upward or downward movement in income over time.

A key component of the inequality narrative in both popular and academic writings is that inequality is endemic to unregulated markets, particularly unregulated financial markets. In Piketty (2014), the argument is clear: those with higher incomes and higher wealth will earn a greater portion of their income from interest on investment, while those with lower incomes and wealth are earning nearly all of their income from wages. Because the return on investment is greater than the overall growth in wages, economic inequality will increase steadily without any corrective action. In other words, the natural tendency of capitalist societies, i.e., societies that allow private investors and entrepreneurs to allocate capital toward more productive uses, is toward greater and greater inequality, that is, a growing gap in living standards between wage earners and those receiving investment income. The premise is that those at the top of the income and wealth distributions will see both growing wealth and growing incomes, which lead to much higher standards of living over time, while those who rely primarily on wage incomes will experience stagnation. The inequality, left unchecked, can lead to oligarchy and civil unrest.

To support this narrative of growing inequality, researches offer data on both income distribution and income mobility. The literature in these areas has grown since the 1990s, partly because of more widely available data in more countries and partly due to new techniques for measuring income distribution. In the past 20 years, Thomas Piketty and Emmanuel Saez (2003, 2004) have innovated a new way of looking at income distribution, which uses tax return data to focus on the share of total income received by the top 1% of the distribution. Doing so has allowed them, for the United States in particular, to demonstrate a U-shaped pattern in income distribution over the past 100 years; in the early 20th century, inequality was very high, fell sharply in the middle of the century, and rose again beginning in the 1980s. Gini coefficients, described in the next section, show a similar U-shaped trend. Mobility data presented by Chetty et al. (2017) suggest a slightly different narrative: adults are less likely to earn more than what their parents earned in the past, which likely contributes to growing income inequality over time.

This chapter argues that although these measures of distribution and mobility likely tell us something about income inequality, changes based on existing measures do not reveal much about changes in underlying economic inequality. The next section discusses the measurement of income distribution using Gini coefficients and presents simple examples of how Gini coefficients fail to capture changes in inequality. The third section discusses the use of income shares to measure changes in inequality and explains how the measurement of income share changes is distorted by both endogenous and exogenous factors. The fourth section examines the relationship between mobility and inequality. The fifth section concludes.

II. Gini coefficients

II.I. The Gini coefficient and the Lorenz curve

The most common measure of income inequality, particularly in international comparisons, is the Gini coefficient. The Gini coefficient requires use of the Lorenz curve (shown in Figure 10.1), which plots the income distribution of

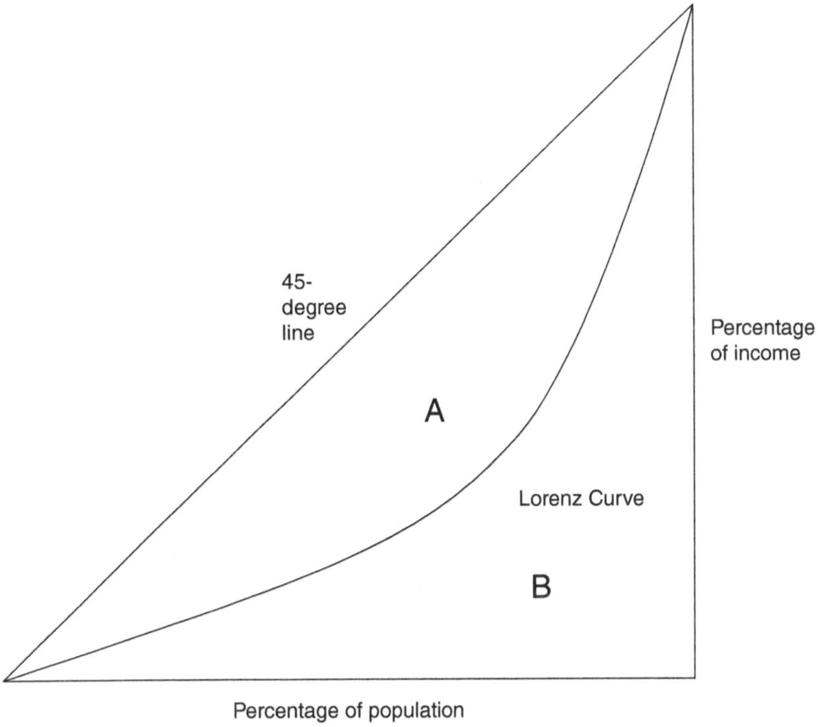

Figure 10.1 The Lorenz curve and the Gini coefficient

a country based on income shares. The vertical axis depicts the percentage of total income in an economy, and the horizontal axis depicts the percentage of the population that receives that percentage of total income. For example, if 5% of the population receive 20% of the income, that would be represented by one point on the Lorenz curve. If 80% of the population receive 99% of the income, that would be another point. The 45-degree line in Figure 10.1 represents a completely equal income distribution – 50% of the population receives 50% of the income, 10% receive 10% of the income, and so on. Such a distribution is possible only if every unit, i.e., every individual or household being measured, has exactly the same income. To measure income inequality, then, the Lorenz curve is compared with the 45-degree line.

The Gini coefficient is calculated as the area of the gap between the Lorenz curve and the line plot of perfect equality, area A, divided by the total area under the 45-degree line, $A + B$. In other words, the Gini coefficient defines income inequality as deviation from a hypothetical economy where all individuals and/or households receive identical annual incomes. Note that this is not the same as defining inequality as, for example, the deviation from an economy where individuals receive some version of "equal pay for equal work," or even one where all workers receive the same hourly wage.

A basic feature of the Gini coefficient is that income growth does not necessarily affect the coefficient so long as the growth in incomes is symmetric. For example, if the Gini coefficient were based on individual incomes and every individual who received income received a 2% increase in income this year, the coefficient would not change. However, if individuals who had received zero income began to receive positive income, the Gini coefficient would likely change.

It is worth noting that the source data for Gini coefficients are typically measures of pretax, pre-transfer incomes. This means that changes in taxes or transfer payments do not directly affect the Gini coefficient for a country unless those data are adjusted, although those changes can affect the incentives earners face. The effect of tax and transfer payment changes on Gini coefficients in the United States are discussed later in this section.

II.II. Individual Gini coefficients

Suppose a business owner wants to estimate the extent of income inequality within his firm and wants to ensure that the new hire for next year, Charlie, does not affect the current level of income inequality in the firm. The owner uses the salaries listed in Table 10.1 for the year 2018 to calculate the firm's Gini coefficient and gets a Gini coefficient of 0.282. Suppose, for the sake of the example, that the firm implements an annual pay increase of 2% for all employees. The owner intuits that without Charlie's hire, the Gini would remain the same for 2019, after the pay increase of 2% is implemented. This is correct, so the owner then intuits that the Gini should remain unchanged if Charlie is simply paid the average of his new colleagues' 2019 salaries, which would be $91,630. However, when the owner calculates the new Gini for the firm, he finds that it has fallen by over 24%.

Table 10.1 Within-firm gini coefficients

Worker	*Y2018*	*Y2019*
Charlie		180,000
Dave	34,000	34,680
George	50,000	51,000
John	80,000	81,600
Chris	100,000	102,000
Randy	125,000	127,500
Rick	150,000	153,000
Gini	0.282	0.282
Average	89,833.33	104,254.29

Because of the small-population bias of the Gini,[1] increasing the number of employees from six to seven should increase the Gini slightly, if the owner gets Charlie's salary just right. However, the owner was not aware that Gini coefficients are relatively more sensitive to changes in the middle of the distribution than they are to changes in the top and bottom portions of the distribution (Jones and Weinberg 2000; Pressman 2013). As it turns out, to maintain the same Gini coefficient from 2018, Charlie would need to receive an income of $180,000. What would intuitively be a mere preservation of equality, i.e., paying Charlie the average salary in the firm, would substantially *increase* equality as measured by the Gini. And what would intuitively *decrease* equality, i.e., paying Charlie nearly 18% more than his next highest-paid colleague, Rick, would merely maintain equality as measured by the Gini. Similarly, if an individual were added below the current bottom of the distribution, for example, with a salary of $30,000, the Gini would *fall* slightly. Intuitively, widening the gap between the lowest and highest incomes should increase measured income inequality, but that is not necessarily the case with Gini coefficients.

II.III. Individuals versus households

Table 10.2 shows the Gini coefficients for the individuals living in a fictional cul-de-sac at two points in time 15 years apart. In 2000, the cul-de-sac has three households: Jack and Diane, and their children Kim and Kal; Joe and Fran, and their children Bob and Sally; and Han and Leah, and their children Kylo and Rey. By 2015, all these six children are grown up and earn incomes. In this example, everyone except Diane, who happens to live in the highest-income

Table 10.2 Individual income-based gini coefficients

Individual	*2000*	*2015*
Jack	300,000	600,000
Diane	30,000	30,000
Kim	0	50000
Kal	0	100,000
Joe	40,000	65,000
Fran	25,000	45,000
Bob	0	45,000
Sally	0	60,000
Han	95,000	125,000
Leah	0	110,000
Kylo	0	40,000
Rey	0	70,000
Gini	0.79251701	0.486940299

household, has received an increase in income. And the individual Gini coefficient drops by roughly 40% between 2000 and 2015.

However, the Gini coefficient drop probably does not match most peoples' intuition about the change in inequality – it seems clear from the table that Jack gained much more than anyone else, and that in absolute terms, the gap between Jack's income and others is greater than before. In 2000, Jack received $205,000 more than the next highest-income earner, Han, while in 2015, he received $475,000 more than Han. Proportionally, Han's income rose a bit more than 30%, while Jack's rose by 100%. The sensitivity of the Gini to the growth in the number and incomes of those in the middle of the distribution is apparent. More importantly, in the example, there is not an obvious connection between the individual incomes and equality of living standards. Diane's income did not rise but her household income rose dramatically, and her standard of living likely improved. Household incomes are more intuitively relevant.

Table 10.3 shows the Gini coefficients in 2000 and 2015 if we measure household income instead of individual income. To make the example simple, the new households in 2015 consist of the grown children from the households in 2000. The income changes are the same as in Table 10.2, but instead of a large drop in the Gini coefficient, it rises slightly from 2000 to 2015. When calculating the Gini for household income instead of individual income, the Gini moves in the opposite direction. In other words, using a different unit of analysis changes the result.

Household income measures complicate our understanding of how Gini coefficients change. A Gini coefficient based on CPS data, for example, uses the household income distribution to plot the Lorenz curve. Just as for individuals, it is true that if all income increases were proportionally identical across all households, the Gini coefficient would not change *but only if there are no other changes in the number of households or household composition*. Imagine, for example, that all incomes remained the same for all individuals but the number of households changed. The Gini coefficient would almost certainly change. Changes in the size and composition of households, especially those near the middle

Table 10.3 Household income-based gini coefficients

Household	*2000*	*Household*	*2015*
JackDiane	330,000	JackDiane	630,000
JoeFran	65,000	JoeFran	110,000
HanLeah	95,000	HanLeah	235,000
Gini	0.36054422	KimKylo	90,000
		KalSally	160,000
		BobRey	115,000
		Gini	0.3880597

of the distribution, can drive changes in Gini coefficients, even if the gains in income are completely proportional.

There is another unit of analysis that has not been discussed: the family. Rather than examine households or individuals, the family may be the most analytically important. It clearly matters for Jack and Diane's adult children that their parents have such a high household income, even though they are no longer part of that household. But if it matters for their children, does it matter for their in-laws? The complications of household measurement over time are compounded when trying to measure changes in family incomes over time.

II.IV. International comparisons

It is worth noting that Gini coefficients are the most common way, and in some cases, the only way of making international inequality comparisons.[2] However, different countries use different source data, and for many recently developed and developing countries, the income (or consumption) data used to create Gini coefficients exist only back to the 1990s or 1980s. The United States is unusual in that these data series can go back to 1913, even though the CPS data go back only to the 1960s. This is because of the existence of SOI data, which has become more commonly used to measure inequality since the Piketty–Saez series was created.

Aside from questions of data quality and the incompatibility of data sources, there is a more basic problem with using Ginis to compare changes in inequality across countries. Consider a case of two poor countries, with relatively low Gini coefficients. The first country, Alpha, has rising average incomes but largely because of high-income immigration. This is similar to the example of the firm adding a high-salary worker. More high-income people could be added to the distribution, creating a larger gap between the lowest earners and the highest but without much impact on the Gini coefficient. The Gini may even fall in this scenario, even though the gap between earners has grown.

The second country, Beta, has rising average incomes because of relatively even growth across the income distribution, but the income growth coincides with an increase in the number of households, and a smaller average household size. For Beta, the Gini coefficient could easily rise. Intuitively, Alpha's distribution has become less equal while Beta's has become more equal. Yet the Gini changes can suggest just the opposite.

Suppose that in a third country, Gamma, has income growth of 10% for the bottom decile of the distribution, relatively flat growth near the middle of the distribution, and income growth of 20% for the top decile. Gamma would surely see its Gini increase, suggesting greater inequality. Percentage-wise, their gains were smaller than for the top 10%, which is why the Gini increases. But the lowest-income people in the economy have moved closer to the middle class.

Gini coefficients do measure inequality in the sense that they quantitatively describe how far an income distribution is from being perfectly equal. However, changes in the Gini coefficient do not necessarily reflect changes in inequality as most people would understand the concept. Intuitively, keeping average incomes about the same would not change inequality, but Gini coefficients are sensitive to changes near the mode of the distribution and will fall rapidly if more individuals or households are added to the middle of the distribution. Also, Gini coefficient changes, like income share changes, reflect changes only among changing statistical groups within the distribution, not between groups of specific people. Hypothetically, even if no individual's total income changes, changes in the Gini coefficient can happen due to changes in the number and size of households, or the composition of households.

III. Income shares

III.I. Income shares and SOI data

Income shares for specific quantiles are the other main tool for measuring income distribution. The most commonly cited version is the income share of the top 1%, but income shares for the top 10%, top 0.1%, and top 0.01% are often given as well, because in the United States, SOI data are most commonly used for these figures, and extensive analyses of SOI-derived income shares have been made possible by the creation of the Piketty–Saez series (Piketty and Saez 2003, 2004).

According to the Piketty–Saez series, including capital gains income, the top 1% of income earners in the United States received 20.3% of total income in 2015 versus 11.1% in 1985 (Piketty et al. 2018). That the income share of the top 1% has nearly doubled over those 30 years is taken as evidence that inequality has nearly doubled, although careful observers may make a milder conclusion that inequality has increased substantially. Note that, unlike Gini coefficients, income shares do not necessarily build in the assumption that perfect equality means that individuals or households receive identical annual incomes. It merely suggests that whatever the standard for equality is, higher income shares for top quantiles signal higher levels of inequality. Piketty and Saez, for example, suggest that the policy response to rising income inequality in the United States should be a return to the high marginal income tax rates of the 1950s and 1960s (Piketty et al. 2014). Note that despite top marginal income tax rates of over 90% from 1951 to 1963, the income share of the top 1% of the distribution was well above complete equality, hovering around 8–9% of the total income during that period (Piketty and Saez 2004).

There are two main advantages to the SOI data in the United States. As previously mentioned, the data allow for the creation of income-share measures going back to 1913, which is longer than other data sources can go by four or more decades. The second advantage is that the data source is very complete and includes nearly every income earner in the United States since 1942, when the number of filed returns first exceeded the number of U.S. households.

However, there are a few disadvantages of the SOI data, particularly as they are presented in the Piketty–Saez series. First, the data are pretax, pre-transfer data. In other words, although the incomes reported in the Piketty–Saez series ultimately come from personal income tax returns, the income number taken is the adjusted gross income taken before taxes. For measuring inequality, this means that the income share of the top 1% is measured as their share of total income before taxes. If the point of the measure is to assess inequality due to the actual incomes *received* by the top 1%, then the pretax numbers overstate one side of the inequality between the top 1% and the bottom 99%. The Piketty–Saez series is also pre-transfer, which means that income numbers do not include all income from transfer programs such as welfare or the nontaxable portion of Social Security benefits. This necessarily understates the actual income received by lower quantiles. When taxes and transfers are taken into account, the estimated shares of the top 1% fall substantially (Auten and Splinter 2017).

The SOI data also use a curious unit of analysis: the taxable unit. Technically, the SOI income figures do not report individual income *or* household income. The series reports the income of a taxable unit, which is determined by the filing status, i.e., "single," "married filing jointly," "married filing separately," "head of household," or "qualifying widow(er) with dependent children." There may be one return per household or multiple returns per household, depending on filing status, and changes in income distribution can be partially driven by changes in patterns of filing status.

Another disadvantage of the SOI data is they are derived from personal income tax returns, and therefore do not include corporate income. A related disadvantage is that the SOI data do not account for differences in reportable income due to changes in the income tax code. The concern here is income shifting, where tax filers may change how much income is reported (as personal income versus corporate income, for example) based on changes in the tax code.

A prominent example is the Tax Reform Act of 1986 (TRA86), which lowered the top marginal rate for personal income below the top marginal rate for corporate income (Burkhauser et al. 2012). The result was the conversion of C-Corporations, which report income as corporate income, to S-Corporations, which result in income being reported on personal income tax returns (Wilke et al. 1996; Wittman and Gill 1998). This change alone leads to an overstatement in the increased income share of the top 1%, as it implies that *shiftable* corporate income was not included in the Piketty–Saez measures prior to TRA86 (Mechling et al. 2017). In short, the reliance on SOI data understated income shares of the top 1% prior TRA86 and overstated the increase in the share of top 1% share after TRA86. TRA86 is just one important change in the tax code. It seems likely that income shifting, combined with other tax avoidance strategies, can explain a portion of the observed changes in income distribution over the entire Piketty–Saez series from 1913 on. Note also that income shifting may even apply to CPS data, as survey respondents may report household income based on personal incomes rather than corporate incomes.

Although these disadvantages have been noted, all can in principle be corrected for; the only limitation is the availability of the data needed to adjust the series. The exception is the unit of measurement itself, namely, households and taxable units, which change endogenously.

III.II. Income shares versus inequality

So do income shares measure inequality? Aside from the previously discussed measurement problems with income shares, there is a deeper problem: income shares measure inequality between quantiles not inequality between people. One can comprehend the change in Jack's income share, or the change in Jack and Diane's income share, as reflecting a change in inequality. At any given moment, the measured quantile, e.g., the top 1%, reflects the income share of the people in that quantile. But in a subsequent moment, or year for annually measured data, the measurement of the top 1% reflects the income share of a *different* group of people.

The group, in fact, can be substantially different: Auten et al. (2013), for example, found that only 30% of those in the top 1% had remained in the top 1% for five consecutive years. The change in inequality between people is not itself captured. An increase in the share of the top 1% may occur while many households within the distribution moved closer together, i.e., many inequalities between people within the distribution may have been reduced. A reduction of inequality can result from people moving from one part of the distribution to another as they move toward each other. New households can change the distribution even as previously existing inequalities are reduced. Additionally, income shares based on SOI data measure inequality between quantiles of taxable units rather than quantiles of individuals or households. Changes in income shares are more precisely described as *changes in the distribution of the income shares of the quantiles within a group of households, which are changing in both number and composition.* Changes in income shares of taxable units could be described as *changes in the distribution of income shares of the quantiles within a group of taxable units, which are changing in both number and composition.* In other words, changes in income shares reflect the changes in the shares of statistical groups, not of stable groups of people.

Income distribution measures also can vary based on the unit of analysis, such as individual or household income data. The conceptual difficulty is that income is typically earned by individuals but expended by households. If income inequality is merely the dispersion of incomes, individual measures more precisely convey the distribution of income. But to the extent that income inequality describes *how* income variation affects the broader economic inequality between people, household income changes arguably better reflect how inequality of well-being changes over time. However, this logic can be taken further; family income is likely important to well-being, even where families are spread among multiple households.

IV. Mobility

IV.I. Intragenerational and intergenerational mobility

Economic mobility is either presented as an intragenerational comparison, i.e., the same individual or household at two points in time, or as an intergenerational comparison, tracking how adult children compare with their parents at the same age.

Economic mobility is the basic mechanism by which inequality can increase or decrease. Trends in intragenerational income mobility can indicate how likely it is that people at separate ends of the distribution in one time period end up closer to each other decades later, and intergenerational trends can indicate whether those raised in low- and high-income households have a tendency to move closer together in the distribution or farther apart. Not coincidentally, most mobility data are derived from the same sources as income distribution data. For example, Auten and Gee (2009) use U.S. SOI data to measure intragenerational mobility among income tax filers, while Chetty et al. (2014) use the same data to measure intergenerational mobility across the income distribution. Meanwhile, other studies, such as Chetty et al. (2017), use census data to construct mobility measures.

For intragenerational mobility, Auten and Gee (2009) report on the top 1% of the distribution in addition to the quintiles, finding that 60% of the top 1% in the beginning year of the study (1996) had fallen to a lower percentile by the tenth year of the study (2005). Their later study (Auten et al. 2013) found that for the top 1% of tax filers in 2005, 35% fell to a lower percentile within one year, and 73% fell to a lower percentile within five years. The numbers for the top 1% of filers in 1991 are 39% and 71%, respectively. In their sample, from 1991 to 2009, one-year persistence was lowest in 1999 (with 48% falling to a lower percentile within a year), but hovering between 30% and 40% for most years in the sample.

IV.II. Absolute versus relative mobility

Relative mobility is measured by tracking movement across the income distribution. The studies are longitudinal, following either individuals at different points in their lives or parents and their children at similar ages. A typical measurement of mobility in the United States, reported both in Chetty et al. (2014) and Auten et al. (2013), examines the percentage of adults who are in different income quintiles than their parents, and specifically the percentage who move up or down one quintile, or two quintiles, etc. Chetty et al. (2014: 145) report that people in the birth cohorts of 1971–1986 with parents in the middle-income quintile have approximately a 20% probability of reaching the top quintile at age 26. Auten et al. (2013: 170) report that 21.9% of children born to parents in the middle-income quintile were in the highest quintile in 2007, when they were between the ages of 35–38.

For relative mobility, both intergenerational and intragenerational studies show flat trends since the 1970s when mobility is measured as movement across the distribution (Chetty et al. 2014, Auten et al. 2013). Upward mobility has been stable, with no clear trend of increasing or decreasing over time. Downward mobility has fluctuated, but it also shows no clear trend of increasing or decreasing over time. Later-year cohorts are not significantly more or less mobile than earlier ones.

Economic growth, however, presents a problem for relative mobility measures. It is clearly true that economic growth, and particularly income growth at the top of the distribution, makes the gap between zero income and the income required to be in the top 1% greater. Although this widening gap has nothing to do with how difficult it is to move up or down within the distribution, it does move the percentile markers farther apart. If, as most researchers do, you report mobility among the five quintiles of the income distribution, you have artificially created four markers for those in the bottom 20% to move past to make it to the top 20%. As incomes grow, those markers move farther apart. If, as Chetty et al. (2014) report, relative mobility among those quintiles is stable, then compared to the smaller economies and populations of the past, current mobility is being understated as the threshold for moving up or down a quintile has increased over time. In other words, the real income change required for moving up or down a quintile increases as overall incomes grow, and especially as incomes at the top grow. But real income changes represent real mobility. The apparent solution, then, is to examine absolute mobility.

Absolute mobility measures simply examine whether people have seen their incomes rise or fall. The trend in intergenerational absolute mobility, as reported by Chetty et al. (2017), is clearly a downward trend. In the 2017 study, absolute mobility is measured only as upward mobility. The study measures the percentage of adults aged 30 who earn more than their parents and finds a consistent decline in upward mobility, for each birth cohort measured from 1940 to 1984. At age 30, 92% of those born in 1940 earned more than their parents, but only 50% of those born in 1984 did the same. That absolute mobility appears to have fallen while relative mobility has remained stable presents a puzzle, one that requires an explanation of what mobility means for changes in economic inequality.

The reason absolute mobility appears to have decreased while relative mobility has stayed flat is that the measure Chetty et al. (2017) use for absolute mobility is confined to upward mobility. Over the entire income distribution, the average percentage of children who earn more than their parents at age 30 has declined, as explained earlier. But the trend is very different for different portions of the distribution. For children with parents who were in the 5th percentile of the income distribution, for example, absolute mobility fell much less between 1940 and 1980 than it did for children of parents in the 80th or

90th percentile of the income distribution. In other words, the overall trend in upward mobility has been that the higher one's parents' household income was at age 30, the less likely it is that their children would have higher household incomes at age 30.[3] Put another way, the children of parents who had relatively high incomes experience more *downward* mobility than the children of parents who had relatively low incomes. Absolute mobility is important, but when considering the impact on economic inequality, downward mobility matters just as much as upward mobility. Upward mobility arguably matters more when discussing well-being, but strictly speaking, if the goal is to understand how inequality between people, rather than statistical categories, is changing, then it matters that some incomes fall while others rise.

In both the SOI and census data, and for measures of relative and absolute mobility, one trend is clear: upward mobility is highest at the bottom of the income distribution and downward mobility is highest at the top of the income distribution. For example, the SOI data show that 59.4% of children born to parents in the top 20% of the income distribution fall out of the top 20% as adults, while 70.4% of children born to parents in the bottom 20% of the distribution rise out of the bottom 20%. The census data show that, on average, children born to parents with lower incomes have a better chance of earning more than their parents than do children born to parents with higher incomes.

This trend arguably contradicts the narrative of growing income inequality. The household income one is born into matters less overall today than it did in the past; parental income is inversely related with upward mobility. Consider the example of the households in the cul-de-sac in Section III. Suppose the highest-earning parents, Jack and Diane, were 40 years old in 2000, and their children, Kim and Kal, were 15-year-old twins. In 2015, both Kim and Kal are 30; Kim lives in a household with $135,000 of annual income and Kal lives in a household with $160,000 in annual income. Even if both of the children's households were to experience average 5% annual increases in real income over the next decade (considerably higher than the U.S. average economic growth over the past few decades), they will, at age 40, still have household incomes considerably lower than their parents' income was at the same age. But for the other households in 2000, those with lower incomes, by 2015 their children live in households with incomes that are much higher than those of their parents at the same age. Recall that in the example of household incomes in Table 10.3, the Gini coefficient rose slightly from 2000 to 2015, and the income share of the highest-income household rose. But their children's household incomes were closer to their peers' because of both upward and downward mobility working at the same time. The question of whether inequality increased is tricky, because the intergenerational trend is one where people of the same age group move together, even as the overall income distribution widens.

The example of the households in the cul-de-sac illustrates a further contradiction: that absolute and relative mobility can appear to move in opposite directions. In absolute terms, i.e., dollars of income, Jack and Diane's household income grew faster than Han and Leah's. Han and Leah arguably were less mobile. But in relative terms, Han and Leah had a steeper profile of income growth than Jack and Diane did. Another question, one which this example cannot directly answer, is which household saw a greater increase in living standards?

V. Conclusion

While a snapshot of income distribution may give some insight on inequality, changes in income distribution do not necessarily (or always?) reveal underlying changes in economic inequality. Inequality is something that only meaningfully exists between people, not statistical categories of people. Attempts to measure changes in inequality as changes in income distribution fail because they measure changes in the distribution itself rather than comparing how individuals or households move together or apart within that distribution.

While mobility is not itself equality or inequality, it is the mechanism by which inequality changes. The mobility data are frustratingly inconclusive. Relative mobility in the United States has been stable for decades, and absolute mobility studies are inconclusive regarding the impact on inequality. Upward mobility at the bottom of the distribution has fallen over time, but downward mobility at the top seems to have risen. The former would suggest a trend toward more inequality over time between individuals, but the latter would suggest less. If anything, the relative mobility data understate mobility changes over time, as overall growth in incomes widens the absolute gap between percentile groups.

The ideal is to measure inequality changes between individuals or stable households. This is unsatisfying, because individual income gives a limited picture of well-being and households are anything but stable in terms of their size and composition. Even the most stable household is highly likely to change over a 20-year period, and most change within a shorter time. But that may be the only answer, as income inequality can meaningfully exist only between people. A second-best option is to measure changes in standards of living across the income distribution, as some researches have attempted, including the chapters written by Manish and Horwitz in this volume.

Notes

1 Gini coefficients for small populations or samples have been demonstrated to have a downward bias (Deltas 2003).
2 The World Inequality Database (https://wid.world) does offer limited international comparisons of income shares.
3 Auten et al. (2013) observe a steep income profile over individuals' life cycle, one which continues to ramp up during an individual's 30s and 40s at the higher portions of the income distribution. They suggest that measuring mobility at particular ages likely understates income mobility for the highest quantiles of the income distribution. Chetty et al. (2014) partially address this objection by repeating their intergenerational absolute mobility calculations for parents aged 35–45 to their children at age 40 in addition to their

baseline calculation of parents at ages 25–35 to their children at age 30. They find a similar trend for the average upward mobility, although the decline in absolute mobility is less pronounced. They find that adjustments for family size also reduce the decline in absolute mobility but do not change the overall trend.

References

Auten, G., and G. Gee. 2009. "Income Mobility in the United States: New Evidence from Income Tax Data." *National Tax Journal* 62 (2): 301–328.

Auten, G., Gee, G., and N. Turner. 2013. "Income Inequality, Mobility, and Turnover at the Top in the U.S., 1987–2010." *American Economic Review* 103 (3): 168–172.

Auten, G., and D. Splinter. 2017. *Income Inequality in the United States: Using Tax Data to Measure Long-Term Trends*. Working Paper. Available at https://mronline.org/wp-content/uploads/2018/12/AutenSplinter-ax_Data_and_Inequality.pdf. Accessed April 1, 2019.

Burkhauser, R. V., Feng, S., Jenkins, S., and J. Larrimore. 2012. "Recent Trends in Top Income Shares in the USA: Reconciling Estimates from March CPS and IRS Tax Return Data." *The Review of Economics and Statistics* 94: 371–388, May.

Chetty, R., Grusky, D., Hell, M., Hendren, N., Manduca, R., and J. Narang. 2017. "The Fading American Dream: Trends in Absolute Income Mobility Since 1940." *Science* 356 (6336): 398–406.

Chetty, R., Hendren, N., Kline, P., Saez, E., and N. Turner. 2014. "Is the United States Still a Land of Opportunity? Recent Trends in Intergenerational Mobility." *American Economic Review* 104 (5): 141–147.

Deltas, George. 2003. "The Small-Sample Bias of the Gini Coefficient: Results and Implications for Empirical Research." *Review of Economics and Statistics* 85 (1): 226–234, February.

Jones, A. F., and D. H. Weinberg. 2000. *The Changing Shape of the Nation's Income Distribution*. Current Population Reports P60–204. Washington, DC: U.S. Census Bureau.

Mechling, G., Miller, S., and R. Konecny. 2017. "Do Piketty and Saez Misstate Income Inequality? Critiquing the Critiques." *Review of Political Economy* 29 (1): 30–46.

Piketty, T. 2014. *Capital in the Twenty-First Century*. Cambridge, MA: The Belknap Press of Harvard University Press.

Piketty, T., and E. Saez. 2003. "Income Inequality in the United States, 1913–1998." *Quarterly Journal of Economics* 118: 1–39.

Piketty, T., and E. Saez. 2004. *Income Inequality in the United States, 1913–2002*. Paris and UC Berkeley: EHESS, NBER. Available at https://eml.berkeley.edu/~saez/piketty-saez OUP04US.pdf. Accessed April 1, 2019.

Piketty, T., Saez, E., and S. Stantcheva. 2014. "Optimal Taxation of Top Labor Incomes: A Tale of Three Elasticities." *American Economic Journal: Economic Policy* 6 (1): 230–271.

Piketty, T., Saez, E., and G. Zucman. 2018. "Distributional National Accounts: Methods and Estimates for the United States." *Quarterly Journal of Economics* 133 (2): 553–609.

Pressman, S. 2013. "Cross National Comparisons of Poverty and Income Inequality." In R. S. Rycroft, ed., *The Economics of Inequality, Poverty, and Discrimination in the 21st Century*. Santa Barbara, CA: Praeger.

Wilke, P., Young, J., and S. Nutter. 1996. "Corporate Business Activity Before and After the Tax Reform Act of 1986." *IRS SOI Bulletin*: 32–45, Winter.

Wittman, S. M., and A. Gill. 1998. "S Corporation Elections After the Tax Reform Act of 1986." *Internal Revenue Service SOI Bulletin*: 80–88.

Index

Note: Page numbers in *italics* indicate figures, **bold** indicate tables and page numbers with "n" indicate the end notes in the text.